Spiritual Wisdom

Spiritual Wisdom

An Evolutionary Insight

Ramesh Malhotra

iUniverse LLC
Bloomington

SPIRITUAL WISDOM
AN EVOLUTIONARY INSIGHT

iUniverse books may be ordered through booksellers or by contacting:

iUniverse
1663 Liberty Drive
Bloomington, IN 47403
www.iuniverse.com
1-800-Authors (1-800-288-4677)

ISBN: 978-1-4759-9289-2 (sc)
ISBN: 978-1-4759-9291-5 (hc)
ISBN: 978-1-4759-9290-8 (e)

Library of Congress Control Number: 2013909541

Printed in the United States of America

iUniverse rev. date: 7/10/2013

To my grandchildren and to all the children of world, who are the guiding light for all of humanity in the future.

Contents

List of Illustrations

Preface

Since completing my education in 1970, I have searched for relationships between scientific and spiritual knowledge. This has involved questioning topics such as the big bang theory of the creation of the universe, the relationship between Einstein's equation of $E=MC^2$ and divine illumination, the unmanifested or undifferentiated nature of God or the Creator, and other scientific and spiritual investigations that are related to understanding the powers of the Creator.

In 1991, after the death of a close relative, I went through a period of melancholy. During this phase of my life, I received inner inspirations to read books and explore spirituality and metaphysics as a means to seeking answers to my questions, but I felt I was not going anywhere. I even traveled to India to seek higher knowledge.

On February 3, 1998, during one of my visits to India, I purchased *The Holy Geeta* by Swami Chinmayananda at the New Delhi Airport. When I returned home, without ever opening the book, I put it on the bookshelf with the rest of my collection of read and unread books. Almost ten years later, in October 2007, I found myself discussing the same troubling questions with a relative, Ashok Kapoor, in Palo Alto, California. After listening to me, Ashok suggested that I should investigate the teachings of Swami Chinmayananda, especially his discourse on the holy scripture of the Bhagavad Gita.

Upon my return home from California, I immediately started reading books by Swami Chinmayananda, including the book I had purchased ten years earlier. (It had been sitting on my bookshelf, unread, the entire time.) While studying the text of *The Holy Geeta,* I developed an intense desire to channel all my energy, resources, and time into an in-depth investigation of the spiritual knowledge contained in the book.

In June 2009, I felt encouraged to write down my thoughts as I studied the book. I developed notes about the knowledge I had acquired based on teachings within the book. After I filled several spiral notebooks, I composed several illustrations and looked for examples that could help me comprehend the knowledge buried within the sacred book.

Since I am a businessperson and not a professional writer, I found the task of compiling and presenting my thoughts in the form of a textbook to be the most difficult task of my life. Moreover, I found it necessary to present my thoughts and findings in a format unlike that which has been used for centuries to discuss the spiritual wisdom included in the book (i.e., the Bhagavad Gita's wisdom presented in eighteen chapters with verse-by-verse interpretations).

First, I limited my thoughts strictly to the knowledge included within the holy scripture based on Vedic knowledge and the Bhagavad Gita. I found this approach to be incomplete; I elected to investigate the spiritual knowledge contained within other holy scriptures in an effort to find similarities and links with other faiths that evolved within other civilizations around the world.

In the midst of my expanded quest for spiritual knowledge, I found *A History of God* by Karen Armstrong. Her book was very informative, and I found it to be of great assistance as a source of references that Armstrong had compiled and included. I used several of these references to investigate specific subjects in depth. In addition to this book, I discovered four additional books to be of great help in understanding the psychological process of self-evolution. These include *Mysticism: A Study in the Nature and Development of Man's Spiritual Consciousness* by Evelyn Underhill, which first appeared in 1910; *Sufis: The People of the Path*, volumes 1 and 2, by Osho/Shree Rajneesh; and *Seeds of Contemplation* by Thomas Merton.

It took more than four years of research, writing, and rewriting to compose this text, which represents the true and most beautiful journey of my life. I hope that readers will find this book invigorating and will further explore, on their own, the various concepts and ideas presented here. The primary purpose of this book is to awaken members of our materialistic society, just like me, to further explore the infinite field of spiritual knowledge and seek inner tranquility and peace. The objective of this book is not to support or promote the Hindu religion or any specific belief; it is to encourage others to explore the field of spiritual wisdom and reexamine the answers we have cultivated based on everything known and unknown. I fully believe that a quest of this nature can bring peace, tranquility, and happiness to any individual, just as it did for me. It does not keep us from being actively involved with the material world, but it enhances our involvement. I also believe that if we make spiritual knowledge an integral part of our everyday lives, we could easily transform our society from one of pure materialism to a modified system that cultivates a *spiritual* form of capitalism.

Acknowledgments

No words can adequately express my gratitude to my family, friends, teachers, employees and bosses, as well as my enemies, who, unknowingly or knowingly, have all contributed to my personal growth and my inner quest to seek higher knowledge. Their influence has transformed my temperament and personality, and it has helped me practice newly discovered principles to successfully develop and expand my business.

In particular, I am indebted to certain spiritual scholars who have produced wonderful writings, not knowing the contributions they have made in helping others, like me, to acquire higher knowledge. I am indebted to Swami Shiv Sewa Nand Ji from Tapovan, Sadhupul, Solan, who provided the guidance I needed to pursue this project. He not only gave me the opportunity to stay at his ashram in the Himalayas for several days, but he also provided me the first opportunity to present my views to his residents and visitors staying at the ashram. This experience of responding to the questions of others as they satisfied their own spiritual quests gave me the true inner confidence to proceed with my mission. My ultimate emotional lift came when Swami Ji, out of his unbounded generosity, recognized my work and assigned me the spiritual name of *Atamnanda*, which means a seeker of inner peace.

The second source of encouragement came when I received a letter from Jennifer, my book's first editor at CreateSpace. She reviewed the first draft of this book and provided many encouraging comments. She stated, "[Your book's] in-depth and venture some investigation and discussion of the spiritual knowledge and guidance found within the Bhagavad Gita, with its special attention to how we might apply its spiritual principles to everyday life, could be enjoyed by any reader with an interest in religious or spiritual studies, and, perhaps more importantly, by any reader seeking guidance on how to live a better life." She touched my soul with the following comments regarding my research: "This book makes the daunting tome of the Bhagavad Gita more accessible, both to students of religion or spirituality and to the average educated reader. ... This is done well, both by repeating themes and by using creative analogies or similes to illustrate crucial points ... to show that spirituality and physicality are not opposites, but instead are more complementary, even seamless, than they may at first appear." Her suggestions and advice made me investigate this subject further and expand my research to include illustrations. For this, I am very grateful to her.

Another source of encouragement came from the letter from Janet A. from CreateSpace. She reviewed the second draft of this book and said, "I am fairly well educated, and I learned some fascinating new things ... which was exciting!" She found the progression of the narrative clear, concise, and logical, but she commented that my approach and my efforts to expound on the Bhagavad Gita were too wordy and were not clear in several instances, especially when I tried to explain the complicated topics covered within the Bhagavad Gita. She recommended reworking the book to convey these messages with clarity by using a direct and concise approach.

In reexamining these complicated topics to make them simpler, I discovered additional information that not only helped me to clarify points, it also helped me uncover additional information I had missed the first time, which helped me better explain such subjects. I am indebted to Janet for giving me her honest and frank opinion and suggestions.

I would like to thank several others who helped me develop this book. My dear friend Judie Braje took time from her busy schedule to read the first draft and provide several constructive comments, suggestions, and recommendations. I also want to thank my sister Manorma Kapoor, her husband Surinder Kapoor, my cousin Rajan Dhawan, and his wife Ritu Dhawan, all of whom provided moral support and assistance during my "journey of eternal joy." Finally I would like to thank all the members of the staff of iUniverse Publishing who helped me bring this book to reality especially the encouragement from Krista Hill who summarized her overall impression as follows "The author is to be commended for writing a book that explores the history of the path to enlightenment and grounds the discussion with down-to-earth examples."

I am extremely grateful to my wife for her enormous patience and understanding, and for giving me time alone to devote to this project. Quite often, this took me away from family responsibilities, and I want to express from my heart that without her assistance, patience, and understanding, this book never would have been possible.

Introduction

The most important aspect of our existence is that every living thing is subject to two forms of evolutionary trends. One is physical, which deals with the investigation of nature by means of science and technology. The other is spiritual, which requires an investigation of nature through perceptive power, commonly achieved through meditative practices. Because of its objective nature, only the physical evolutionary process has been studied and documented extensively.

Even though spiritual nature has existed for centuries, because of its subjective nature, it remains difficult to comprehend and investigate. Understanding spiritual aspects of nature requires the use of individual subtle faculties; therefore, the documentation of the spiritual evolutionary process remains undefined. The unveiling of the spiritual evolutionary process is called eternal wisdom; even without recognizing it, it remains the underlying quest and longing of every human being to know the spiritual evolutionary aspects of our creation.

I have elected to explore eternal wisdom in four categories: (1) mythological wisdom, (2) inspirational wisdom, (3) transcendental wisdom, and (4) absolute truth.

Mythological Wisdom

Initially, mythological wisdom was derived from the holistic visions received by highly evolved spiritual human beings. A great number of people experienced such wisdom during the Bronze Age, and it inspired them to cultivate faith in the supreme powers of causations, which are invisible, infinite, indescribable, immortal, and invincible in nature. Because of its immense power and invisible nature, humanity accepted, without any caveat, the almighty force and named it "God"—the ultimate power responsible for the causation and demise of the universal system.

Throughout early recorded human history, individuals with mythological wisdom determined there are three main elements of this divine power: Creator (the Lord supreme), creations (Universe), and the primordial force (the life force) that provides the link between the Creator and creations. The primordial force is defined as neutral in nature, but depending upon the actions it can transform from neutral to divine (holy) or demonic (evil).

Through the powers of the primordial force, the unmanifested bodies changed into manifested bodies, and manifested bodies changed into unmanifested bodies. Our universal system thus consists of different unmanifested, semi-manifested, and manifested physical bodies, including our planetary system and all living beings, moving and not moving.

Based on available information, such mythological knowledge was recorded within the earliest epics of *Enuma Elish* in Babylon between 115 and 170 BCE. Later, information from this epic was included and made part of the first book of Moses: Genesis. Subsequently, it became part of the holy scriptures of many religions, including Judaism, Christianity, and Islam. *Enuma Elish* describes the presence of these different universal systems, and it describes the first creation on earth.

According to *Enuma Elish,* the origin of life on earth started when the Creator formed a dwelling from the earthen (clay) material to house the immortal primordial force in the form of a living spirit. In spiritual terms, life started with the entry of the primordial force to create living things that are able to move and perform actions and activities. In mystic terms, the Creator introduced living things through introducing the "breath of life" into a fist of clay. Ultimately, this evolved into different shapes, colors, and sizes, and it grew from infancy, to early stage, to middle stage, to old age, after which it died.

Humanity further believed that, after death, the material part of the embodiment returned to earth and to the elemental phase, and the immortal, living spirit departed to a higher universe. After some time, the living spirit will return to earth as a living thing. Egyptian pharaohs fully believed in this mythology and preserved their physical bodies in sacred places for the living spirit to return.

As part of mythological knowledge, the power of the Creator, the primordial force, was believed to be ultimately responsible for the demise of everything; therefore, such powers were considered demonic and evil. To attain longevity, peace, and tranquility, various groups elected to perform personal and other kinds of sacrifices, such as the offering of oblations in the form of gifts, and the practice of continued personal devotion through hymns, prayers, chanting, and other forms of worship.

Inspirational Wisdom

During the Axial Age, the concept of inspirational wisdom evolved as humanity learned to practice logical and practical thinking. The concept of inspiration-based wisdom evolved as intellectual or real-world knowledge became an integral part of individual lives. Furthermore, higher intellect developed as changes took place in power structures from dynasties to king-warriors, which developed in tandem with advancements in trade among nations and the advent of organized educational systems, such as the teaching of science.

Throughout the inhabited world, individuals questioned the premises of myths and their associated rituals and practices that had been adopted by society to please the Supreme Being, such as idol worshipping, killing of innocent animals, and overall control of spiritual powers by the selected few. These questions led to gradual change as individuals used logical and practical methods to explain Mother Nature instead of relying on a mystical approach. This led to the development of practical thinking and the cultivation of philosophical fields of inquiry.

Further advancements led to subjective ways to investigate and understand the natural world. Individuals learned to invoke inner higher powers through concentration, meditation, and contemplation, commonly referred to as yogic practices. These practices were used to understand the workings of the Supreme Being responsible for the origin of life on earth and to explore peace and tranquility. Well-known books were based on this knowledge, such as the Book of the Dead, the Book of Solomon, the Talmud, the Tao, Shinto, the Rig Veda, and many more. Some of these have been lost along with their civilizations, such as the Mayan Indians.

Of all the most prominent is the Rig Veda, which probably is the oldest. During the period from 1700 to 1100 BCE, in the hills of the Himalayas, Aryans compiled these scriptures. Aryans later migrated from the Himalayas to the Indus Valley and then spread into various parts of the Middle East, especially Prussia. The original mythical knowledge of Mesopotamia adopted the Aryan knowledge. This led to a greater expansion in spiritual thinking as it migrated into the northern parts of Europe, Greece, other parts of the Middle East, and as far into Asia as northern China. Ultimately, during the Axial movement, it gave birth to a spiritual revolution that led to the formation of many cults, faiths, and religions, such as Zoroastrianism, Hinduism, Buddhism, Jainism, Sikhism, Confucianism, Taoism, Sufism, Hasidic Judaism, Christianity, and Islam.

With enlightenment attained through such spiritual evolutionary movement, spiritual scholars began to distinguish between two kinds of demise of individual embodiment, labeling one as permanent (death) and the other as impermanent (sleep). The enlightened souls came to realize that both are similar in nature, but in one case, the physical body's demise is permanent, and in the other, the physical body's demise is impermanent. In death, the manifested form disappears into its original elemental form and loses its identity. Such demise only comes to embodiments or physical bodies made from inert materials.

Therefore, enlightened souls determined that the cultivation of attachment to material objects is the source of disappointment and anguish. Some individuals came to realize that the demise of every inert or physical body is predefined and predestined based on its composition, structure, and environment.

Spiritual scholars accepted that the immortal living spirit

residing within the embodiment is predestined to leave the embodiment as part of the astral body while the remaining parts of the embodiment disintegrate and merge with its original source, the nature. However, the immortal living spirit, through its association with the mortal physical body, develops affiliations that generate blemishes that contaminate the astral body and generate incrustations on the living spirit. Just like associations with the earth, it suppresses the opulence of a diamond.

As a result, the immortal and pure living spirit is unable to merge with the eternal soul, and the living spirit is subject to cycles of life and death until the astral body is purified. When it is, that allows the living spirit to attain liberation and merge with the eternal soul. Therefore, the living spirit, though immortal, is subject to transient changes as it passes through different forms of embodiment. Thus, even physical death or total disappearance of individual embodiment is merely a transient phase. The changes caused by physical death are only realized and experienced through the sensory organs of living things, which in turn are responsible for dualities such as pleasure and pain, anger and peace, heat and cold, love and hate, happiness and sadness.

Enlightened souls during the Axial Age discovered that wisdom attained through inner inspiration was one of two kinds: lower or higher. Lower spiritual wisdom relates to understanding the forces working behind the manifested bodies; attaining such knowledge can be accomplished by studying spiritual scriptures, meditation, learning from other spiritual teachers, or even through challenging scientific discoveries and scientific knowledge. With this knowledge, individuals can unveil the limitations imposed by Mother Nature.

Higher spiritual knowledge entails comprehension of the

supreme powers operating and controlling unmanifested and unconsolidated parts of the universal system. With such knowledge, a seeker can unveil the limitations imposed by the perpetual essence to protect the true nature of the Creator. To comprehend these unidentifiable immortal forces controlling every aspect of supreme power, including the powers of Mother Nature, the seeker has to cultivate powers beyond intuitive, perceptive, and mystical abilities.

To go beyond intuitive, perceptive, and mystical abilities, a seeker must learn to stabilize one's mind from its usual oscillating state to become firm to acquire single-point focus through the process of meditation, devotion, and abandonment of all forms of thoughts and desires to achieve purity of the astral body. Once a seeker has achieved such a state, he or she can receive direct guidance from the living spirit to access perpetual essence, protecting the true nature of Creator that is providing the ultimate substratum to all its manifestations.

Transcendental Wisdom

With further advancements in transcendental wisdom, enlightened souls determined that the ultimate death of a living thing is not the physical death; rather it is the ultimate liberation of living spirit to unite with the eternal soul of the Creator, called *moksha*. With the understanding of such absolute truth, enlightened souls discovered that there is an unchangeable form within every changeable form. The living spirit is the source of oneness in everything. In every change, it provides a new substratum for all causations. For example, rain, snow, and steam are all forms of water, or its chemistry, which is the combination of hydrogen and oxygen, and the vital force of that bond. There is nothing else by which to explain rain, snow, and steam other than temperature change. The inner illuminated souls thus observe among these three changes a substratum water (H_2O), which remains unchanged.

Within this framework, spiritual scholars recognized the oneness within duality or multiplicity, and thus visualized the *absolute truth*—that all changes are immaterial and superficial. This realization brought an appreciation of the true meaning of life and death. With the acceptance of this absolute truth, individuals' views of life changed. The fear of death (which constantly haunts most living beings) was removed. The spiritual scholars who made this connection accepted the immortal role of the living spirit that is neither born nor dies; it only changes its form and not the substance. With such inner illumination, they acquired the ultimate strength to face their own demise (in the form of physical death) without fear, agony, or grief. By knowing that only physical matter or the material form is destroyed at the time of death, and the living spirit remains living until it merges with its perpetual essence to attain eternity, the concept of the rebirth of the physical body after death, as believed in the past, became baseless.

It was determined that the inert part of the embodiment being mortal returns to its elemental phase—just as gold jewelry (and, at some stage, even gold itself) loses its identity when melted, once the physical body and causal body go into their elemental form, they become part of the earth. Similarly, the subtle faculties and causal body after death are freed to join the vital energy that prevails throughout the universal system—just like, as a balloon pops, the air within the balloon merges with the atmosphere and becomes infinite, invisible, indestructible, invincible, and indescribable. Both the inert matter and the vital force go back to their origins once they have served their purpose.

Absolute Truth

Further advancements eliminated the fear associated with the supreme power of causations as being a demonic force. Love, faith, and respect for the Supreme Being as the source of all causation developed respect for the Creator as divine and not a devil. It brought further advancements in individual thinking and led to further discoveries in the fields of science, technology, and metaphysics, which led to the understanding of underlying forces responsible for the sustainability of the universal system and thus started to unveil the eternal wisdom called *Sat* or *absolute truth.*

With such perceptive thinking, individuals not only overpowered the limitations imposed by the power of nature, they also came to comprehend the four aspects of the supreme power of causations: vibration, time, space, and cosmic atoms. The scholars identified the power of vibration as the source of the generation of electromagnetic waves. They identified time and space as the source of extension and expansion created by the gravitational forces. The eternal energy, which prevails as the primordial force, is now identified as the force responsible for the creation of attraction and repulsion or magnetism that transformed "inert" atoms into "cosmic" atoms. Further, they identify this as the source of illumination and brilliance. Even today, many of these physical and nonphysical phenomena of illumination are constantly being observed and investigated by scientists and spiritual scholars.

At a higher level, spiritual scholars have determined that the living spirit residing within every living being contains the eternal wisdom, and any living beings can acquire, comprehend, perceive, and explore such knowledge through the invocation of individual living spirit. They determined that spiritual awakening is the only way to comprehend the inner workings of various segments of our universal system, including the development of individual embodiment. These powers of causations are all infinite, invisible, indestructible, immortal, and inconceivable; therefore, humans can only go so far to comprehend them through intellectual knowledge or scientific investigation.

In *A History of God,* Karen Armstrong shows that many human beings, from the Bronze Age to today, have attained spiritual wisdom; some have even gone beyond to acquire the *absolute truth.* Such individuals are respected as the true envoys of the Creator and have earned the utmost respect for their love of humanity, their selfless natures, and their ability to explain the unexplainable. With the attainment of spiritual wisdom and/or absolute truth, such individuals acquired noble temperaments. Their teachings are used even today to bring prosperity and long-term peace and harmony. Such envoys constantly help human beings who have become victims of the unbound materialistic desire to conquer and control lands and possessions of others. They even helped animals and other creatures that have fallen victim to malicious circumstances caused by humanity or Mother Nature.

These envoys use the support of immortal and indestructible divine powers that they acquired through eternal truth to kill or overcome demonic forces and reinstate faith, righteousness, and morality into their respective societies. Even today, such spiritual souls are respected as messiahs, prophets, *rishis,* sages, mystic souls, swamis, mahatmas, gurus, or spiritual teachers. Historical records show the human quest to find *absolute truth* reaches a new climax during periods of unrest and chaos.

Source Book

For centuries, the Bhagavad Gita has been recognized as a source of transcendental knowledge throughout the world. This knowledge is expressed in the form of a dialogue between Lord Krishna—the spiritual teacher, the Avatar, or God—and Arjuna, a friend, devotee, warrior, or seeker of knowledge. Arjuna, like any common human being, is facing the inner conflict between materialism and spiritualism, morality and greed, good and evil, and divine and demonic, which is described in the form of a battlefield that every human faces in life.

Arjuna, as a confused warrior, seeks advice from his friend Krishna to cope with the current situation or live in this material world full of conflicts. Arjuna faces conflict from his friends, relatives, teachers, and other innocent people and is caught in the middle of a conflict or war that is unjust—but has become necessary. The choice is between killing and overpowering the ruling evil forces and becoming a ruler of this unjust kingdom or walking away from this conflict and not worrying about the situation.

In this epic, the transcendental wisdom is passed from the teacher (God) to his student (devotee) in the form of a conversation or questions and answers with the objective to transfer the absolute truth in an abstract form by Krishna to

Arjuna. The knowledge transmitted requires personal analysis; therefore, each individual reading the Gita will come to his or her own interpretations.

The wisdom was originally developed by *rishis* as part of revelations and later were composed in the form of prose or hymns and transcribed into text and recorded as Upanishads. In the Bhagavad Gita, it is organized into eighteen chapters that were originally recited in the form of songs, called Songs of God. Later, it became a part of the Hindu epic called the Mahabharata. Over the years, the teachings from the Bhagavad Gita led to the development of the Vedanta that provided codes of covenant for the Hindu faith and several other religions.

Due to its complexity and the potential for multiple forms of interpretation or misinterpretation, the Bhagavad Gita requires an intensive, in-depth investigation to unveil the *absolute truth* encrypted within each word of the hymn and within each hymn itself. The Bhagavad Gita has been investigated, studied, interpreted, discussed, and even published in more than a hundred ways. Even after all such investigations, the book continues to unfold new knowledge and present new challenges.

This one book is still highly regarded as one of the best sources of spiritual wisdom. Many Indian leaders, including M. K. Gandhi (Mahatma/Freedom Fighter), Dr. S. Radhakrishanan (India's first president), J. L. Nehru (India's first prime minister), and Yogi Aurubindo Ghosh (the leading Indian nationalist) have used this book in their daily lives.

Around the world, well-known scholars, including Aldous Huxley, Albert Einstein, Dr. Annie Besant, J. Robert Oppenheimer, Ralph Waldo Emerson, Carl Jung, Heinrich Himmler, and Herman Hess, have studied and numerous times commonly quoted the book.

As a holy scripture, the world's well-known philosophers, scientists, metaphysicists, and transcendentalists have used this book as a reference. Immanuel Kant said, "[Vedic] knowledge [is] transcendental, which is concerned not with objects but with our mode of knowing objects." In *Walden*, Thoreau described the Gita as a transcendentalist's debt to Vedic thoughts.

Other well-known personalities have used this book as part of their investigations and writings. These include Henry David Thoreau, Margaret Fuller, Amos Bronson Alcott, Charles Timothy Brooks, Orestes Brownson, William Ellery Channing, William Henry Channing, James Freeman Clarke, Christopher Pearse Cranch, John Sullivan Dwight, Convers Francis, William Henry Furness, Frederic Henry Hedge, Sylvester Judd, Theodore Parker, Elizabeth Palmer Peabody, George Ripley, Jones Very, and many more.

In her new book *Great Transformation*, Karen Armstrong stated, "The Bhagavad Gita, as one of the last texts of the Axial Age, marks a moment of religious transition." She further states that the Bhagavad Gita has probably been more influential than any other Indian scripture, since it does not negate the spirituality of the Axial Age, but instead makes it possible for everybody to practice it. The spiritual masters used this book to develop practices such as self-awakening, self-realization, self-development, self-perfection, self-enlightenment, and self-illumination.

Humanity thinks it has come a long way—not knowing that the true journey has not even started.

Part 1: A History of Spiritual Evolution

A Brief Historic Review

A study of the history of religions as described in *A History of God* by Karen Armstrong shows that human beings have sought spiritual wisdom from as early as the beginning of the Bronze Age. Many have come to realize the powers of bliss and even have advanced beyond to become true envoys of the Creator to reinforce morality and bring peace and tranquility to the world. Armstrong's book clearly shows that the quest for knowledge has not been limited to any specific region.

History shows that this process of spiritual evolution starts once a living being accepts his or her spiritual ignorance and realizes the existence of the invisible supreme power, the ultimate source of all causations. Only humanity has fully developed subtle faculties of cognizance, the mind, intellect, and conscience, which jointly provide humans the unique ability to explore the unknown and comprehend the true relationship among causation, nature, and the Creator. Therefore, humans are the only living beings blessed with the ability to experience spiritual wisdom or attain absolute truth.

Humankind has already come a long way on the path of spiritual evolution; it appears to have started during the Bronze Age with the development of practical knowledge. In the Iron Age, our ancestors made significant progress in terms of transforming practical knowledge into intellectual knowledge; however, because of the need to progress in the material world, they acquired intellectual knowledge at a rapid pace—sometimes at the expense of spiritual knowledge. This led to an increase in mental anguish, emotional unrest, and further deterioration of righteousness. In the current era, we have expanded our intellectual knowledge into technological knowledge that is now being extensively used to learn more about the Creator and its creations.

Chapter 1
Mythology: Bronze Age

During the period from 120,000 to 24,000 BCE, Neanderthals lived on the earth. The Neanderthals possessed traits far more similar to animals than humans. According to archaeological records, the Neanderthals disappeared during the Stone Age and were replaced by modern humans, who first appeared in Ethiopia as archaic *Homo sapiens*. These early humans nursed the elderly and practiced ritual burials. Beyond the immediate requirements of procuring food, making coverings for the body, and building shelters, the culture included the practice of specific rites relating to death and burial. There is no established record of any major spiritual activities or revelations during the Stone Age.

The first record of holistic visions received by human beings recorded in caves around 4,000 BCE during the early Bronze Age. Within the ancient sacred scriptures, such revelations indicate there was a form of communication between divine powers and human beings. The information was transcribed in an abstract form and passed on from one generation to another until a much later date. There is no doubt that the sacred knowledge received as part of these revelations gradually changed as it was transferred from one cult to another. This information was largely used in the form of prayers, oblations, sacrifices (personal, and of other living things), plus the building of temples and shrines to honor the Creator and its divine powers.

Mesopotamian Region

One of the oldest available sacred texts of such holistic visions is clay tablets. In the tablets, such script was recorded in cuneiform around 2,600 BCE when the first highly evolved human beings experienced holistic visions describing the formation of earth. The cuneiform script described the origin of life on the planet in detail. These seven tablets, called *Enuma Elish*, describe how human-like beings appeared on earth and ultimately became the rulers of this planet. These people were different from common human beings; they were immortal and had divine or mystical powers of creation.

The Sumerians, who prevailed within the Mesopotamian region during that era, discovered the information. This information led to the development of the first available written mythology. This mythology is referred to as the "Epic of Gilgamesh of Babylonia." A copy of this historic document ended up in the library at Nineveh in the seventh century BCE. Archeologists uncovered it in the 1800s, and now it resides in the British Museum.

These seven tablets describe—with some accuracy—a power struggle, a civil war of sorts, among different divine powers that caused a catastrophic cosmic environment that brought into balance the supreme power of causation. This has been discovered by modern-day science through technological advancement—the origin of our universal system, the formation and alignment of planetary systems, the different stages of the earth's stabilization, and the origin of life on earth.

The ancient epic describes two kinds of primeval waters that prevailed on the planet: fresh flowing waters (rivers) and a body of stagnant water (oceans). The fresh flowing water coming from the ground was named *Apsu,* and the stagnant water or salty water of the oceans on the earth was named *Tiamat.* The divine power prevailing on the planet, described as wind, was called *Ea.* The wind power not only made tremendous noise or babel, but it also caused floods, storms, hurricanes, and tornados, which they named *Mummu.*

The wind, in combination with its related powers, was considered one of the most powerful divine forces on the planet. The other major divine power in the sky was an illuminated body like the sun, which they named *Marduk.* The sun was even more powerful than all the other powers residing on or above the planet. *Marduk* came to help and protect all the lower divine powers from the chaos, created because of continued disputes in the lower powers of *Apsu, Tiatma, Ea,* and *Mummu.* The lower powers gave *Marduk* the power to rule over the planet and appointed *Marduk* the king of the earth.

Marduk created a shield, the sky, to protect the divine lower powers prevailing on the planet from the powerful cosmic forces of radiation, gravitation, ultraviolet rays, and meteoritic showers. Further, *Marduk,* the sun, used its superior powers to organize planets and stars into a planetary system and established seasonality by organizing the orbital system that regulates the movement of the moon, providing light during the night when the sun is unable to do so. The lower gods or powers gave their allegiances to *Marduk* to protect the split that *Marduk* created between the cosmos and earth to protect the lower powers that prevail on the earth from demonic forces that prevailed within the cosmic region. This split also created a region beyond the sky where the eternal soul of the Creator, named *El*, provided a protective shield or a transitory home for individual living spirits that humanity identified as the "heaven in the sky" or *swarga*. Below the protective shield resided earth, which they called *Ki* or *Antu*. The lower divine powers and embodiments—consisting of the eternal soul in the form of living spirit—were able to coexist in harmony with the living force or lower divine powers. According to *Enuma Elish*, in Babylon (Mesopotamia) the residence of the *demigods* was established.

Based on this mythology, Mesopotamian civilizations accepted Babylon as the home of *Marduk* and thus built the first temple to worship the sun god. (Interestingly, even today, the hottest place on the earth is El Azizia in Libya, where the scorching temperature reaches 136 degrees Fahrenheit with the ambient surface air temperature recorded at 93 degrees Fahrenheit.) Sumerians respected the lower divine powers as *demigods* and believed all the higher powers or *deities* prevailed beyond the shield.

The Sumerians called *El* the High God of the Canaanites; they worshipped *El* as the Creator and the supreme power. *El* was responsible for the maintenance of peace and tranquility among these powers and was responsible for the causation, existence, protection, prosperity, and ultimate annexation of all these powers.

It is further described that High God *El* started the beginning of humanity on earth by creating an embodiment from dust (inert material) and placing divine breath or divine blood (living spirit) in it to start the first pair of living beings. According to *Enuma Elish*, each pair of emanations consisted of a divine male and divine female; at the beginning, there was no gulf between humanity and divinity (except that divinity was regarded as immortal and humanity as mortal).

With the passage of time, human beings changed, grew weaker, and became more attenuated as they moved further from the original divine source of creation. I believe this may represent the beginning of both physical and spiritual evolutionary trends. According to *Enuma Elish,* all these creations and transformations carried out in six divine "days" or six primordial epochs.

Based upon the mystical revelations of *Enuma Elish,* it led to the development of mythology to construct temples and perform devotional worship and sacrifices to please the divine powers and prevent them from performing evil acts. The mythology of *Enuma Elish* greatly influenced the civilizations living within the Mesopotamian region—and ultimately led to the development of the highly cultured civilization of the Canaanites.

Abraham later organized this group, which was known as the Israelites. Their reach eventually spread to all the surrounding regions and heavily influenced the development of Egyptian, Greek, and Persian, Byzantine, and Roman mythologies.

Middle East

In the Middle East, within the Old Iranian region, another mythology developed, which was based upon a divine vision received by a holy man named Zoroaster. This holy man introduced the concept of one God, the true Creator of the universe, whom he named *Ahura Mazda*. The holy man proclaimed that *Ahura Mazda was* the true source of all goodness and was worthy of the highest worship.

The holy man further proclaimed that demonic forces

called *devas* were created by *Angra Mainyu* to deceive humans and make them believe that *devas* were divine powers. Thus, humans were led away from the path of righteousness and subjected to the hostile spirit, the source of all sin and misery in the universe.

Ahura Mazda is superior to *Angra Mainyu*. This led to splitting the kingdom into two sections. One group, the *Mazdayasnians* (monotheists), followed the ideology of One God; the other group, who called themselves *Daevayasnians* (polytheists), followed different deities. The *Daevayasnians* became less powerful, and they moved away from Prussia, eventually joining the Indo-Aryan group to become part of *Brahmanism*.

The *Mazdayasnians*, however, stayed within their native soil of Iran and flourished as successful rulers, including the dynasties of *Achaemenidas*, the *Parthians*, and the *Sassanids*. The Muslim rulers who came from Arabia eventually overpowered these dynasties when they introduced Islam as the ruling faith. They later moved to India.

China

Further to the east, a Chinese mythology developed, which defined that in the beginning there was nothing on earth except for formless chaos. This chaos amalgamated into a cosmic "egg" for about eighteen thousand years and gave birth to duality called *yin* and *yang*. When *yin* and *yang* are in a state of perfect balance it produces harmony, which they called *Pangu*, the balancing power or the Creator of the universe.

A *Pangu* is a primitive hairy giant with horns on his head and wearing furs. *Pangu* created the universe by separating *yin* from *yang* with a swing of his giant ax, creating the earth (murky *yin*) and the sky (clear *yang*). To keep them separate,

Pangu stood between them and pushed up the sky. This task took eighteen thousand years; with each day, the sky grew ten feet (three meters) higher, the earth ten feet wider, and *Pangu* ten feet taller. In some versions of the story, *Pangu* created four prominent beasts, namely the turtle, the qilin, the phoenix, and the dragon.

According to scriptures, after the eighteen thousand years elapsed, *Pangu* disappeared. His breath became the wind; his voice became the thunder; his left eye became the sun; and his right eye became the moon. His body became the mountains and extremes of the world; his blood created rivers; his muscles became the fertile lands; his facial hair became the stars and the Milky Way. His fur became the bushes and forests; his bones became the valuable minerals; his bone marrow became sacred diamonds; his sweat fell and became the rain; the fleas on his fur were carried by the wind and scattered throughout the earth in the form of different forms of fish and animals.

Nuwa, the goddess, then used the mud of the riverbed to form the first humans. The first humans were individually crafted and very smart. *Nuwa* became bored of making each human individually, so she put a rope in the riverbed to soak it and then lifted it above the water, and the drops of mud that fell from it became new humans. These new humans were not as smart as the original unique humans were.

In Chinese shrines, stereotypical "caveman" regalia with long hair and leopard-skin tunics depicted as *Pangu* and as a symbol, such as the *baguna,* are associated with *Pangu* in these shrines.

Central America

In Central America, the Mayan people lived from 2,300 to 1,000 BCE. They developed into a complete, self-contained civilization. The *Popol Vuh*, the "Book of People," was established as their holy scripture. This scripture encompassed a wide range of subjects, including creation, ancestry, history, and cosmology.

The time of creation was nothing but dark and silence; like a peaceful night, there was no mobility at all. The divine spirits, the ancestors of creation, surrounded the water with light, but they all hid behind a cover of soft green-and-blue materials like feathers. They were super human beings. They were named *Gucumatz* and *Tepeu*, and above the earth in the sky was a "Heart of Heaven," which they called *Hurricane*, or "God prevailed."

In the darkness of night, *Gucumatz* and *Tepeu* received individually a message from the Heart of Heaven or so-called revelations. They agreed to unite their words and their thoughts, and they meditated until it became clear to them that when dawn broke, new life would appear on the earth, which would become trees, animals, and humankind. They witnessed three creations; the first they named *Caculha Huracan*, the second *Chipi-Caculha*, and the third, *Raxa-Caculha*. They determined jointly that these three represented the Heart of Heaven on earth. *Gucumatz* and *Tepeu* considered these the divine powers of the sun and the moon that were created to provide life and light and produce food and nutrition for all created beings.

They witnessed the creation of an empty void, and then water receded to form the sea, which made the space for the earth to appear as a solid. This was all done with the blessings of *Huracan*. Then there was light, which was followed by a dawn in the sky. The earth developed, and instantly there was a mist, and then there was a cloud of dust, and then the mountains appeared from the water and grew, and valleys formed. The groves of cypresses and pines put forth shoots together on the surface of the earth.

Gucumatz was filled with joy as he thanked the three divine powers—*Caculha Huracan, Chipi-Caculha,* and *Raxa-Caculha*—and said, "Your coming has been fruitful."

"And," they answered, "our work, our creation, is now finished."

There was no glory or grandeur in their creation and formation until the first human beings appeared. From these human beings, "hero twins" were born of *Vucub-Caquix*. The twins were named *Hunahpu* and *Xbalanque*. Their children, *Zipacna* and *Cabracan*, established the propagation process on earth. By using white and yellow corn, the gods created dualities, such as day and night, and calmness and wind. The twin hero wives then created more offspring.

Based on the mythology of *Popol Vuh*, these creations ultimately led to the development of a civilization called *Quiche*. The people of *Quiche* traveled into the mountains and found *Quetzalcoatl*, the feathered serpent lord, who provided them with the prominence to dominate and institute elaborate rituals and build temples and shrines. Later, many cities were established, and significant architectural structures emerged; fortifications were added later. Anthropologically, a classic period of civilization prevailed within Central America roughly between 1,000 and 790 BCE.

Indian Subcontinent

On the Indian subcontinent, according to Hindu mythology, the creation started with the formation of *Hiranyagarbha*, meaning the golden egg or universal embryo from which all manifestations originate and ultimately terminate. *Purana,* an ancient holy scripture, describes that after the great dissolution of the earlier universal system, there was darkness everywhere and nothing was moving. Out of this tranquil darkness, a supreme power, called *Svayambhu,* arose to create the golden womb, *Hiranyagarbha*, commonly known as *Brahma,* and then the supreme power itself entered into the golden womb as *Vishnu*, an eternal soul. This started the process of creation or manifestation. This process of origination, sustenance, and dissolution established *Trimurti*, consisting of *Brahma*, *Vishnu*, and *Shiva*. This multi-headed, multi-eyed, multi-footed, multi-armed, multi-limbed being was called *Hari*, the Lord Supreme—the undifferentiated substratum from which every manifested and unmanifested, visible and invisible form developed and continues to create, sustain, and dissolve.

Within the hills of the Himalayas, the spiritual scholars, the *rishis*, established that everything that exists between earth and heaven is contained within the golden womb. The supreme power, in its abstract form, can only be perceived by humanity through devotion, undivided attention, worship, and selfless sacrifices. Even though individuals can ignore its existence, the supreme power as the Creator never ignores or neglects its creations, including humanity. The supreme power always remains unmanifested and can only be seen as manifested through its divine creations, such as the light in fire, the sound in wind, the taste in water, the germination of seeds in earth, and, ultimately, as the mighty force of Mother Nature's natural creative phenomena.

This Vedic knowledge goes beyond the definition of the supreme power as the source of causation. It further expands to explore the fundamental elements of its causation and their purposes in life. As an illustration, Vedic knowledge explores the subjective aspects of each creation as the splendors or glories of God's creative ability to comprehend absolute truth defined as spiritual wisdom, such as the heat, glow, and other subjective aspects of fire.

An example of Vedic knowledge is an understanding of how the rising sun illuminates the glow of dawn and brings happiness to the individual souls at the same time that the rays of the sun take moisture from the surface of the ocean. The sun's rays transform the moisture into dark clouds, which, during particular months of the year, proceed with stunning speed, thousands of miles up in the sky at a height of four thousand to twenty thousand feet, supercharging the water particles with electricity to produce thunder, lightning, wind, and storms. These natural phenomena return the water molecules to the ground in the form of rain and snow, which ends up joining the ocean from where they started, thus completing a full divine cycle.

All this knowledge, compiled over many centuries into the Rig Veda, extended from the Indian subcontinent to the Middle East and further into the Ural Mountains. Even in areas beyond the Sintasha-Petrovka area, home to the Andronovo, people adopted the Rig Veda mythology, which included 1,028 hymns and 10,600 verses.

Within India, the Rig Veda were expanded to ten books called *mandalas*. These ten books included all the information originally composed by poets from different priestly groups over a period of several centuries, dating back to the period of roughly the second half of the second millennium BCE.

Chapter 2
Ideology: Iron Age

The Iron Age brought several modifications to existing mythologies with the large-scale migration of people from one part of the world to another. This not only resulted in the exchange of prevailing mythologies among highly evolved individual souls, but it also made humanity recognize peculiar characteristics among the various mythologies, including similarities and conflicts. This migration of people and the subsequent exchange of mythologies and ideologies led to an intellectual revolution that had a profound influence on human thinking, which gave birth to different interpretations and led to newer concepts. These included the acceptance of one God as the ultimate source of causation and the acceptance of supreme powers as the primary force of causation that influences each individual's life and destiny.

These aspects of spiritual thinking brought changes in economic, social, and political developments, including shifts from dynasties to independent rulers, monarchies into marketplaces, legends into logic, and the proving or disproving of philosophical views, which led to the development of intellectual knowledge and science.

Mystic scholars became spiritual teachers or prophets as they disseminated evolving new ideologies to the people. Independent rulers recognized the charismatic or magnetic personalities of holy sages and elected to incorporate them into their modified ways of ruling kingdoms. Humanity's desire to honor and worship divinity and deities—to acquire peace and tranquility—became an integral part of ruling kings and dynasties.

Recognizing their own limitations and abilities to learn and grasp subjective concepts and spiritual knowledge led many people to follow these prophets. Individuals became devotees or followers and spread the message of prophets to others with personal experiences, parables, and well-defined ritual practices. The fundamental change such ideologies professed was that humans did not have to fear the Creator or divine powers. Instead of being a fearful image, they started to change the image as they transformed God to be reasonable and understanding. They accepted God as a protector and helper to provide individual prosperity—for spiritual and material gains. The image of God changed from evil or demonic to noble and understanding of human needs.

Mesopotamian Region

The mythology introduced by *The Epic of Gilgamesh* of Babylonia led to the development of an enhanced culture based upon spirituality and gradually started to shift to materialistic values as the societies advanced within the Mesopotamian region. Two different accounts of the origin of life developed: one was based on creation, and the other was based on the great flood. This led to the division of the Canaanites into two groups—one worshipped the YHWH as the God, and the other worshipped the Elohim as the God. By the eighth century BCE, this led to the formation of the Kingdom of Judah, which worshipped YHWH as God. The Judeans believed that humanity (Adam) came out of the earth; therefore, there was no direct link between divinity and humanity. The Kingdom of Israel worshipped Elohim, or *El,* as God. They believed that God created living things by breathing life into an embodiment made out of clay or inert matter; therefore, all living things were inherently connected through the eternal spirit of God.

Indian Subcontinent

In India, spiritual scholars added two additional Vedas: the *Yajur Veda* and the *Samsa Veda.* The *Yajur Veda* included archaic prose mantras and, in some parts, verses borrowed and adapted from the *Rig Veda.* Its purpose was to make the knowledge practical and usable for other seekers of knowledge. Each mantra accompanied an action plan to supplement the described sacrificial rite. The *Samsa Veda* included 1,549 verses; only seventy-eight came from the *Rig Veda.* The spiritual scholars further modified the entire composition to fit the practice of rhythmic singing unlike the abstract reading of verses. Some of the verses repeated more than once to make it soothing to the ears and to help individual worshippers develop personal interest in following the rituals, spiritual practices, and liturgy.

The fourth, the *Atharva Veda,* incorporated the fast-growing needs of civilizations, and it included 760 verses; only 160 remained the same as in the *Rig Veda.*

These Vedas led to the urbanization of the *Harappan* civilization along the Indus River. Later, this developed into the Indo-Aryan civilization that spread throughout the northern part of the Indian subcontinent and extended all the way to the east into Prussia.

China

In China, the ideology incorporated three forms of divinity: *Yuanshi Tianzun, Lingbao Tianzun*, and *Daode Tianzun*. Each divinity represented three deities or heavenly kings—Yu Huang, Beiji Dadi, and Tianhuang Dadi—and eight immortal demigods that ruled the earth. These eight immortal demigods are He Xiangu, Cao Guojiu, Tie Guaili, Lan Caihe, Lu Dongbin, Han Xiangzi, Zhang Guolao, and Han Zhongli.

This reformed ideology spread into many neighboring countries, such as Korea, Japan, Taiwan, and Singapore. This ideology was further modified to include the belief that one should give up one's life, if necessary, either passively or actively, for the sake of upholding the cardinal moral values.

Chapter 3
Doctrine: Axial Age

Further advancement in humanity and the development of philosophical thinking led to the development of doctrines. During the period from 800 to 200 BCE, now formally recognized as the Axial Age, these new doctrines brought a major societal shift as revolutionary ideas of individual spirituality came to the forefront. In addition to the realization of absolute truth by revelations, individuals believed they could attain spiritual wisdom directly through invocation of a living spirit and/or the perpetual essence of the Creator. Individuals no longer needed to depend upon divine revelations.

Humanity started to take responsibility for individual actions and activities as more people began to accept that individuals could influence the future or even control their ultimate destiny. As a result, dependence upon external powers or holistic visions started to diminish with the growth of a new sense of personal responsibility. The use of a logical and reasonable approach to comprehend the influence of internal and external nature on individual temperament gained control. Practicality and logic became an integral part of civilization. During this period, many highly learned scholars throughout the world archived their forays into inner enlightenment, and they started to preach a logical and reasonable approach to exploring the supreme powers of causations through theology.

Middle East

One of the first prophets to preach theology was the Hebrew prophet Isaiah in 800 BCE. While serving the Kingdom of Judah, his teachings compiled and presented in the form of the Book of Isaiah. Well-recognized prophets, such as Jesus Christ and Muhammad, quote the book, and his teachings have become part of the Torah (the Hebrew Bible). In the Quran, even though Isaiah is not specifically mentioned by name, his teachings are recognizable, including the exhortation that outward observance of and service to the Creator is not enough, but that humans must discover the inner meaning of their faith.

Isaiah teaches that God wants humanity to take responsibility for its actions and incorporate compassion, morality, and righteousness into daily life instead of worshipping demonic behaviors by oblations and sacrifices covered with blood. Isaiah's teachings look at life in a more practical way, and the admonition to perform actions and activities with compassion for all living beings was incorporated within the Torah (Exodus 4:11).

Further evidence of the development of theology comes from the ancient Greek civilization, which began in 600 BCE and continued through the Hellenistic period, until it was incorporated into the Roman Empire. During this period, the Greeks incorporated a variety of subjects—including political philosophy, ethics, metaphysics, ontology, logic, biology, rhetoric, and aesthetics—in the development of their theological practices.

The influence of ancient Greek theology gave birth to

Hellenistic philosophers, including the world-renowned philosophers Socrates, Plato, Aristotle, and Pythagoras. A sixth-century mystic philosopher, scientist, and a true man of wisdom, Pythagoras was specially influenced by the ideology introduced by Indo-Aryans via Persia and Egypt. Pythagoras said, "The human soul represents a fallen, polluted deity that incarnated in the body as a tomb and is doomed to perpetual cycles of rebirth." He further professed the reincarnation of the soul, repeatedly, into bodies of humans, animals, or vegetables until the soul becomes immortal.

Pythagoras became an elaborate legend; both Plato and Aristotle later followed him. As a supernatural figure, people believed he had the ability to travel through space and time and communicate with animals and plants. He established the Pythagorean School in Athens that influenced many students seeking higher knowledge. He helped people invoke intellectual thinking and thought-provoking ideas and philosophies. Socrates, Plato, and Aristotle held open discussions on a number of subjects, including logic, mathematics, philosophy, science, astronomy, and theology. Intellectuals traveled from Italy, Egypt, Cyrene, and countries farther afield to acquire higher knowledge and wisdom at this institute. Ancient Greek philosophers later provided a new way of thinking to Islamic philosophers and became the prime impetus of the Western or European Renaissance.

Indian Subcontinent

Within the Indian subcontinent, the transformation of ideology came in the form of the Vedanta doctrine and led to the creation of the Upanishads. The first Upanishad, called *Isa*, elaborated in detail the concept of the eternal soul that resides within each manifested body, including embodiments, which provide a dwelling to house the living spirit, a part of the eternal soul. As part of the immortal soul, the living spirit provides living beings the ability to acquire knowledge; therefore, it is called "the seat of knowledge."

The second Upanishad, called *Kena*, elaborates the true nature of the immortal living spirit that continues to prevail in an unmanifested, invisible, and incomprehensible form, directing all the activities of divine creations. The third Upanishad, called *Katha*, follows to elaborate the process of attaining liberation of living spirit or eternal sanctity. The *Katha* also covers the process of attainment of *absolute truth* and ultimate union of living spirit with the eternal soul. Therefore, it refers to the "death of the teacher."

The fourth Upanishad, called *Prasna*, deals with the source and functioning of the living force that creates the link between living things and the Creator. It is also responsible for the causation of Mother Nature that directly or indirectly influences individual temperament. The fifth Upanishad, called *Mundaka*, identifies two forms of spiritual knowledge; one is objective, and the other is subjective. The sixth Upanishad, called *Manduka*, elaborates the purpose of subtle faculties such as the mind, intellect, wisdom, conscience, and the astral body—and their purposes in life.

The seventh Upanishad, called *Taitteiya*, elaborates on the impact of the transition of matter from its objective to subjective forms, such as "from food to joy." It discusses how individual desires transform living beings' needs into wants, wants into greed, greed into ego, and ego into arrogance. The eighth Upanishad, called *Aitareys*, deals with the interrelation between attachment to material things and the impact on individual personalities and relationships with other living things.

The ninth Upanishad, called *Chandogya,* outlines the process of rituals, worship, oblations, and sacrifices used for the renunciation of selfish desires. The tenth Upanishad, called *Brhadaranyaka-Brahman,* deals with the cycles of life and death and overpowering the shackles of nature to attain eternity.

The development of such doctrines encouraged a young man named Siddhartha Gautama, a son of the king, to leave his family and all of his wealth to discover "enlightenment." In 600 BCE, he became a devotee of spiritual wisdom and proceeded to unveil the *absolute truth*. He grew up in the northeastern part of India where Vedic Brahmanism sought eternal truth, and Hindu priests or Brahmans controlled it. As a young man, Siddhartha did not agree with this teaching and decided to search for eternal truth by himself. After many years of suffering and living with the continual suppression of human desires, he eventually adopted a path of moderation. Instead of living from one extreme to the other, such as self-indulgence or self-mortification, Siddhartha started to perform undivided divine devotion through meditation and contemplation. He found a place to sit under the *pipal* tree and vowed not to arise until he had found eternal truth.

After a reputed forty-nine days of meditation, at the age of thirty-five, Siddhartha realized—through inner enlightenment—the cause of suffering and determined the necessary steps to eliminating such sufferings. By giving him the title of "Buddha," the enlightened soul, Siddhartha earned the honor of being the first enlightened soul of the century. His findings became the Four Noble Truths that later became the heart of Buddhist teachings. For the remaining forty-five years of his life, the Buddha traveled to China and other parts of Asia to teach his findings.

China

Within mainland China, Buddha's teachings were incorporated with the ideologies of Confucius, which were already being modified to incorporate the doctrines of Taoism.

Chapter 4
Spiritualism: Inspirational Age

Increasing advancements and developments in science and technology accompanied by inspirational or motivational thinking, which started in 200 BCE, rapidly displaced doctrines that had spread throughout the world. With the growth in motivational thinking, increasing numbers of people started to accept the two fundamental aspects of existence: matter and spirit. Ideologies that could not support the combination of matter and spirit had to change. Scholars started to discover how the creation of the universe and principles of faith could explain the unexplainable. This led to the spiritual evolution based upon inner inspirational movement to comprehend spiritual wisdom buried within the ancient scriptures.

Middle East

Within the Middle East, Greek philosophies, which had already provided pragmatic ways to delve into the meaning of life, led the Hellenic culture to adopt spirituality or inner motivated spiritual thinking as eternal wisdom. The eternal wisdom attained by the Greeks of Alexandria reflected some of the earlier work of Solomon, which was included in the Book of

Proverbs (one of the books of the Old Testament). This book, compiled in the first or second century BC, suggested humans must respect the glories of God, and YHWH as the symbol of God. Even though elaborated as more pragmatic, the original sources of King Solomon's teachings remained an important part of Greek spiritualism.

According to the Book of Proverbs, God devised a master plan at the time of the creation of this universe that provided humans the ability to glimpse into God's creation as well as into the affairs of all other living things. The major difference between the Jewish and the Greek concepts of the attainment of absolute truth resides in the method of realizing that truth. Jewish scholars following the Kings of Judah continue to believe that absolute truth can only be attained through revelations, such as messages directly received from God (YHWH). They believed that God is from heaven and man is from earth; therefore, there was no kinship between God and humans, and they worshipped the powers of the temple. Greek philosophers believed there was a direct or kin relationship between humans and God; therefore, any human being, through his or her own efforts, could attain spiritual wisdom and come to realize the *absolute truth* through revelation.

After the Roman army burned the Temple in Jerusalem, they made the city of Jerusalem into a Roman city and sent the Jews back into exile. The Jewish community broke up into various sects, which revolutionized the inspirational thinking already simmering within the Jewish community. The Essenes and Qumran adopted to live in monastic-style communities that extended beyond the Dead Sea. They believed God resided within brotherhoods instead of manmade temples, and they worshipped the "temple of the spirit." They believed in purifying themselves through baptismal ceremonies and communal meals, and they practiced forgiveness as a means to purify sins instead of making animal sacrifices to please God.

Another group, known as spiritual Jews, believed that God was present in the humblest homes. They looked for signs of God's presence in the smallest details of daily life. They learned to practice invocations of the living spirit instead of going through priests or temples. They started praying as a group, practicing loving-kindness, and performing charitable acts and selfless services, which they called *Mitzvah*. They believed God (YHWH) was the ultimate divine entity who directed humanity from heaven, without any direct link. They further believed God (YHWH) was intimately present within humankind and remains an integral part of human life to the minutest detail.

During the period from 45 to 30 BCE, the conflict between the Greeks and the Jewish people regarding the proper way to invoke God—the Greeks through enlightenment and the Jews through revelation—reached its peak as Vedanta philosophies introduced into Prussia by the Indo-Aryans started to be adopted within Greek schools of higher knowledge.

Philo of Alexandria, a renowned, prominent, and highly respected philosopher, followed Plato. While he remained a devout Jew, he introduced *logos* to help alleviate the dispute between the two schools of thought. Philo of Alexandria used metaphor to support his *logos* to fuse the differences and harmonize the Greek philosophy with the Jewish theology. He combined Jewish methods of interpretation with the *Stoic* philosophy and suggested that destructive emotions were the result of errors in judgment; any man with moral, righteous, and intellectual perfection could overcome such emotions and therefore not suffer from anxiety, inner unhappiness, or other negative emotions. He saw no incompatibility between the Jewish God and the God of the Greeks, even though he considered elaborate Jewish allegories to be an embarrassment.

As a Jew, Philo believed that God revealed himself to his disciples or prophets; as a philosopher, he accepted that there was an active and ongoing relationship between cosmic conceptions and human liberation of spirit. He was of the opinion that it was the moral duty of the virtuous to comply with the laws of nature; as a Stoic philosopher, he accepted this as a way of life. He also believed the best way to know the true nature of a person was to examine how he or she behaved—not just what the person said. Furthermore, he supported the thought that we can never know God in its true form; however, he did believe that God communicates with humanity through its supreme powers.

Philo introduced two aspects of God. One relates to the essence or spirit of God, which is entirely incomprehensible and remains shrouded in impenetrable mystery; he called this *ousia*. He defined the other aspect of God as existing in different manifested forms of energy through which God appeared. He believed that highly evolved individuals could comprehend such powers, which he defined as *dynameis*. *Ousia* and *dynameis,* working in unison, were the *kingly powers*, through which God revealed the order of the universe, *logos*, and exposed or revealed himself through a state of bliss that was bestowed only upon selected members of humanity. Philo believe that humans could catch a glimpse of divine reality through these blessings.

Philo also believed God had a master plan of creation to materialize the formation of our universal system. He defined this plan as being a part of *logos*. No human, under normal conditions, could reach God or attain the highest divine truth, and humans could only capture God through an ecstatic state.

Like Plato, Philo saw the soul as being in exile, trapped

within the physical world by matter, and waiting to ascend to God, the true home, leaving passion, the senses, and even language behind, all of which bind humans to the imperfect world. Once an individual achieves ecstasy, the soul lifted above the dreary confines of the ego to a larger, fuller reality. Later, when their rabbis recommended, all the other Jews, who had lived in *diaspora*, endorsed such a pragmatic approach.

During this period, a charismatic Jew known as the faith healer named Jesus began his career by following the newly discovered path of spirituality. Many of his followers perceived him as a new Moses, a new Joshua, or the founder of Israel. After his death, his followers believed he was divine and started to worship with the understanding that Jesus was God in human form; this led to the formation of the faith known as Christianity. Later people started to refer to Jesus as the Son of God, but Jesus never claimed to be God. Jesus went out of his way to emphasize that he was a frail human who would one day suffer and die like other common human beings. His followers later accepted him as the one true God.

The Romans helped enhance the image of Jesus with the creation of a new holy scripture. The New Testament included the ancient wisdom of the Jewish Bible, the Old Testament. The New Testament propagated Christianity as a newfound religion to gain control of Rome from pagans who had become a great threat to the Roman Empire.

Within the Arabian region, for many generations *Quraysh* was the dominant tribe. They were a branch of *Banu Kinanah* and descended from *Khuzaimah*. This tribe remained completely disunited until Qusai ibn Kilab first consolidated it through war and diplomacy. Qusai became the self-declared first king of the region where Muhammad ibn Abdullah, or Muhammad, the founder of Islam, was born in AD 570. As Muhammad, he provided evidence of attainment of inner inspiration to acquire spiritual wisdom and ultimate *absolute truth*.

According to Islamic belief, at the age of forty, Muhammad adopted the practice of meditating alone for several weeks every year in a cave on Mount Hera, near Mecca. According to several sources, during one of his visits, he received divine bliss through an angel, Gabriel. Upon receiving this revelation, Muhammad became deeply distressed, and the revelation was paused for three years, during which Muhammad gave himself to prayers and spiritual practices. When the revelation resumed, he was reassured, and then he commenced preaching. Though the revelations were accompanied by mysterious seizures, Muhammad was able to distinguish the divine messages as part of revelations.

The key theme of the Quran is that every human should worship the Creator, ask for his forgiveness for sins, offer frequent prayers, assist others, particularly those in need, cast off cheating and the love of wealth, and never kill an innocent life. Muhammad started preaching three years after his first revelations. He taught that the only way to salvation was by publicly proclaiming, "God is one," and surrendering to him completely. He later moved to Medina where he helped unite several conflicting tribes.

After eight years, he took control of Mecca, and his followers increased to more than ten thousand. He died in AD 632, and all his revelations later consolidated into what became the Quran, the holy scripture of Islam.

The Islamic faith is based on the ideology that "God is one," and it encompasses all the primordial faiths and revelations that were received by other prophets in the past, including Abraham, Moses, and Jesus. According to historic records, many believed that Muhammad belonged to the group called *Hanif* and was one of the descendants of Ishmael, son of Abraham, which ties his early heritage to the Israelites or Canaanites. The spiritual thinking of Islam elaborated during the eighth and ninth centuries to encompass Islamic laws pertaining to religious rituals, personal hygiene, burial of the dead, and the mystical aspects of one's individual relationship to God. These were called *hadith.*

The two largest denominations of Islam are *Shisum* or *Sunnisum*, each of which follows a different set of *hadith.* Both have played a major role in the development of Islamic sciences, philosophy, laws, and culture. Sufis, who are known as Muslim mystic souls seeking the inner meaning of life, follow different customs, *sunnah,* which are based on principles of attainment of ultimate unity with God. Sufis respect Muhammad as both a prophet and as a perfect saint, and they consider him their spiritual ancestor.

The basic difference between Muslims and Sufis is that Muslims believe they are on the pathway to God and will meet with God upon death, whereas Sufis believe they are on the pathway to God and it is possible get closer to God by embracing the divine presence in this life. The chief aim of a Sufi is to seek divine bliss by working to restore within the body a primordial state of being or *fitra*, described in the Quran as the pure state at the time of birth.

Indian Subcontinent

In the Indian subcontinent, the growth in spiritual thinking led to the development of schools based on specific Yogic Sutras, including *Brahma-Sutra, Sariraka, Vyasa-Sutra, Badarayana-Sutra, Uttra-Mimamasa*, and *Vedanta-Darshana.* Reinterpretation of the Upanishads led to the creation of these sutras and the formation of the Vedanta school. Each was based upon the interpretation of the sutras. The basic premise of each individual school was to provide spiritual wisdom for the fulfillment of human quests to acquire *absolute truth*.

Each school developed yogic practices based on mental concentration, meditation, contemplation, and devoutness as means to invoke the inner living spirit to attain higher knowledge and ultimately acquire *absolute truth.* To invoke the living spirit, specific codes of covenant were defined, such as divine devotion, love for humanity, and practicing morality and righteousness. The process of *Bhakti yoga,* a well-defined method of self-perfection, ultimately became a common practice. The sutras contained within Bhakti yoga established substratum that ultimately helped develop a coherent and logically advanced civilized system called Hinduism.

Vyasa introduced the Brahma sutra doctrine of "One and only one," and all other scholars accepted the Brahman as the *absolute truth*. However, each elected to give a different name to the same entity, such as *Ishvara*, *Baghawan*, *Paraatama*, and so on. Because of its perplexing nature, several interpretations developed, of which only six were considered important. Ultimately, only three were predominately used, creating the *Advaita* school of thought, the *Vishishadvaita* school of thought, and the *Dvaita* school of thought.

The Hindu sage Ramakrishna describes the concept of Brahma as follows: There were two birds; one was perched at the highest branch, serene, majestic, and divine. The other bird was at the lowest branch, restless and unhappy, eating fruits that were sometimes sweet, but sometimes they were sour or bitter. These best illustrate the underlying concepts of such interpretations. Every time the bird on the lower branch ate a bitter or sour fruit, he looked at the bird on the top branch and climbed one branch higher to get closer to that content bird.

Eventually, the lower bird reached the top and realized that he was now the same as the divine bird that he had wanted to be. He soon realized that, at all times, there was only one bird; the restlessness of his mind had created the illusion of two birds and the consequent sense of separation. The fruits in this story represent the karmas, the restlessness is the human soul, and the majestic bird denotes the absolute, the God.

The *Adaita* school of thought, propagated by *Adi Shankra,* ultimately led to the development of a scripture called "The Song of God." It provided the fundamental guidelines for individuals seeking higher divine knowledge to comprehend the supreme power or Creator and to attain freedom from the shackles of this material world or from the cycles of life and death. "The Song of God" later incorporated with the Hindu spiritual epic *Mahabharata.* It is now referred to as *The Bhagavad Gita,* the source of eternal wisdom. The Bhagavad Gita is now used by Hindus to worship Lord Krishna, the Hindu god of wisdom and internal happiness.

China

In China, Lao-Tzu introduced Tao ideology which, like Buddhism, explains the primordial force that provides the natural order of all existence. Tao principles are ineffable and have qualities that prevent it from being defined or expressed in words. The principles of Tao can only be experienced through practice, but they cannot be defined by any physical form or in any material way.

Much of East Asian philosophical writing focuses on the value of adhering to the principles of Tao and outlines the various consequences of failing to do so. Taoism intrinsically relates to the concepts of *yin* and *yang,* where every action creates counteractions, which are an unavoidable movement of every manifestation.

Chapter 5
Materialism: Egocentric Age

Materialism has displaced spiritualism only to accommodate the growing human desire to acquire and build a materialistic society or to maintain a capitalistic lifestyle. Today, most people fulfill their spiritual needs through following an organized religion. Most live with the misconception that religion is the same as spiritualism. There is no denying that spiritualism and organized religion are related. In truth, spirituality encompasses everything covered within organized religion; however, no single organized religion encompasses every aspect of spirituality.

Organized religion accounts only for a fraction of spiritualism, and it does not address the human need for spiritual wisdom or explore the subject of *absolute truth*. It even refrains from supporting the individual quest to discover the unknown aspects of nature other than what scientific investigation has already proven or established as fact. Even most of the teachers or spiritual scholars of religion do not comprehend the divine powers of the Creator responsible for our creation, sustainability, prosperity, and annihilation—or understand the true meaning of eternal wisdom.

To put it simply, organized religion is more like understanding the workings of a light bulb, whereas spiritualism is like comprehending everything about electricity—and what is operating behind the light bulb.

In spiritual terms, eternal wisdom is comprehending *absolute truth* or unveiling the supreme power of the Creator. Absolute truth is a multi-layered body of knowledge; an invisible layer of ignorance protects each layer. For this reason, revelation of the absolute truth is attaining knowledge through unveiling each layer of ignorance. This process is called self-perfection or spiritual evolution. It is similar to peeling an onion to find the core; each layer is separated from the next layer by a thin membrane that acts as a barrier to attaining eternal truth.

First Barrier

The first barrier of ignorance is manmade; it is commonly identified as the individual ego. In practical life, as soon as humans come to comprehend a certain aspect of material or spiritual knowledge, an invisible power is born. This immediately creates an artificial barrier of ignorance, called human ego. Just like a dense dust storm, the creation of ego blocks an individual's power of rational thinking and leads him to believe he is better than others are; therefore, he or she does not need to go further.

Second Barrier

Over time, the individual ego transforms into arrogance and becomes a self-generated second barrier of ignorance, which limits the individual's ability to explore further or attain higher knowledge. The individual thus wrongfully stops seeking—without realizing that arrogance is only a transitory barrier that he has created because of a lack of knowledge. It is similar to an individual driving on a highway; the limitation of human vision makes it appear that the road is getting narrow ahead, and it merges with the sky at the end. This illusion appears real until the individual elects to continue driving, and it ends up moving even farther away. Similarly, the path of knowledge to spiritual wisdom is a continuous process; however, due to the transitory ignorance created by human arrogance, most individuals elect to accept such breaks within the continuous process as the final ending and never proceed past the ego.

Third Barrier

The third barrier of ignorance is created by a lack of understanding of the complex laws of nature, operating to maintain equilibrium and balance and bring harmony and tranquility. These laws of nature are complex and cause duality and sometimes multiplicity. Both the material way and the spiritual way are part of these laws of nature. Just like the head and tail of a coin—one cannot exist without the other. Unfortunately due to ignorance, humans consider these two approaches as alternatives and select the material way, which is easy to follow and can provide identifiable rewards. Humans elect to ignore the spiritual way, which is difficult to attain and brings rewards that are subjective and doubtful. Such selection creates imbalance and causes inner conflicts that gradually develop into anguish, mental turbulence, depression, and melancholy. History has shown that such imbalance on a large scale can lead to war, major social upheaval, the downfall of empires, or major natural disasters.

Fourth Barrier

The fourth barrier of ignorance originates from the misconceptions created by mental or intellectual limitations; if something cannot be proven by science or technology, it must not exist or it cannot be true. Human misconceptions can over time transform into beliefs—and then they become facts. For example, before it was scientifically proven that the earth is round, the misconception that the earth was flat was accepted as fact. Another example is darkness, which for generations was considered evil; now it is accepted as nothing more than a shadow or a proven scientific phenomenon.

Fifth Barrier

The fifth—and the biggest—barrier of ignorance originates from a lack of faith in the supreme power. Humanity today views the existence of the invisible and incomprehensible supreme power as a figment of human imagination; therefore, humanity sees no need to explore or investigate such power. The source of such ignorance comes from the shrouds created by the supreme powers to separate the mortal from the immortal and material from the spiritual. These shrouds generate doubt or uncertainty within the human mind and lead the individual to disobey or defy codes of covenants. This entices the individual to follow the path of immorality. Lack of faith also causes individuals to perceive having powers greater than supreme power; therefore individuals learn to disregard the existence of a living spirit residing within the embodiment.

The best way to comprehend the existence of living spirit is through the investigation of the state of consciousness. For example, during the energetic state of being (the active state), the human embodiment is under the direct influence of material nature. During the pre-sleep state (the awakened state), the embodiment goes into a resting phase where it starts to come out from the direct influence of material nature. During the preconscious state of being (the sleeping state), the embodiment goes through a transitory separation between human embodiment from the influence of the material nature. Then, during the subconscious state of being (the deep sleep state), the living spirit establishes a transitory link with the individual embodiment, and it brings the embodiment into a state of balance to provide the necessary tranquility or peace.

Many individuals even today cultivate faith and devotion to go beyond this state of consciousness to invoke the power of the living spirit and seek guidance and wisdom. Some even go further through a meditative state to attain ecstasy or inner tranquility. There are spiritual scholars who use single-minded focus and undivided devotion to attain freedom from the embodiment and have out-of-body experiences.

In the following chapters of this book the underlying principles are explored in detail to unveil the secrets of eternal wisdom.

Through history, we learn our past.
Through experience, we acquire knowledge.
Through devotion, we realize the eternal truth.

Part 2: Elements of Spiritual Wisdom

Highly evolved spiritual souls have found that, without spiritual wisdom, it is impossible to go beyond the material world to unveil the invisible, incomprehensible, infinite, and immortal nature of the supreme powers. Humanity currently focuses upon intellectual knowledge as a means to uncovering the secrets of Mother Nature. The intellectual knowledge comes from an understanding of practical and physical aspects of actions and activities; however, it does not help individuals comprehend the subjective or spiritual aspect of actions and activities. For example, through intellectual knowledge, we can learn all about the physical and chemical properties of water, but how water germinates life remains unanswered.

Within the holy scriptures, the Vedas, the Upanishads, and the Bhagavad Gita, spiritual wisdom is subgrouped as lower spiritual wisdom and higher spiritual wisdom.

Lower Spiritual Wisdom

The lower wisdom relates to an understanding of the living spirit residing within the body.

It also encompasses its relation to the everyday life of individual living beings. Such knowledge encompasses understanding individual actions and activities and learning to bring individual lives in balance with the codes of covenant. Spiritual scholars and prophets have used such wisdom to justify the establishment of different religions and sects.

Higher Spiritual Wisdom

Higher spiritual wisdom relates to understanding the relationship of the living spirit with the eternal soul or the perpetual essence of the Creator residing outside the human embodiment.

This wisdom is mystic in nature and requires nonphysical means, such as control of individual subtle faculties and subtle actions, such as single-point focus, concentration, meditation, and contemplation.

A combination of the two prepares an individual to attain bliss or acquire higher perceptive to comprehend the invisible relationship between the individual living spirit within the body and the eternal soul, the primordial force that is prevailing throughout the universe. Through an invisible network, it connects all the creations with the Creator or what forms the trinity. The understanding of this relationship is called the *absolute truth,* which in spiritual terms in the Vedas is defined as the eternal truth, *Sat.*

With the attainment of eternal truth or *Sat,* one can unveil the mysteries of the supreme power of all causation prevailing within and outside our universal system. In this book, lower spiritual wisdom is also referred to as *spiritual knowledge,* and the higher wisdom is referred to as *transcendental knowledge.* They are not alternatives; they are complementary and successive. For example, to comprehend the *transcendental knowledge,* one has to acquire *spiritual knowledge.*

Section I:
Spiritual Knowledge

The process of comprehension of spiritual knowledge starts with the acceptance of the existence of a supreme power, even though there is no clear consensus as to who the ultimate Creator is. For centuries, out of respect, humanity has opted to honor such supreme power as the God or the true Creator who is responsible for the creation of the universe and everything else that prevails within it. Within the Abrahamic conception, God is monotheistic; in the Christian conception, God is Trinitarian. In the Islamic conception, God is the Absolute; within the Hindu conception, God is one but can appear differently and is given names that vary by region, sect, and caste. Fundamentally, the name of God is truly a by-product of individual perceptions that an individual assigns to an unknown entity that can provide support to an individual to fight inner conflict.

The Creator itself is neutral in nature; therefore, it can change depending on individual preference, confidence, belief, and ultimate faith. It is just like water; it is neutral in taste but has the infinite ability to quench thirst. To meet individual specific preferences, people put different flavors in water; some prefer to drink Pepsi, Coca-Cola, limewater, beer, wine, or whisky. In *absolute truth*, we are all drinking water, and its substratum remains a combination of two molecules of hydrogen and one molecule of oxygen.

The Vedas teach that the Creator shields itself by its own nature; infinite, invisible, immortal, and incomprehensible powers protect the nature of the Creator; therefore, it will always remain unknown and beyond comprehension even with advanced science and technology. Further, the only way to comprehend or realize it is through personal experience.

A well-known Hindu spiritual scholar, Ramakrishna, best described the relationship between a living being and the Creator as similar to a silkworm in its cocoon. A silkworm is encased in the cocoon spun by its own effort; similarly, we are entangled in the meshes of our own desires, and thus we get lost within our own creations. Just as a silkworm gradually metamorphoses into a butterfly and breaks open its cocoon to come out and never return, we only learn to realize our true nature when we develop into the fullness our Creator meant us to be. When that happens, we never return to our old nature.

The Bhagavad Gita illustrates the relationship between creation and the Creator in the form of an invisible and indestructible eternal tree called the *ashwattha* tree. The *ashwattha* tree grows upside down from a space far beyond the sky; it grows to extend right down to the earth or ground. The tree continues to receive its nutrition from a substratum above the roots; the nutrition trickles down to the tree trunk and extends right into the earth.

In the Gita, the *ashwattha* tree is born from substratum from which it receives the eternal energy that provides various parts of the tree the ability to flourish and grow. The part closest to the substratum is the eternal soul that gives birth to the roots that form the tree. It is comparable to the celestial part of our universal system that is in its initial phases of development. The branches of the tree that are closet to the earth represent the terrestrial part of the solar system that forms environments to permit leaves, flowers, and fruits to grow and provide nutrients for living things.

Just like leaves, flowers, and fruit, we all survive for a short time to serve our respective obligatory functions; once our function is complete, we all disappear. Eventually, based upon our inherent characteristics and DNA, we appear again as creatures, animals, birds, and living human beings to perform our responsibilities.

Similarly, the Quran describes the Creator as a force that is responsible for the causation of the universe and for the maintenance of equilibrium without any incongruity or discord. It describes the Creator's hands as its kingdom; the Creator's will is its power. The Creator does whatever the Creator desires to maintain harmony between the different parts of the universe and safeguards it against ruin. The Quran further describes that the Creator uses different devices to maintain harmony and balance at different levels of manifestation. It is suggested that we must respect such powers and worship the powers of the Creator to continue to yield the beneficence that each divine power is specifically designed to generate.

According to the Vedas, the process of knowing spiritual wisdom requires individuals to understand the basic elements of spiritual wisdom. Through investigation of the holy scriptures, I have identified five main elements—faith, covenants, creation, omnipresence, and encirclement—that establish the foundation for lower spiritual wisdom or spiritual knowledge. To further elaborate upon these elements, I have used the information included within the Upanishads and the Vedas and used the discourses published by many authors in specific reference to chapters 2, 7, 15, 16, and 17 from the Bhagavad Gita.

Faith is the true foundation of every aspect of spiritual wisdom.

Chapter 6
Faith

Initiation

Human faith, the first element, appears at first in the form of confidence. Once an individual receives rewards from performing actions or activities, confidence begins to be transformed into trust. Over time, the performance of selfless actions transforms individual trust into faith, and performance of selfish traits transforms individual trust into the cultivation of attachment to material possessions that transforms confidence into ego.

Faith and ego represent two sides of a coin. Selfless acts instill an altruistic character, and selfish acts instill an egotistic nature and character. An altruistic nature transforms an individual's quest to unveil the invisible power of the ultimate Creator, Almighty God. The faith itself fuels and ignites the fire to seek spiritual knowledge. Individuals in this process go through three levels; each level reflects the individual's involvement and his or her commitment to knowing the absolute truth.

Highest Level

At the highest level, an individual displays the desire to abandon all forms of attachment to materialistic possessions and materialistic longings. Individuals perform every activity and function in true devotion to the Creator and nothing else. Humanity respects them as holy prophets, noble souls, and sages. Even after death, their deeds and contributions to society are remembered for centuries.

Second Level

The second highest level includes individuals who are passionately committed, both mentally and spiritually, to pursue life by following the divine covenants. They remain unselfish as they obligate themselves to serve others and help advance society as well as protect other living beings. Humanity respects them as noble rulers, kingly warriors, and spiritual masters. They are, however, prone to be dualistic in nature; their faith can easily transform from divine *yakshas* into demonic *rakshasas.*

Third Level

The third level includes energetic people who elect to follow selfish goals and become very possessive of their material gains. They use their possessions to benefit only themselves and accumulate material wealth, power, position, and control to pursue personal motives. Such individuals exploit others who they deem beneath them, including innocent, hardworking, conscientious people, such as skilled workers, farmers, manual laborers, and others who perform services. They use faith as means to enhance their personal goals. Such people ultimately become victims of their greed, and they lose perspective of true spirituality.

They often end up idolizing someone or something just to fulfill their spiritual needs. When they go even further down and lose total respect for faith, they become thieves and murderers and perform other criminal acts without any remorse. They even elect not to believe in divine worship; instead, they choose to follow specific convictions, personal beliefs, voodoo rituals, or black magic. Ultimately, they develop evil or demonic personalities, or *rakshasas*.

Functionality

In terms of functionality, individual temperament determines individual personality. The external environments influence each human being differently at different times. The impact of external environments is defined as a trait of nature *(gunas).* The *gunas* arouse different types of reactions within the human mind, depending upon individual temperament. They generate impulses that are unique in nature, and they produce distinctly different performances among different living beings.

Even though the process followed by living beings may remain the same, depending on individual personal circumstances, time, and place, the outcome can vary from individual to individual. The continually changing external environments create different stimuli, and the impact on individuals varies from person to person. Therefore, each of these *gunas* creates multitudes of emotions where each emotion influences individuals in a different manner. With proper observation and analysis, an individual can determine what type of *guna* is governing his or her life at any given moment.

There are three kinds of *gunas: sattwa* (good), *rajas* (middle), and *tamas* (bad). The impact of any specific *guna* depends on an individual's spiritual development or faith. In terms of progression, the *sattwa guna* arises with the detachment from traits of the *rajas guna*, and the *rajas guna* arises only after the elimination of all the ignorance associated with the *tamas guna*. The three *gunas* remain active at all times; only when one *guna* becomes predominant do the other two *gunas* become less active, but they continue to function even when they have become dormant. Whichever *guna* is predominant; its characteristics will dominate the individual's personality. There are nine openings in the physical human body, including two ears, two eyes, two nostrils, a mouth, a sex organ, and an organ of excretion; through these nine apertures, the living spirit interacts with the natural world. The first seven apertures receive and display the presence of *gunas* within the human body. Of the other two organs, one acts as the source of purification through the excretion of waste, and the other produces sexual desires to encourage reproduction. From nine openings, individuals exude the dominance of specific *gunas*. When one *guna* rises to the top in a human personality, the two other *gunas* do not disappear; they start operating on a secondary level.

An individual under the influence of the *sattwa guna* displays a personality of unassuming purity, stainlessness, transparency, and an inherent essence of greatness. The influence of such a *guna* brings genuine happiness and contentment, and it further ignites the inner quest to go beyond and attain unity with the perpetual essence. When an individual's living spirit is in tranquility, the individual personality reflects dominance of the *sattwa guna*. It exudes purity, nobility, genuine compassion, happiness, physical comfort, and love. When it exudes greed and selfishness, it reflects the dominance of the *rajas guna*.

When it exudes demonic traits, it reflects the dominance of the *tamas guna*.

Longevity

The influence of *gunas* is like a metal wire tightly wound on a spool. For example, if the wire remains coiled for a long time it acquires the memory, which over time, becomes an integral part of the wire—and the wire remains coiled even after it is unwound from the spool. Similarly, individual personality traits acquire residual memories that do not die with the demise of the physical body. They become part of the astral body and transfer from one life to the next life; once carried for several life spans, they even become inherent traits. Such traits carried from one life to another, just like DNA, become part of the genes and are transferred from one life to another life.

These residual memories create an inert barrier, limiting the ability of the living spirit to provide individual embodiment, knowledge, and guidance to perform actions in conformance with laws of morality. As part of acquiring faith, the individual learns to invoke the living spirit and acquire spiritual knowledge through which they learn to control the mind and desires and overpower individual subtle faculties to allow the living spirit to manage and guide individual embodiment. If an individual does not follow such a path, the individual continues to chase the same pattern or can spiral downward on the path of birth and death.

According to the Bhagavad Gita, cycles of birth and death go on until the astral body becomes free from blemishes of residual memories, and the living spirit is liberated from the astral body to join the eternal soul. Therefore, spiritual scholars consider birth and death as points of transfer within the spiritual journey of individual living beings.

Even though there is no physical relationship between the old and new physical bodies, the activity performed during the previous life establishes the substratum for the new life. This process is similar to a traveler changing hotels along the journey to attain eternity.

At the time of death, if individual astral bodies have overpowered even the influence of *sattwa guna*, the astral body departs as spiritually evolved. It is destined to acquire new physical bodies with the potential and opportunity to reach a higher level within the process of spiritual evolution. Similarly, astral bodies that are predominantly under the influence of the *rajas guna* are placed within families that are already established and prosperous. This way, they can quickly realize that the material world provides temporary happiness and enjoyment, and they quickly cultivate a longing for freedom from materialistic bondage through self-realization. If they still do not make any further progress, they are subject to the same future—or even go backward. Some even become lazy and inactive; they lose *rajasic* predominance and come under the influence of *tamasic* predominance. Gradually, they recede to the extreme lowest stages of the *tamas gunas* as they learn to act and behave more like animals and spend their whole lives eating and sleeping.

Standing

At the current level of spiritual evolution, the majority of humans appear to be born with a living spirit that is not totally transformed into a transcendental spirit. Their spiritual temperament falls between the *rajasic* and *tamasic*. From birth, the aspect of spirituality comes mixed with a demonic nature. Their souls, from birth, are prone to materialism and egocentrism; at the same time, they are able to comprehend the existence of divine powers and have the ability to comprehend the concept of the invisible, incomprehensible, undefined nature of the Creator.

The majority of such individuals find it very difficult to worship the invisible form of the Creator, and they find the concept of faith very difficult to accept. Out of fear or for selfish reasons, they choose to worship demigods or some form of physical object they can visualize in their minds. They learn to respect the laws of holy scriptures and pursue established religious organizations based on the scriptures or teachings of spiritual masters. They find the practice of undivided divine devotion unnecessary, and therefore, all their actions and activities focus on the acquisition of material resources and the performance of services to fulfill individual responsibilities.

They do get involved in activities to serve the community or fight noble causes, and they will even give their lives for a moral cause, but in most cases, they perform these activities with some form of selfish objective. They find some form of selflessness in everything they do. Many individuals who are born with the mental disposition of a *rajasic* nature often get themselves trapped in the possessive powers associated with this temperament; they use worship and faith as a means to disguise their underlying motives. These hypocrites deceive themselves; they are never able to rise above the basic level of faith and continue to be born life after life without making any progress in the cycle of human spiritual evolution.

It is evident that some people are even born with an impure mental disposition with *tamasic* traits. They are born with the mental disposition to seek only sensory gratification. They become victims of demonic forces and evil powers. They come under the control of cult leaders, and they prefer to perform devotional observance to dead spirits and other forms of evil forces. They remain misinformed, law-breaking criminals; they are malicious and unable to recognize the existence of divine powers or the divine spirit. They continue to live miserably and cause pain not only to their physical bodies but to all other living beings.

As described in the Bhagavad Gita, faith does not rule one's nature. The mental disposition does not rule one's faith—even though they are intertwined and influence individual temperaments, it is possible, though not easy, to change one's nature by remolding or changing one's faith. Therefore, with the shift from one faith to another, most individuals experience a change in their personality, convictions, and temperament.

In general, individuals with a *sattwic* temperament represent wholesomeness, passivity, morality, and goodness; their quality of faith leads them to follow spiritual and mystical practices to worship the Creator. Individuals with a *rajasic* temperament represent diverse, obsessive, selfish, and passionate desires; due to different beliefs, they follow organized religion and practice worship specific to demigods or idols. Faith by itself does not relate to the physical body in their estimation; therefore, any change in individual faith does not physically change the individual being. However, a change in faith does affect the individual's mental disposition and brings subtle changes in the individual's nature and behavior.

Sages always teach that, to improve one's actions, one must improve the true force behind the action. The mental activities create desires. One can stabilize the mind through faith. On the contrary, the lack of faith causes individuals with a *tamsic* temperament to display a lazy, demonic, or lethargic nature. They follow cults, practice voodoo magic, engage in thoughts of the supernatural, worship evil spirits and spirits of the dead, or are fascinated with ghosts and demonic powers.

Many do not recognize the existence of divine powers or the divine spirit; they live as atheists.

In general, it is the desire of every human being to have the temperament of a *sattwic* personality, and many individuals with *rajasic* or even *tamasic* temperaments try to display a *sattwic* personality by imitation. They are able to display such façades only for some time; they are not mentally equipped to cope with the inward spiritual vitality associated with the true *sattwic* personality. This leads to physical discomforts, doubts, and inner weakness. They often develop mental illness and waste their energies needlessly; the process in no way helps cultivate true faith or the mental temperament of a *sattwic*. This senseless torture often leads to an unnatural temperament and causes the individual to adapt demonic actions and activities. They can lead the individual to an even lower temperament than the *tamasic* and make such individuals behave like animals.

It is natural for living beings to detach from the materialism; therefore, the living spirit provides to each divine manifestation, including divinity, demigods, archangels, humanity, and even some very advanced members of the animal kingdom, the ability to attain higher knowledge and overcome such weakness.

History shows ancient prophets who cultivated undivided faith in the powers of the Creator attained this level of wisdom. This higher knowledge was received by humanity directly through inspiration or indirectly through messages from demigods in the form of covenants, which led to the development of commandments and austerities to help individuals cultivate faith, seek higher knowledge, invoke the living spirit to attain transcendental knowledge, and cultivate a true *sattwic* temperament. Periodically, humans have developed specific processes and practices to attract others to join a particular cult or organized religion. Such practices may bring temporary peace and happiness, but they also can lead to torture in individual organs in the physical body—and even indirectly stop the living spirit residing within the body from providing guidance.

Cultivation

The type of faith that feeds and nourishes an individual's temperament depends on four basic elements of that individual's life. The first includes the fulfillment of individual necessities to survive, such as which foods to eat *(sarvasya)*. The second has to do with the nature of sacrifices *(yajna)* that an individual aspires to make to know the truth. The third is the texture of individual strictness *(tapas)* one follows to integrate the functioning of the physical body, the causal body, and the astral body to comply with covenants and attain divine wisdom or revelations. The fourth has to do with the quality and quantity of charitable acts an individual performs *(daana)*. Each of these represents a transitory level that gets absorbed into the next higher level until the temperament is completely transformed—and the living spirit is linked to the eternal soul. Each of these four elements is subject to three traits: purity *(sattwic)*, passion *(rajasic)*, and dullness *(tamasic)*.

Cultivation of Individual Faith

The Three-Fold Faith

Faith "Sattawic'	Faith "Rajasic"	Faith "Tamasic"
Temperament *Pure*	**Temperament** *Passionate*	**Temperament** *Dull-witted*

Basic Elements

Faith "Sattawic'	Faith "Rajasic"	Faith "Tamasic"
Food Intake *Fresh* *Oleaginous* *Agreeable* *Pleasant*	**Food Intake** *Bitter* *Sour* *Saline* *Pungent*	**Food Intake** *Stale* *Tasteless* *Putrid* *Rotten*
Sacrifices *Selfless* *Morality* *Duties* *Dedicated*	**Sacrifices** *Selfish* *Ostentatious* *Vanity* *Glamorous*	**Sacrifices** *Devilish* *Immoral* *Hoarding* *No rituals*
Austerity *Physical Body (Celibacy)* *Causal Body (Firmness)* *Astral Body (Serenity)*	**Austerity** *Physical Body (Hypocrisy)* *Causal Body (Oscillating)* *Astral Body (Transitory)*	**Austerity** *Body (Self Torture)* *Causal Body (Demeaning)* *Astral Body (Wicked)*
Charity *Timely* *Discrete* *Selfless* *No obligations*	**Charity** *Convenient* *Display* *Selfish* *Return expected*	**Charity** *Wrong place* *Unworthy* *Disrespect* *With insult*

Illustration 1: Cultivation of Individual Faith

Food (Sarvasya)

The intake of food is essential to life, and it directly influences the level of human energy. It influences individual abilities and temperament, including laziness, being active and energetic, contentment, greediness, and even demonic tendencies. The primary purpose of food is to provide energy—and anything beyond that serves only the sensual needs. Individuals make food choices based on the signals received from the human thought processes; selected food contributes to the development of individual temperament. For centuries, sages have suggested that one can learn to modify individual temperament with the modification of food intake. Food intake is grouped into three categories.

Sattwic Foods

Sattwic foods include those food products that purify the physical body and provide vitality and longevity. Seekers of higher spiritual knowledge eat only foods such as milk, milk by-products, natural sugar, simple carbohydrates, fruits, and vegetables. They refrain from eating foods that induce any form of sensual desire; they only eat unprocessed food in its purest form.

Rajasic Foods

Rajasic foods include those food products that create sensual desires and generate the urge to acquire or own material things. This type of food builds physical strength and includes meals produced from the slaughtering of animals as well as full-flavored spices and oily or fatty materials. Eating these foods creates restlessness and mental anguish and contributes to a passionate desire for sensual activities. These foods also contribute to physical pain, bodily unrest, and mental aggression and grief.

Tamasic Foods

Tamasic foods include food products that contribute toward laziness, lethargy, and ignorance—and bring out latent demonic attitudes. This type of food generates inherent odor and includes liquids that are not fresh and commonly are of a fermented nature, such as beer, wine, and liquor.

Sacrifices *(Yajna)*

Sacrifices relate to the offering of oblations in the form of detachment from material things. Sages have found that the practice of offering sacrifices helps humans transform egoistic personalities into altruistic personalities. The sacrifices can be grouped into three categories:

Sattwic Oblations

Sattwic oblations include sacrifices that are offered strictly in accordance to guidelines established within the holy scriptures—and nothing else. Such services free individuals from any form of desire or expectation and are conducted with the unsolicited desire to help or for the betterment of humanity in general. With such services, an individual is able to invoke the supreme powers of the Creator. They perform such sacrifices in secrecy without any form of physical display or personal attention.

Rajasic Oblations

Rajasic oblations include sacrifices that are offered to cover selfishness and use sacrifices or oblations to display a commitment to higher powers. These oblations are based upon individual obsession and the passionate desire to acquire material gains, fame, and nothing else. Therefore, these include ostentatious prayers, building of temples, and donating to charities for personal gains.

Tamasic Oblations

Tamasic oblations include sacrifices that are normally used to honor and worship demonic and evil powers and to show off superiority over righteousness and morality. These include the slaughtering of innocent animals as a gift to please the evil spirits.

Strictness *(Tapas)*

There are individuals who elect to go beyond these sacrifices and practice celibacy to serve the supreme power or eternal soul. Through such sacrifices and devotion, they are able to access the powers of the divinity and cultivate the temperament that gains genuine respect as the sanctified soul, such as Jesus Christ, Muhammad, Buddha, Lord Krishna, Moses, or Abraham.

Sattwic Strictness

Such strictness is followed by sanctified souls who have fully accepted that the Creator prevails beyond the universal system—and everything else is in his image or represents his power. These sanctified souls control their subtle faculties in such a manner that their speech causes no excitement, and it is truthful and pleasant. They maintain tranquility and serenity of mind through self-control. They overpower delusions, created through the traits of divine nature, such as different shapes, colors, forms, races, and beliefs and accept everything as created equal. It is only through balancing the individual mind that they are able to understand that these differentiations are only illusions and not reality.

Rajasic Strictness

Saints and *mahatmas* who practice principles of nonviolence and worship the supreme powers that prevail within the manifested parts of the universe or the solar system, such as deities, demigods, archangels, and even divine envoys, practice such strictness. They acquire wisdom through revelation or through enlightenment. They study holy scriptures, and they follow principles of morality. They seek the union of the living spirit with the perpetual essence to attain absolute truth, and they strive to control the powers of inner consciousness by practicing meditation, contemplation, and undivided devotion. This cultivates good-heartedness and transforms their humanly love *(chit)* into divine love *(chitta)*. With such good-heartedness, they bring inner happiness to others. Such noble souls receive honor and respect from humanity as *mahatmas*, saints, or spiritual leaders.

Tamasic Strictness

Tamasic strictness in those with *rajasic* temperaments who practice austerities with selfishness turns their powers of goodheartedness *(yakshas)* into demonic powers *(rakshasas)*, and the individual's temperament transforms from *rajasic* to *tamasic*. When this happens, the individual cultivates faith in evil spirits and deliberately hurts people and other living beings. Physically, the living being remains the same; only the individual temperament transforms.

Charities *(Dannas)*

With the invocation of an individual's inner living spirit, the faith of that individual takes on a new perspective. Performances of charitable activities become part of the natural divine covenant, originally created by the supreme power to keep the universe in balance. The principle of charity *(dannas)* was established at the time of the manifestation of our cosmic system. As faith takes on a new perspective, individuals realize this principle as part of inherited instinct. Individuals start to express such change through natural expressions, such as "Every sacrifice is another gift," "Saving one life saves many lives," "Giving is divine; grabbing is sin," and "Charity is next to God."

Individuals come to accept that everything on earth is blessed with certain hidden qualities and certain weaknesses; each blessing is assigned a specific purpose to help others who are deprived of such abilities. Therefore, charity is an act of willingness to share whatever one has with another who lacks such a divine gift. There are three kinds of charities: *sattwic, rajasic,* and *tamasic.*

Sattwic Charity

If such an activity is performed without any expectations—and is performed for someone who is unable to attain the gift or pay it back and is not associated with any form of public display—the charitable act becomes *sattwic.*

Rajasic Charity

If charity is given with some form of expectation or return, it immediately changes from being pure, *sattwic,* into *rajasic*, or impure.

Tamasic Charity

If the charity is given with evil thoughts or motives, is given to the wrong person, is given at the wrong place or the wrong time, or is given without any humility, the charity immediately transforms to *tamasic.*

In terms of accomplishments of faith, there are two kinds of people. The first group includes individuals who are born with astral bodies that are free from blemishes or residual memories. The second group includes those who are born with astral bodies contaminated with blemishes or residual memories. Irrespective of the condition of the astral body, the individual's commitment and devotion determine his or her ability to overpower the traits of human nature and formulate a modified individual temperament. If an individual practices the four elements of individual life as described above, the individual temperament is modified, and he or she goes above the purest *sattwic* temperament, the individual receives eternal bliss—and his or her soul is sanctified.

This allows the individual's living spirit to establish a link with the eternal soul, which causes the individual's body to go through a transformation, which in spiritual terms is expressed as a *revelation* or an experiencing of the *absolute truth.* The individual acquires a new outlook reflected through the aura as a brilliant radiance. The enhancement of the individual's personality brings happiness to all who encounter such an illuminated soul. If the individual practices three austerities with underlying selfish objectives of recognition, glory, honor, or ostentation, they are unable to receive this inner radiance. They will only receive ostentatious forms of honor and welcome, which generate transient forms of peace and tranquility.

Individuals who are able to cultivate faith—and are able to go beyond the *sattwic* temperament—come to comprehend the three phases of the Creator: undifferentiated, differentiated, and embodied. This first phase represents the Creator in the form of unity, which in spiritual terms is defined as *divinity,* or the true image of the Creator. The second phase includes the differentiated or duality, which in spiritual terms is defined as *deities* or presence of the Creator in the form of opposites, such as positive and negative or male and female. The third phase includes the appearance of the Creator in multitudes of embodied forms, ranging from unmanifested *(demigods),* semi-manifested *(archangels),* to fully manifested *(divine envoys),* and living things *(living spirit).*

Sanctification

As part of this sanctification, a devotee first overpowers his or her human nature, and then he or she attains detachment from the powers of the living force that is responsible for the creation of multiplicity and duality. Devotees unveil the mysteries of the Creator through attainment of *absolute truth* and realize that the Creator is the "one and only" controller of all supreme powers.

In the Bhagavad Gita, this unification is defined as *"Om-Tat-Sat."* In the New Testament, it is expressed as the Trinity of the Father, Son, and Holy Spirit. In science, this is described as the mass (M), energy (E), and electromagnetic waves (EM) producing illumination. It is the same phenomenon that led Einstein to formulate his famous equation of $E=MC^2$.

All these expressions represent that Almighty God is "one and only one"—even though it takes on different forms, ranging from unity and duality to multiplicity. This is likened to how milk can take the form of butter, cheese, or yogurt, but none of those forms can exist without the milk.

According to the Vedas, a combination of these three words, *Om-Tat-Sat*, represents the three ultimate phases *(nirdesha)* of the existence of the Creator or its supreme power. In practical terms, it also reflects the three forms of manifestations: eternal, unborn, and born.

Om **(Unborn)**

The first word, OM, according to holy scripture represents the unborn vibration, the ultimate source of all creations and existence. It prevails throughout the universe and even extends beyond the universe. It is provides the ultimate substratum to all creations, including the entire universe.

In terms of science, OM is comparable to *dark matter,* which is hypothesized to account for a large part of the total mass of the universe. It is not possible to see dark matter—even with the most sophisticated telescopes; evidently, it neither emits nor absorbs light or other electromagnetic radiation. Its existence and properties are inferred from gravitational effects on visible matter, radiation, and the large-scale structure of the universe. According to scientific estimates, dark matter constitutes 84 percent of the matter in the universe and at least 23 percent of the total energy density.

Tat **(Born)**

TAT represents the perpetual essence or the supreme power of the Creator that is infinite, invisible, and inconceivable—and prevails throughout the universal system. *TAT* represents the living force and the living spirit, the two aspects of the perpetual essence responsible for the manifestation of physical bodies. In the Hindu religion, uttering the word *TAT* is commonly is used to invoke the living spirit to attain divine blessings and acquire knowledge; therefore, it is always used as part of a sacrifice of austerity—as well as part of the performance of every action and activity. *TAT* is also used in prayers to attain divine strength for detachment, renunciation, and abandonment of the materialistic world.

In scientific terms, *TAT*—within the cosmic and celestial part of the universe—reflects the supreme powers responsible for the causation of gravitational, electromagnetic, and magnetic waves.

Sat **(Eternal)**

SAT is a symbol that represents the absolute truth or the ability to know the supreme power that prevails beyond the universe, above which there is nothing. There are many who practice to attain *SAT* without undivided devotion. They do not realize that without undivided devotion, seeking *SAT* is similar to an action performed without intent; it generates only movement and achieves no other result. Similarly, faith without undivided devotion is *Asat*. One cannot hope to attain eternity without undivided devotion.

Morality is divine; only humans make it demonic.

Chapter 7
Covenants

Covenants

Covenants, the second element, are nothing more than principles established by the primordial forces to keep the universal system in equilibrium. They allow every creation to exist in conformance with the laws of balance, poise, and the capacity to endure changes in environments. The covenants at the human level include morality, righteousness, and kindness. They have been passed through the powers of the living spirit from divinity to deities, deities to demigods, demigods to divine angels, divine angels to divine kings, and finally to living beings. The process of comprehending covenants is accomplished through understanding the mystic powers of attraction and repulsion.

The mystic power itself is neutral; however, as stated earlier, it has two aspects. One is called divine *(yaksha)*, and the other is demonic *(rakshasas)*. They operate opposite of each other, and they are trying to overpower one another at all times. The law of equilibrium keeps them in balance through physical and spiritual activities.

For centuries, scientists and sages have studied the divine principles of equilibrium. Their findings are compiled in books of ethics. These books are regarded as sacred testaments. Irrespective of faith or religion, all these books emphasize the same basic principles; even after centuries of continued usage, revisions, and interpretations, only some exceptions have been made to fit special situations. Even after changes in culture, human values, and technology, the fundamental principles have remained the same, and teachers of these scriptures still emphasize the same elements to attain balance, peace, and tranquility.

Code of Conduct

The principal aspect of a covenant is the code of conduct that affects the course of an action. The main element that influences the transformation of desires is attraction or repulsion, which transforms want into greed. This power of transformation in the Vedas is defined as the powers of *maya,* the ultimate source of delusion and illusion. St. Thomas Aquinas defined this as "a sin against God." Dante classified this power as lust, gluttony, sloth, greed, wrath, envy, and pride—the Seven Deadly Sins. Fundamentally, each one of these is associated with the cultivation of an attachment to an anticipated result. In the Gita, it is defined as the underlying force that transforms selfless acts into selfish acts. It can be also expressed as the force that determines the result of a coin toss.

A seeker practices the highest yoga (*vibhaga yoga),* which delineates the relationship between elements and the attributes of nature. It offers an explanation of the inquisitiveness of the seeker to know who is the Creator of the world, who is running nature, and who created all living things. Individuals prepare an embodiment to free individual living spirits to merge with the perpetual essence of the Creator. The seeker fully understands that, at all times, the demonic forces are continuously operating against the divine forces and influence living things at various levels.

Lowest Level

At the lowest levels, these forces appear in their demonic forms of materialistic desires, which cause individuals to perform *akarma* yoga. They cause attachment and create greed. When greed is not controlled, it transforms into egotism and gives birth to jealousy and competitiveness, and it can entice individuals into performing selfish actions. At such a level, they remain harmless and short-lived.

Highest Level

At the higher levels, these demonic forces transform individual *akarama* into vindictive behavior, *irsha,* and it transforms egotism into anger, arrogance, and ultimately leads the embodiment to perform demonic acts. Individuals start to acquire things belonging to others and gain control of others. The demonic control clouds thinking, just as dense smoke overpowers the burning flame. The demonic forces take full direct control over the individual's astral and causal body. Individuals perform brutal acts of torture, murders, and mass killings.

To keep demonic forces subdued, a seeker learns to follow the code of conduct and cultivate a respect for all of creation manifested through the supreme power. Concurrently, the individual must follow a path of nonviolence to cultivate love and respect for the living spirit residing within every living being. A seeker respects and honors the different supreme powers regulating the universal system. A seeker follows the principles of undivided devotion and personal austerities and sacrifices. With these practices, the individual's temperament is modified as he or she comes to realize the true nature of divine and demonic forces. A seeker also comes to understand that human temperament is of a transitory nature, but it can be transformed through the modification of individual actions and activities.

A seeker learns that each desire generates additional desires; therefore, desires never end and generate a compounding impact. A simple desire to acquire material objects can very easily lead to the path of possession and an unbound quest to accumulate wealth and power. This will lead to controlling others and their possessions. Individuals can demonstrate a commitment to morality and righteousness through false pretenses and perform services just for image; every spiritual activity they perform is full of hypocrisy.

Individuals perform superficial acts of morality to fend off any evil spirits. Even though these demonstrations are moral, the activities remain selfish. Each action remains full of maliciousness and wickedness; the underlying desire is to obtain rewards. For such personalities, the selfless acts remain of no value. Individuals cultivate stronger selfish desires, which have no possibility of giving up the attachment to material gains and acquired powers and thus they eventually cultivate evil temperaments.

There are selected individuals who fully understand the shortcomings of materialistic attachment, and they learn to perform selfless acts and adhere to modes of goodness. They diligently strive to comprehend the elements of morality and seek self-awakening, thus reversing the process of empowering the demonic powers.

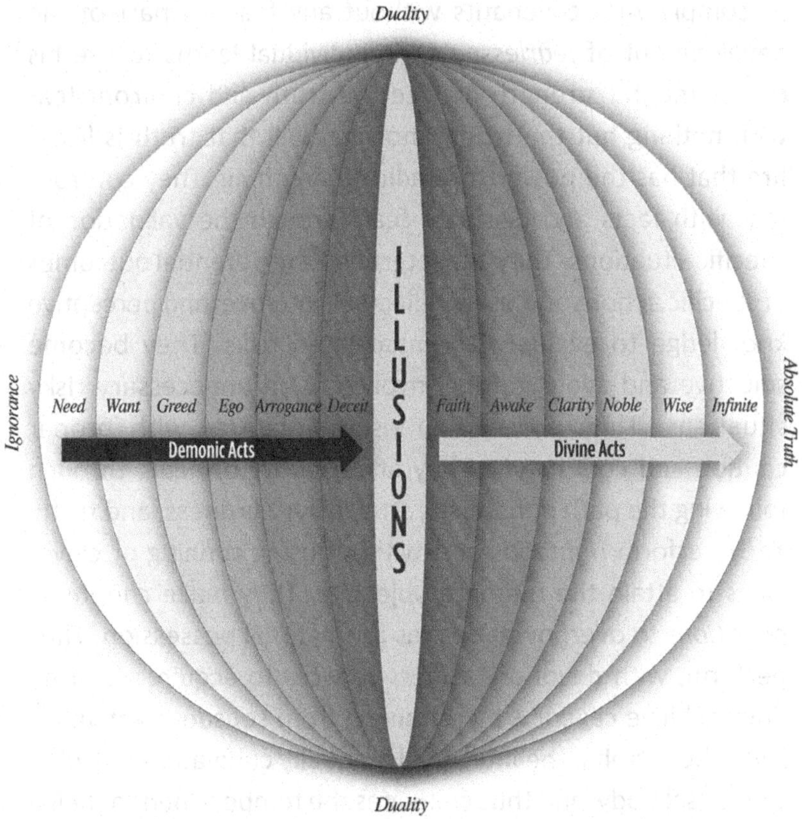

Illustration 2: Impact of Codes of Conduct.

Elements of Covenants

The divine code of covenants—morality, righteousness, and humanity—consists of twenty-five traits. These traits are interrelated and interconnected. To understand these elements, they can be grouped into three categories: a better way of life, higher knowledge, and liberation.

Better Way of Life

In terms of a better way of life, the most important trait is to comply with covenants without any fear. As part of the development of *fearlessness,* an individual learns to use his or her mental strength to face the truth and confront fear with nothing but the truth, knowing well that truth is like a fire that has the power to eradicate anything. They confront fear with facts and dissipate fear through the validation of specific situations. They predetermine the potential outcomes of specific actions and use intellectual, intuitive, and perceptive knowledge to evaluate the associated risks. They become selective and avoid getting involved with unnecessary risky situations. They proceed in risky situations with proper caution and cool heads. They attain *purity of heart* through following the path of honesty, straightforwardness, and truth. They perform *righteous acts* without using cunning or clever ways to attain the ultimate objective. They make *charitable donations* to overpower desires for material possession. They perform, with devotion, *selfless services* to acquire altruism. They achieve *celibacy,* by refraining from sensuous activities. With these traits, the individual gradually cultivates control of the causal body, and thus cultivates the temperament of being *straightforward* and learns to face situations.

Higher Knowledge

To attain higher knowledge, the individual starts with *holy scriptures* and seeks the guidance of a spiritual teacher. Individuals continuously practice concentration, meditation, and contemplation to cultivate a *steadfast mind.* With a steadfast mind, individuals learn to acquire spiritual knowledge and come to comprehend the true purpose of the living spirit residing within the body. With the attainment of higher knowledge, the living being comes to appreciate the principles of *nonviolence.* No individual can acquire this trait of nonviolence without development of a positive mental attitude and not being a bully or thinking of causing harm to any living being. As a part of nonviolence, one learns to adhere to the truth and always expresses things without false pretenses.

The steadfast mind also helps individuals cultivate the ability to restrain *anxieties* through overpowering the negative impulses arising within the mind. Individuals, through control of anxieties, are able to control logical thought processes. The eleventh trait is *inner peace,* which automatically arises with the control of an individual's subtle faculties to bring about the demise of anxieties by performing unselfish acts.

Liberation

The process of liberation starts with the covenant of attainment of *renunciation* from materialistic desires and the possessive nature, which gives birth to the thirteenth trait, *gentleness,* which when further refined brings out *compassion,* the fourteenth trait, within the living being. Compassion, along with all the other traits, brings the individual to the fifteenth trait, *generosity,* which eliminates any quest to acquire properties and things owned by others. This allows one to become more altruistic. Ultimately, this leads to inner *contentment,* the sixteenth trait; as the individual's ways of thinking are refined, the seventeenth trait, *nobility,* sets in, and every word spoken by the individual becomes refined and devoid of maliciousness and gloating.

With all these traits, the individual becomes *modest,* the eighteenth trait of morality, in his or her way of living and dealing with others. These eighteen traits work together to bring about the nineteenth trait, whereby the individual mind comes to an *unswerving position* and is no longer subject to oscillations and the individual learns to express bodily actions and activities with sternness and achieve the twentieth trait, called *humbleness.* Even after all these changes, the individual still does not reflect any major physical change; however, these twenty traits start to bring major internal changes within the individual's astral body, which are reflected through the cultivation of an aura or *inner glow,* the twenty-first trait. Facial expressions display internal contentment, and individual personalities start to exhibit powers of *magnetism,* the twenty-second divine trait. The individual, through inner powers, is able to *isolate the sin from the sinner* or the ability to separate action from the performer and is able to judge them separately, the twenty-third trait.

The cultivation of these twenty-three traits of covenants together fortify and overpower duality and are able to see hatred and love being diffused to become one. The spiritual soul can see only *goodness* in all. With this divine bliss, the sacred soul acquires the heavenly powers—*sanctity*—to fight back any demonic powers that come in the way of divine action.

Demonic Powers

The biggest enemy of morality remains individual desire. Each desire consists of a material aspect that motivates the individual to perform acts. This material aspect has a unique feature that generates self-multiplication; just like waves in the ocean, as soon as one desire is fulfilled, another desire is born. With the fulfillment of that desire, it leads to the creation of several more desires. This process keeps on repeating, generating desire after desire.

Every material desire is associated with an element of greed, which compounds as the material desires to progress and grow. These desires are like a fountain that keeps on regenerating—

transforming unfulfilled thoughts into demonic thoughts, which ultimately become demonic forces. If these demonic forces are not controlled, they have the power to transform the individual character, personality, and temperament—and turn a nobleperson into an evil one.

Unfortunately, once humans acquire intellectual knowledge, they develop a practical justification to support a certain lifestyle; they defend these selfish desires as a means of having prosperity, knowing well that they only provide transitory happiness. The task here is not to have needs or greed, but to restrain the growth of thoughts that lead to such desires and cultivate an attachment to material gain. Once again, it is very important to understand that possession is not bad; possessiveness is evil. Further, through higher knowledge, one understands that the fulfillment of materialistic desires only brings transitory happiness. Similarly, the fulfillment of only divine desires, without an ultimate goal, could make a person into a victim of an uncontrolled passive lifestyle.

With selfish motives—and without any commitment to spirituality—everything the individual performs becomes for the glory of that event. All their actions become full of vanity, arrogance, and an outlandish display of their abilities. Ego, arrogance, passion, and anger gradually lead them to believe that acquired power is better than that of the divine powers; therefore, such evil-spirited individuals quickly become malicious and cruel to the whole society and start to destroy the divine creations.

Once these individuals become uncontrollable and destructive, they believe they control every living being, thing, and divine creation. Even history has proven that every living being who has participated in such demonic activities is subjected to go through the evil life until they have paid for their evil acts and are finally brought back to understand and seek spiritual wisdom and appreciate the principles of morality.

There are evil individuals who refuse to accept the divine powers even after being subjected to brutality or many cycles of life and death. They finally face the challenge of the ultimate powers when such overpowering individuals or regimes are subject to annihilation through the supreme power of demigods or higher authorities. This marks the appearance of the illuminated soul or the divine envoy, which appear like a human being. They overpower and destroy these demonic souls, provide freedom to innocent living beings, and reinstate the divine covenants according to the Bhagavad Gita. These demonic individuals regress down the path to spiritual evolution and ultimately end up serving life cycles similar to an animal.

Massive demonic activities are carried out by rulers of power, such as political leaders, kings, and emperors who obsessively conquer others' possessions by force and exploit the life of innocent humans and living things in order to accomplish their obsessions. Such warmongers become bewildered with fancies, and they end up indulging in all kinds of personal gratification at any cost. Ultimately, they become mentally unstable, entangled by the snare of delusion and hallucinations. The demonic forces take over the intellect and judgment. They lose any logical way of thinking as the gratification of lusts takes full control of their subtle faculties. Then they become victims of demonic powers and end up getting consumed in their own demise.

The process of demonic control can be grouped as follows:

Initiation

Among humanity, this first reflects the loss of faith. This

occurs when an individual becomes enamored with acquired intellectual and materialistic knowledge, and starts to acquire material wealth or seize power. In doing so, the individual cultivates egocentric personality. Individuals thus go through transitory periods of demonic behavior. They end up using arrogance and self-conceit to hide their true natures. They exaggerate their accumulated wealth, acquired power, social status, family heritage, and connections. When their hypercritical position is challenged, they immediately revolt with bursts of anger and they lose control of their faculties. They commonly perform physical acts of violence, or at least bursts of vulgar expressions to show off their acquired power. As their behavior pattern takes full control of their subtle faculties, it creates a disconnect and creates a form of veil that limits the individual's ability to perform righteous acts or follow the path of morality.

Enhancement

Such an individual becomes merciless and prone to evil forces as they come under the shackles of devilish bondage. They become prone to rebel against those who are following the path of morality because they believe the righteous are there to deprive them of a materialistic life. They even deny the existence of any higher spiritual aspect of life. They regress further and take on satanic traits, becoming ruthless. They perform devilish, wicked, and malicious acts, which bring nothing but grief to society by causing increased restlessness, dissension, and destruction, creating large-scale disasters.

Transformation

When an individual comes under the shackles of demonic powers and becomes a threat to the divine principle of equilibrium, the ultimate supreme powers of the Creator transform its neutral or divine nature *(yakshas)* into the demonic nature *(rakshasas)*, and they kill such demonic forces to bring into balance the laws of equilibrium.

Gateway

The holy scripture discusses three gates through which evil and demonic powers overpower any living being. They are passion, greed, and anger.

Passion

Here, passion relates to lust or satisfaction that primarily comes from sexual desire. Passion in the form of drive is energy used to keep the individual productive and contributes toward physical and spiritual evolution. When such passion is carried out too far, it turns from divine to demonic and brings out an evil power that takes control over the individual's strength to maintain purity and cleanliness. Under such situations, sexually transmitted diseases become an epidemic and spread like a brush fire, destroying a large part of humanity.

Greed

The greed-related phenomena are designed to bring prosperity, but when they become uncontrollable, it opens the doors for the evil powers of *maya* to step in and turn greed into obsession, which takes control of all human subtle faculties and gives the human demonic qualities. This challenges the individual's intellect, makes the human immoral, and subjects him or her to pain, anguish, melancholy, depression, and sometimes even self-induced death. The anger reflects the loss of contact with the powers of the living spirit, which brings a momentary blindness or mental dysfunction.

Anger

When anger is not controlled, it turns into a demonic force called rage, which creates a long-lasting mental dysfunction. This rage clouds the individual's eyes just like a dust cloud that leads to an accident or destruction. Rage is the true source of human demise; it causes a temporary or permanent disconnect between the individual and his or her conscience or living spirit.

There are two paths to suppress the demonic forces. The first way is to understand the elements of covenants and to learn to transform selfish thoughts into unselfish desires. This requires individuals to identify, control, and make concerted efforts to transform sensual, selfish, and possessive desires into true powers of compassion. Since such activities do not generate attachment, one can suppress and avoid evil forces of destruction through compassion. Even compassion by itself is not enough; therefore, the second path, devotion, must accompany compassion. As a part of devotion, the individual learns to perform regular worship through study of the holy scripture, prayers, and offering oblations as a gesture of thanks to the Creator for providing everything. This way, the individual attains support of the spiritual powers and does not have to fight the battles alone.

A dogma can be conceptualized—but never confirmed.

Chapter 8
Dogma

The Universe

Dogma is the third element of spiritual knowledge; in spiritual or religious terms, it refers to the core principles of a specific religion, faith, or cult. Proposed disputation or revision effectively means that a person no longer accepts the given religion as his or her own—or has entered into a period of personal doubt. The ideology is usually based upon scripture, which starts with the origin of our universal system and how the universal system, including all living things, is continuously regulated and managed by the powers of the Creator. In part 1 of this book, I discussed various mythologies that describe the genesis of the universe. Interestingly, all such mythologies represent a similar explanation of how the universe was formed.

According to the Vedas, the creation of the universal system started when the unidentifiable consolidated matter was segregated into two parts—undifferentiated and differentiated—by the supreme powers of the Creator of such substances. This separation initiated the process of creation of our universal system. Many years after this initial separation, the differentiated part of segregated matter was divided into two parts, resulting in unmanifested matter and manifested matter. During this process, the Creator, as the supreme power, continued to operate various parts of this segregation through an ultimate eternal power, called *divinity,* or the perpetual essence. With perpetual essence, the *divinity* that is worshipped in the Hindu religion as *paramatma* or the Lord Supreme *(Brahma)* continued to operate and control all the manifested parts of the universe.

Inaccessible Region

The spiritual scholars have determined through inspirational wisdom or revelations that the universe itself could be grouped into fourteen different spheres *(lokas).* Seven spheres constitute the upper part of the universe, and the other seven constitute the lower part of the universe. The seven spheres that constitute the upper part of the universe are called *Vyhrtis,* and the seven spheres that belong to the underworld are called *Sapta.*

Of the seven spheres that constitute the upper part of the universe, the highest sphere is called *Satyaloka,* the sphere of absolute truth, *Sat.* The next below the *Satyaloka* is called *Tapoloka;* it represents the ultimate home of the eternal soul. The sphere *Tapoloka* is nothing more than the true reflection of the seventh sphere.

Both these spheres are unapproachable and incomprehensible by even the unmanifested bodies, such as deities, demigods, and divine angels—or any living being, including those who have attained sanctity or achieved a divine status. Nobody has been able to define these spheres, especially the seventh sphere, which remains nameless, or

Anama. These two spheres are the opposite of the two lowest spheres of the underworld; *Nagaloka* is the sphere of evil powers where everything represents the ending.

The sixth sphere is the *Tapoloka*; it is considered the sphere of perpetual essence, from which everything originates. It also represents the ultimate home of the eternal soul where the *divinity*, the true image of the Creator, resides. This sphere is unapproachable; even deities, demigods, and divine angels cannot enter it. In the Vedas, this sphere is described as *Agams*, meaning inaccessible. The Creator prevails beyond these two spheres, and these two spheres serve as the initial barrier between the Creator and its creation, the universal system.

The Universal System

Our universal system consists of the next five spheres. The *Janaloka* is the sphere of illumination, which is full of brilliance and radiance, producing activities such as electromagnetic waves that light up the entire universal system. Within this sphere, the perpetual essence is separated into two components—living force and living spirit. The living force, defined as the *brahma*, is comprised of the powers of repulsion, the negative charge, and its complementary power of attraction, the positive charge. The living spirit, defined as the *brahman*, is the omnipotent force, such as gravitational force, that provides the eternal power of adoration. This sphere consists of complex forces, and understanding such forces requires comprehension of eternal truth. Only divine spirits, such as divinity, deities, demigods, archangels, and divine envoys who have attained freedom from the attachment caused by the living force, can attain such absolute truth to comprehend the divine wisdom. No living thing or living being has the ability to conceptualize these powers as long as they remain attached to the material nature or are being influenced by the powers of the living force.

The next sphere, *Maharloka,* is the home of the living force, where a combination of the inert matter of innumerable atoms of inorganic substances, referred to as *Purusha,* and the omnipotent force or vital energy responsible for the causation of motion through the powers of vibration, referred to as *Prakriti,* prevails. The interaction of these two forces results in the formation of physical mass that has the ability to produce actions and activities as well as give birth to duality, multiplicity, illusions, and delusions. It creates shadows, causes darkness, and creates ignorance within living things, including humanity. In the Vedas, this is defined as the ultimate powers of *maya,* which has the ability to separate spiritual thinking from material thinking. Any individual who has gone beyond to acquire the perceptive powers comes to comprehend the powers of *maya* through the streamlining of individual subtle faculties.

This sphere could be comparable to the celestial universe, where magnetic fields and many other forces, such as kinetic, potential, dynamic, electromagnetic, thermal, chemical, and nuclear are formed. Several spiritual scholars have identified within this sphere the operation of four axes of causation—vibration, space, time, and atoms. Within this sphere, forces of attraction and repulsion cause atoms (basic units of matter that consist of a dense central nucleus surrounded by a cloud of negatively charged electrons) to collide with one another to form gross mass. It results in the formation of cosmic bodies and manifestations of physical bodies.

The cessation of physical bodies produces other forms of physical and nonphysical forces and thus creates mystic auras or astronomical phenomena, such as seasonality, cyclicality, creation, and destruction that physically and psychologically influence each creation. This part of the universe is governed by the living forces that are of material nature, *maha-prakrit,* and are commonly referred to as the cosmic or manifested part of the universal system.

The next sphere—*Swarloka,* the home of the living spirit—produces an aura that is very similar to magnetic aura, called spiritual attractions. These attractions are all part of the *paramatama,* the eternal soul of the Creator, which is responsible for the creation of an aura also identified as divine love. This is the sphere of astral bodies where no physical or manifested bodies can prevail. This sphere is considered an ethereal part of the universal system. Within selected religious scriptures, this region is defined as purgatory.

The next sphere, *Bhuvarloka,* includes the sections of our planet; the sky, ground, and upper crust are protected from the cosmic rays by the shield created by the sky to create earth's atmosphere for living beings to survive and provide stimuli to perform actions and activities. Within this sphere, living beings are subject to spiritual evolution; once they reach a fully evolved position they could attain freedom and travel without the limitations of time, space, and the physical body. The lowest sphere of the seven spheres, *Bhuoka,* is where only gross material manifestations, such as material bodies, mystical creatures, and monsters that require limited or no direct light to survive, prevail. The gross bodies of living things existing in such circumstances do not advance or even acquire the most basic levels of intellect or knowledge.

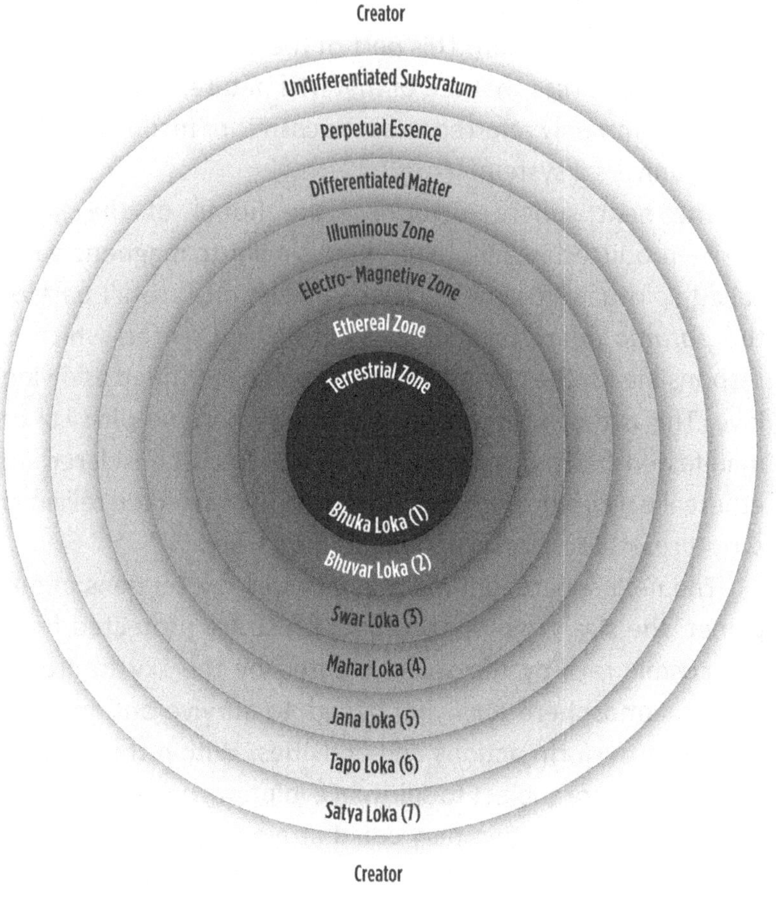

Illustration 3: Seven Spheres of Universe.

The Living Things

The second aspect of creation is to understand the structure of living things prevailing within the universal system. Each creation on the planet consists of five sheaths or coverings that operate as devices to respond to the external vibrations generated by the activities of nature as well as the vibrations generated from the primordial force that are stored within the astral body as residual memories. These vibrations react with each other and send sensory signals that ultimately convert vital energy into an action or activity.

These five sheaths are called *koshas.* The first sheath is referred to as *annamya kosha.* This sheath represents the physical part of the body that is responsible for receiving all forms of nourishment *(anna).* With the help of these nutrients, the embodiments remain active and aware of the surrounding or external world. The second sheath is called *pranamaya kosha.* Within this sheath, atmospheric air is processed by living beings to produce elemental air capable of supplying oxygen to various parts of the physical body, such as the eyes, ears, nose, mouth, limbs, wings, arms, and legs. The breath *(prana)* is commonly recognized as the life force; within this sheath, it sends sensory signals that are received through the fifteen organs of perception (five physical organs, five sensory organs, and five organs of perception) to activate the subtle or the causal body.

The next sheath, *manamaya kosha,* represents the individual mental faculties composed of organs of the senses, *manna.* With the activation of *manna,* individual perceptive powers activate individual subtle faculties (the awareness, the conscious mind, the intellect, the wisdom, and the inner conscience). These faculties send signals through the nervous system to generate specific desires to perform an action or an activity. The next sheath, *jnanamaya kosha,* represents the region of the magnetic aura. Electric charges or magnetic sensations that are necessary to acquire knowledge and wisdom originate from this region. This sheath, home of *buddhi,* is responsible for the activation of individual ability to attain self-perfection and *enlightenment.* The last sheath, *anandamaya kosha,* represents the ultimate state of inner tranquility and peace. Through this sheath, humanly love *(chit)* transforms into divine love. *Chitta* and individual embodiment experience inner *illumination.*

The spiritual development displayed through individual temperament includes dormant living spirit, awakened living spirit, active living spirit, enlightened living spirit, and illuminated living spirit. This is observed in the form of knowledge, including ignorance, common sense, intellect, wisdom, eternal wisdom, and absolute truth. It is reflected through individual actions, such as how one handles inner conflict, maintains inner peace, acquires tranquility, and attains ecstasy or divine bliss. This eternal love is called *annanda.* Some spiritual scholars have suggested these sheaths are counterparts to the major glands in the body; however, this association has not been scientifically proven or otherwise verified.

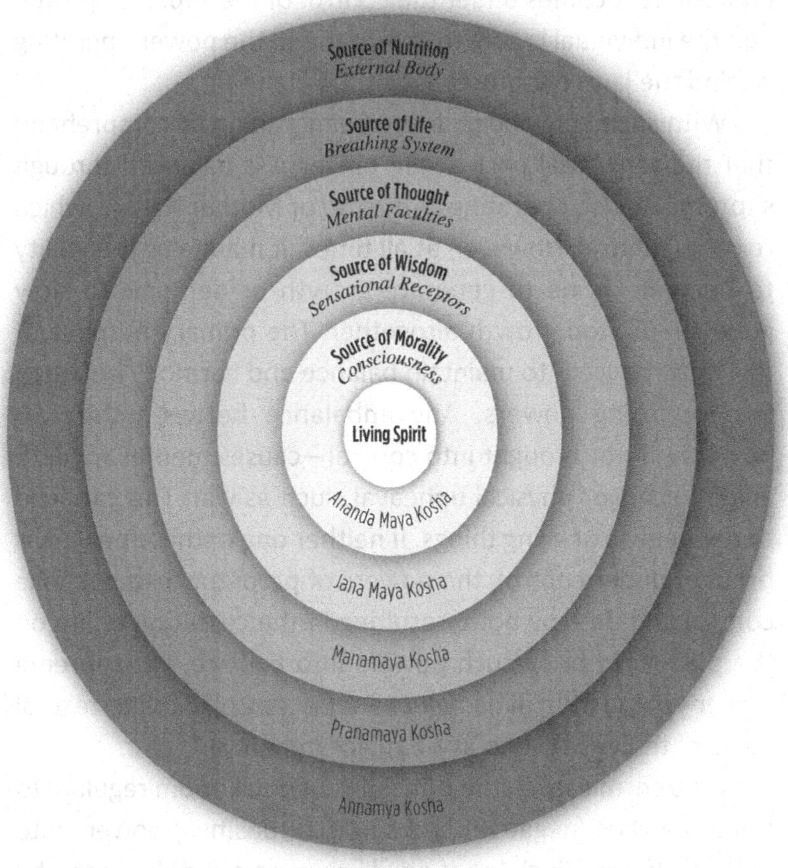

Illustration 4: Five Sheaths of Embodiment.

Nature

According to spiritual scholars, some aspects of the universal system remain mystical to humanity until an individual has gone through a complete transformation and acquired spiritual wisdom. At that point, the sanctified soul and the human body attain a spiritual level to become a saint or *devata*. Individual bondage to the powers of darkness or *maya* is totally abolished, embodiment comes under the control of the supreme power, and the individual is able to comprehend the power operating behind the laws of nature.

With such knowledge, living beings come to comprehend that the terrestrial part of the universe is balanced through supreme power, operating as *prakriti* or Mother Nature, which remains neutral. However, at all times, it maintains the ability to become divine to generate growth or demonic to slow growth—or stop growth altogether. The primary purpose of this dual nature is to maintain balance and harmony between two opposing powers. Any imbalance between the two powers—if not brought into control—causes mental anguish, anger, or major physical upheaval, such as war. This can lead to the demise of living things. If neither one of these powers is brought under control, the powers of perpetual essence take control and destroy both, resulting in the cessation of life on the planet. To bring such powers into balance, the supreme power—in the form of *demigods*—take control of the terrestrial parts of the universe to avoid major upheaval.

On a cosmic level, the principles of equilibrium regulate to bring material (negative) and spiritual (positive) powers into balance. If the principles of equilibrium go out of balance, the supreme powers—in the form of *deities*—take control to bring things into balance to protect against colossal cosmic events. On a celestial level, the deities can take control.

Similarly, to regulate the transformation of undifferentiated substratum into differentiated substratum, the *divinity* takes control. If divinity cannot control, the supreme power takes control to bring the end of differentiated parts of the universe, including the demise of the *divinity*. Thereafter, the evolutionary process ends—until the Creator creates a new divinity and starts the process of differentiation all over again. This concept of balance bringing tranquility is best illustrated within the Tao principle of *yin-yang,* introduced by Confucius during the Axial Age in China.

The powers of causation are omnipotent; only humanity has the faculties to realize such powers.

Chapter 9
Omnipotence

Conceptualization

Another element of *spiritual knowledge* is comprehension of the omnipotent aspect of the supreme power. With this, seekers come to conceptualize the existence of the living spirit within each embodiment and its relationship with the eternal souls prevailing throughout the universal system. To comprehend this element, individuals come to accept the need to cultivate the ultimate concentration necessary to unify every aspect of an individual's mental ability to conceptualize the divine field of manifestation (*purushottama yoga*).

Using this form of yoga, the individual acquires the ability to go beyond and overpower human physical limitations and subtle faculties to comprehend such almighty powers of causation. The Bhagavad Gita suggests, when a living being is able to acquire such supremacy over the individual subtle faculties, including the conscious mind, the powers of devotion are able to activate the dormant subtle faculty of the sixth sense or the third eye. Only through the activation of this faculty can an individual grasp the true interrelationship between the visible and invisible, moving and not moving, manifested and unmanifested, perceptible and imperceptible, and perpetual essence and the living spirit residing within the individual's embodiment.

It is through invocation of the living spirit one can attain such power to comprehend the absolute truth, called *Sat*. In the medical field, the comprehension of the sixth sense is associated with the pineal gland, which is only partially developed in the human body. It is situated between the two hemispheres and refers to the seat of direct perception, intuition, imagination, visualization, concentration, self-mastery, and extrasensory perception. In spiritual terms, the *third eye* is referred to as the seat of the eternal soul that remains dormant until fully activated.

In terms of physical and spiritual evolution, humans have not yet fully evolved; the next phase of human physical evolution could possibly be the full development of the pineal gland, which will permit humanity to go beyond transcendental knowledge to acquire absolute truth—without much difficulty. Once humanity reaches such a level, experiencing the powers of divinity and understanding the entire workings of the universal system will become second nature.

Experience

Until now, only a select few illuminated souls have gone beyond to unveil the presence of the eternal soul at various levels of the universal system. Based on mystical experiences, it has been determined that the eternal soul controls and regulates each and every aspect of the universe. This supreme force was created as an image, and the image prevails as long as the divine power prevails. The Creator continues to prevail even after the disappearance of such power or the *divinity.*

The *divinity,* through its mystic supreme powers, maintains full control of all aspects of creation, sustainability, progress, and the ultimate cession of every part of the universal system. Many times, humanity mistakenly confuses the *divinity* to be the Creator, not knowing it is only a self-regulated illusion—and that it exists only as long as the powers of the Creator want such divinity to exist.

Illuminated and sanctified souls, such as Moses, Jesus Christ, Muhammad, Gautama Buddha, and Nanak, fully understood that *divinity* is only an image created by the Creator; therefore, in addition to divinity, they always honored, respected, and worshipped the infinite, inconceivable, invisible, and incomprehensible form of the Creator as their father.

According to the Bhagavad Gita, in order for an individual to experience the ultimate powers of the Creator, the individual has to surrender to the five subtle forces that are controlled and managed by *divinity*:

1. The individual has to surrender all forms of pride and delusions that can potentially lead to making a wrong judgment.
2. The individual has to surrender all human emotions that can potentially lead to binding the individual; these include love, passion, emotion, and affection.
3. The individual has to surrender all remaining egotistic bonds by transforming thoughts and desires from *me* to *mine*.
4. The individual has to surrender the duality created by powers such as darkness and light, love and hate, pleasure and pain.
5. The individual has to surrender or annihilate every form of desire, thus bringing the individual soul to its original form of purity.

Pervasion

The living spirit—at all times and in each form of existence—remains invisible, independent, and unattached to the physical body. Nevertheless, it has the ability to be enhanced or to transform from a dormant spirit *(jiva)* to a living spirit *(atma)* to a transcendental spirit *(mahatma)* to an illuminated spirit *(purushottama),* and finally to evolve attaining sanctity to merge with the perpetual essence and losing its identity, thereby attaining eternity *(prabhuatma).*

As long as the living spirit resides within the physical body, it enjoys its association with the material nature, but it remains unattached at all times, just like spectators enjoying a game without becoming a part of the play or being a player. However, the living spirit's agents or sensory organs of perception, just like sports fans, develop an affiliation with the material nature and cultivate an attachment that leaves images on subtle faculties. In time, these images develop into residual memories. Over a long period, they become long-lasting images, *vasana,* which influence the individual's evolutionary development—both physically and spiritually.

At the time of death, the individual spirit, along with associated residual memories, departs as an astral body, leaving behind the physical body to decay and merge with inert matter. This is like how the fragrance departs from a flower at the time of death and becomes part of the wind, leaving behind the inert part of the flower to decay and merge with the material nature. The fragrance remains part of the breeze until a new flower germinates to house that fragrance. Similarly, the residual memories, encrustations, and instincts remain part of the individual spirit until a new embodiment is created by the divine nature to house that spirit or soul.

This process is commonly referred to as eternity or *moksha* in the Eastern faiths and resurrection of the spirit in Western faiths. This process of combining the living force with the living spirit to create living things has been going on for centuries. As part of the creation of living things, the astral body provides the living spirit with a newly created embodiment, and the physical body provides the embodiment with a combination of the two, which creates the causal body. Throughout the process of attraction and repulsion, the body generates knowledge in the form of intellect and wisdom, which brings physical and spiritual evolutionary growth.

After overpowering the barriers created by the powers of the *primordial force* or *divinity,* the individual is able to pierce through the divine veil and comprehend the absolute truth. With absolute truth, an individual comes to understand different segments of the universe and realize how each sphere interconnects with each other and derives its powers from the respective divine object, such as *deities*, *demigods*, and *archangels*.

A seeker spiritually rises above the highest spheres to merge with the perpetual essence of the Creator. This ability to go beyond the spheres differentiates humanity from plants and almost all members of the animal kingdom.

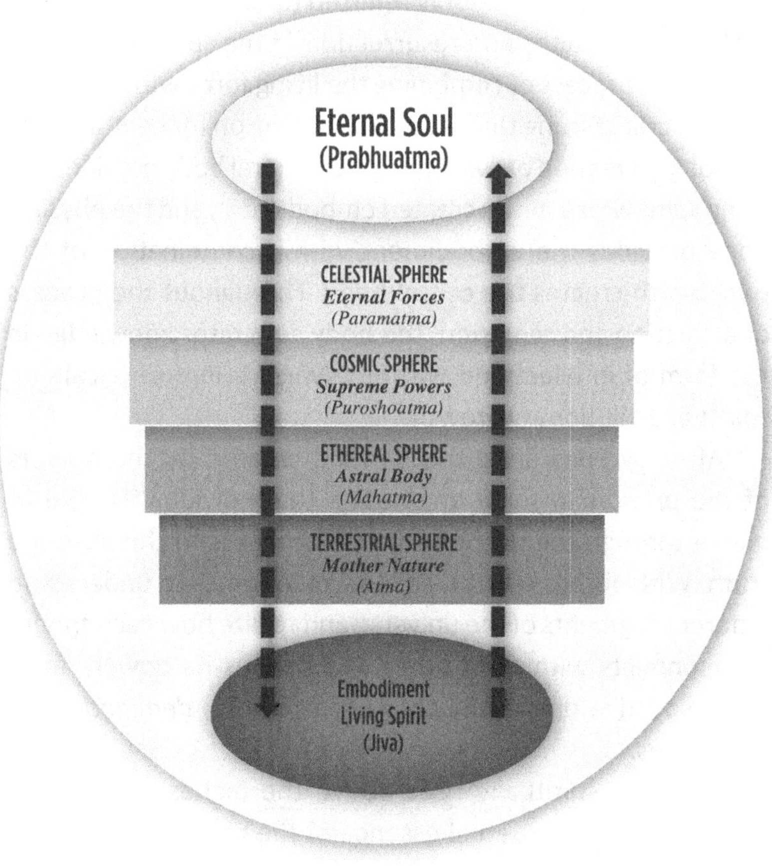

Illustration 5: Pathway to Resurrection of Eternal Soul.

Vital Energies

Vital energy is part of the *primordial force* that provides living beings the ability to survive. This energy is supplied by three main sources: the sun in the form of strong rays during the day; the moon in the form of cool rays during the night; and the air in the form of breath during the day and night.

This vital energy regulates and manages the food intake and functioning of an individual's digestive system, whether the food is received in the form of solid, air, or liquid and digested by means of chewing with the teeth, swallowed through the throat muscles, sucked by facial muscles, or licked by the tongue.

Within the physical body, the oxygen produced through vital energy transforms external stimuli into thoughts and desires, which cause the body to perform physical actions and activities. The physical body absorbs and regulates this vital energy through the powers of the intestinal tract, and it throws out the undigested and unnecessary by-products through the excretion process.

The retained energy is converted from a dynamic nature into producing sentient nature (sentient energy), and induces the sensory organs to be able to perceive and react to the impulses. This brings the body into awareness of its surroundings and causes the individual to realize the impact of his or her actions and activities—and comprehend the associated materialistic values or consequences.

This causes the development of attachment to the materialistic world and gives birth to need, greed, and the desire to own and control things (and sometimes others). These materialistic attachments generate ego to generate images and reflections. However, when sentient energy is used to perform altruistic actions, it transforms the sentient energy into subliminal energy.

The subliminal energy helps discard images and reflections retained within the subtle faculties. Depending on the quality and strength of those images, such energy helps eliminate memories and allow the subtle faculties, such as mind and intellect, to acquire spiritual knowledge. With the help of wisdom and codes of covenant, individual actions and activities cause individual embodiment to perform actions in conformance with the laws of nature.

According to the Vedas, the retention of memories within the astral body also behaves just like the human brain; defective, useless, or false knowledge is displaced to make space for new and valuable information. The residual memories retained within the astral body are replaced with spiritual knowledge. The process of invocation causes an individual to perform loving actions, compassionate acts of kindness, cultivation of personal affection, affinity to nonviolence and tolerance, charitable acts, and selfless services. It purifies the astral body from blemishes from past demonic actions and activities.

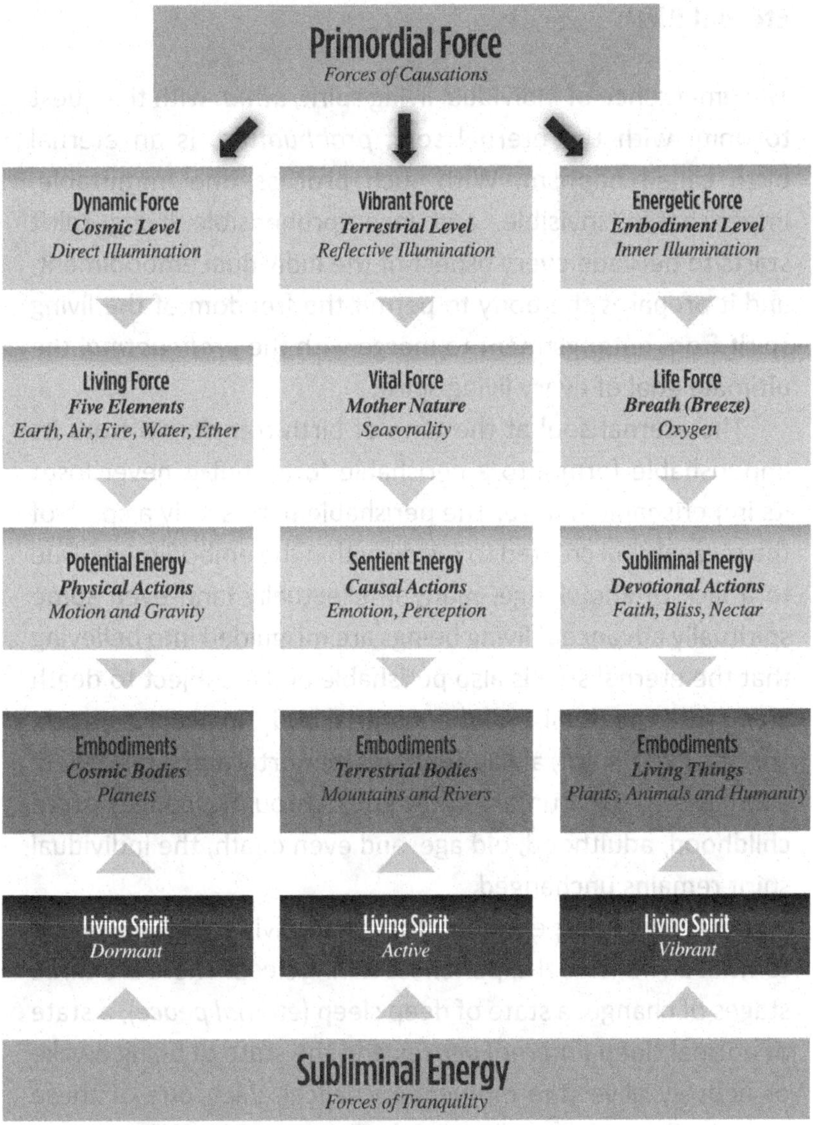
Primordial Force
Forces of Causations
Dynamic Force
Cosmic Level
Direct Illumination
Vibrant Force
Terrestrial Level
Reflective Illumination
Energetic Force
Embodiment Level
Inner Illumination
Living Force
Five Elements
Earth, Air, Fire, Water, Ether
Vital Force
Mother Nature
Seasonality
Life Force
Breath (Breeze)
Oxygen
Potential Energy
Physical Actions
Motion and Gravity
Sentient Energy
Causal Actions
Emotion, Perception
Subliminal Energy
Devotional Actions
Faith, Bliss, Nectar
Embodiments
Cosmic Bodies
Planets
Embodiments
Terrestrial Bodies
Mountains and Rivers
Embodiments
Living Things
Plants, Animals and Humanity
Living Spirit
Dormant
Living Spirit
Active
Living Spirit
Vibrant
Subliminal Energy
Forces of Tranquility

Illustration 6: Transformation of Primordial Force into Subliminal Energy.

Eternal Birth

The emergence of individual living spirit, *atma*, with the quest to unite with the eternal soul, *prabhuatma,* is an eternal birth called baptism. With such process, the immutable, imperishable, invisible, and incomprehensible living spirit starts to pervade every aspect of the individual embodiment, and it prepares the body to permit the freedom of the living spirit from entanglement to merge with the *prabhuatma,* the ultimate goal of every living spirit.

The eternal soul at the time of birth transforms from its imperishable form into a perishable form, but it never loses its imperishable nature. The perishable part is only a spark of the eternal soul created to reside within the embodiment. Due to a lack of knowledge, many intellectually (and even some spiritually advanced) living beings are misguided into believing that the eternal soul is also perishable and is subject to death along with the demise of the material body. In absolute truth, *Sat,* the living spirit, always remains immortal and unattached; even when the human body goes through changes from childhood, adulthood, old age, and even death, the individual spirit remains unchanged.

Any changes experienced through the living spirit are similar to what an individual experiences during sleep. There are three stages of change: a state of deep sleep (*eternal peace*), a state of normal sleep (*internal peace*), and the state of being awake or actively alive (*the momentary peace*). Each one of these stages reflects the condition of the living spirit's affiliation with the inert matter and influence of the divine nature.

The best way to comprehend these phases is through close examination of one's sleep patterns. During deep sleep, one's spirit is essentially free from the influences of subtle faculties, and the link between one's spirit and the powers of divine nature is temporarily disconnected. At this stage, one's mind goes into a transient phase. As soon as the human subtle faculties become active, they start to react to the stimuli originating from internal residual memories; thus, one's mental position changes from a tranquil state to an active state.

During this stage, one experiences dreams, whether good or bad. At this stage, one's body remains physically inactive because the subtle faculties are not being influenced by external stimuli originating from the powers of the divine nature. As soon as one's subtle faculties start to react with the stimuli, however, the physical body connects with the external powers of divine nature and becomes active. It then goes into an energetic phase and performs actions and activities that generate desires.

In all these stages, the individual spirit remains the same—only its outer appearance changes. Just as a wooden stick dipped into chocolate or ice cream develops a new form and new taste, the wooden stick itself never changes its true nature or loses its fundamental character; it only enhances the abilities of coated materials.

An individual who has attained spiritual wisdom fully comprehends the relationship and underlying process of the interaction of the physical body with the inner living spirit. In all such transformations, it remains omnipresent, providing the substratum to all its creations—just as the ocean itself always remains calm, even though it provides the energy to all forms of turbulence, including each wave or current. Even though waves continue to form and prevail as if they were independent of the ocean, as soon as their energy is exhausted, they quietly merge with the ocean and lose their identity.

Even ocean water, with the help of solar heat, evaporates

and changes its physical form. The water separates itself from the body of the ocean to become a cloud in the sky; it again changes its physical form when it turns into rain or snow. Then it joins the river and ultimately rejoins the ocean, losing its individuality and identity. At every stage, the ocean, even though invisible, remains part of each new form of water.

Neither waves nor vapors can exist without the ocean water; similarly, the individual soul cannot exist without the living spirit, and planetary bodies cannot exist without inert matter. Furthermore, as it is described in the holy scriptures of various religions, the upheaval of the oceans ultimately gave birth to the land, which became responsible for the growth of life on earth and started the processes of physical and spiritual evolution. The ultimate substratum for all these creations remains the supreme power or the Creator; without it, there would be no turbulence in the oceans, and the powers of causation would not exist without the Creator.

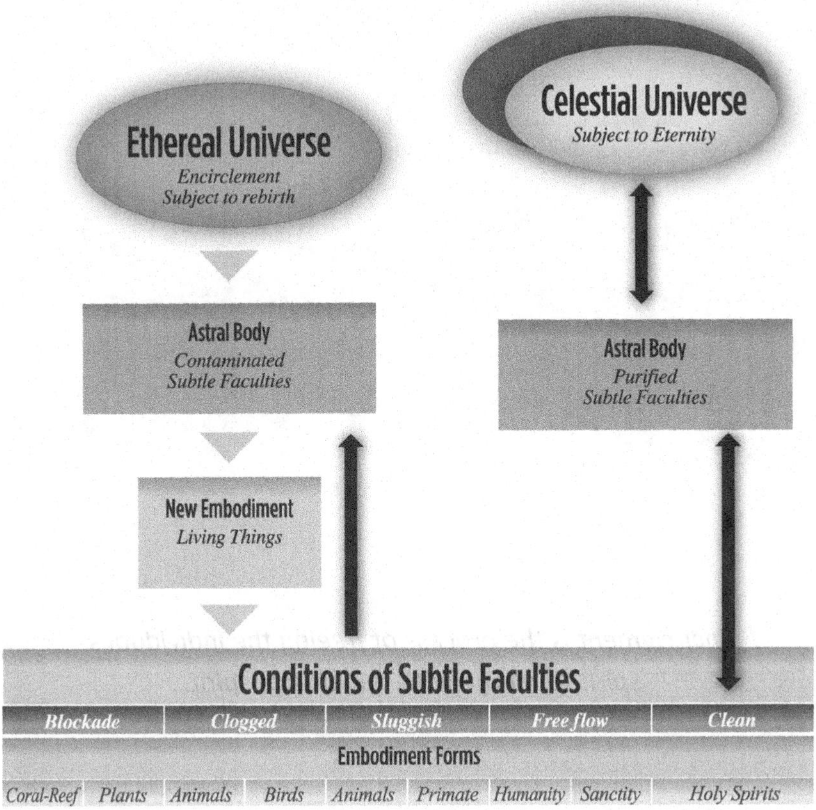

Illustration 7: Pathway to Eternal Birth.

Encirclement is the process of freeing the individual's spirit to merge with the eternal spirit.

Chapter 10
Encirclement

Process

The fifth element of *spiritual knowledge* is encirclement. Supreme powers created this to help living things purify their astral bodies through eradication of prior life memories, blemishes, and residual memories. Since no living being can survive without performing actions, every living thing produces memories, blemishes, and residual memories that become a part of the astral body. While alive, these generate internal stimuli and cause every action to produce a reaction, which generates an image that ends up recorded within the astral body.

Depending on their nature, quality, and strength, they create invisible impressions or blemishes within the astral body that hinder the living spirit's ability to provide guidance to the living being. The strength of the shield depends upon its conformance with the code of covenants, and the strength of the images produced determines the quality of blemishes left behind.

Such blemishes transfer from one life to another, just like

DNA, and they establish the substratum for the newborn at the time of birth. Each life cycle provides an individual the opportunity to purify his or her astral body, accomplished by invoking the powers of the living spirit. With the invocation, an individual's work is transformed into vocation, career into calling, determination into devotion, and competition into collaboration.

In spiritual terms, the individual is able to transform selfish actions *(akarma)* into selfless actions *(karma),* and transform selfless or obligatory action *(karma)* into devotional activity *(dharma)*. *Dharma* can then be used to transform humanly love *(chit)* into eternal love *(chitta)*; through eternal love, it can provide freedom to the individual's living spirit (through *bhakti*) to merge with the eternal perpetual essence of the supreme power and attain eternity *(mukti).*

In the beginning of this process, the lower subtle faculties, such as mind and intellect, are overpowered by the conscience, then the living spirit overpowers the higher subtle faculty conscience, and finally the living spirit itself is overpowered by the perpetual essence, making living spirit part of the eternal soul. This whole process is called encirclement.

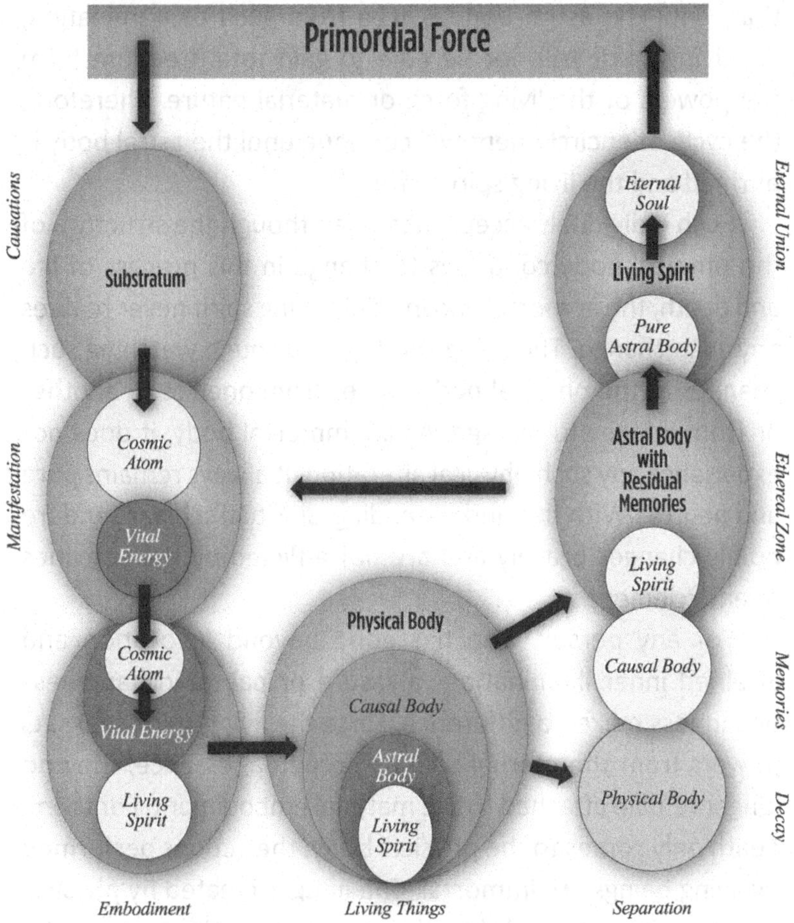

Illustration 8: Process of Encirclement.

Impact

Any living being who comes to understand the principle of encirclement will learn to appreciate the true purpose of birth and death—and thus no longer grieve. They see no big difference between being alive and being dead. They accept the gift of life as an opportunity to cleanse individual astral bodies from blemishes and residual memories. They accept that, until the astral body is free from such contamination, the living spirit will not be able to gain total freedom from the powers of the living force or material nature. Therefore, the cycle of encirclement will continue until the astral body is purified and the living spirit is freed.

Such individuals accept that, even though the structure of the physical body continues to change in this process of life and death, the immortal and invisible living spirit never realizes any such change. The living spirit goes through watching such changes as the physical body passes from one life to another or from infancy to old age. As an immortal body, it does not experience any such physical alteration. It always remains pure and neutral. With this understanding, spiritual scholars endure bodily changes bravely and are not afflicted by the activities of encirclement.

For any person who has gone beyond invocation and attained inner illumination, pleasure or pain and happiness or sadness make no difference. Since the living spirit seeks its powers from the eternal soul or perpetual essence, they no longer remain attached to the material embodiment. For them, death only comes to the physical body; the actions performed by living beings are immortal. The images created by physical actions are destroyed, but the spiritual inactions cannot be destroyed; they become immortal like the living spirit.

As part of the eternal soul, no weapon can cleave it, no fire can burn it, no water can moisten it, and no wind can make it dry. With such confidence, the sanctified souls never waver from performing the actions necessary to fulfill obligatory and devotional responsibilities; they consider nonperformance of action an act of defiance of the code of covenant.

Section II: Transcendental Knowledge

Transcendental knowledge is legendary because it deals with the comprehension of knowledge that is beyond normal human abilities. In the holy scriptures, this mystic knowledge is described as comprehension of the true nature of the supreme powers *(mahaprakriti)* of the Creator. With this knowledge, an individual encompasses the true knowledge regarding the creation of the primordial force. In the past, attainment of such knowledge was recognized as a divine experience or mythical revelation, a form of legendary experience attained by few.

These experiences were so supernatural and awe-inspiring that they were justified as direct messages from the God or the Creator. For centuries, humanity has worshipped primordial energies by giving them different names. The names assigned to such powers reflect its supreme ability, strength, and influence.

The influence and experience of such primordial energies by humanity has ranged from wild inspirations expressed in the form of revelations described as bacchanalian revelry, or a form of deep calmness expressed in the form of tranquility.

It also appears in the form of ecstasy shown by individuals through dancing, singing, and revelry.

In the South Sea Islands, the primordial force is called *Mana,* which is observed within plants, rocks, and animals—like radioactivity or electricity. Similarly, in old Latin, the impersonal primordial force is identified as *Numina.* The ancient Babylonians called this *Ishta,* and the ancient Canaanites called it *Anat.* Egyptian civilization identified this as *Isis,* and ancient Greek civilization called this *Aphrodite.* Within the Indian subcontinent, Aryans referred to it as *Indra,* and ancient Sumerians called this *Iana.* Even today, within Arabian civilization, the primordial force is referred to as *jinn.*

The transcendental knowledge is very complex and difficult to comprehend. To help understand such knowledge, I have elected to define the elements of transcendental knowledge as follows: the primordial force, the living force, the living spirit, the Trinity, and the tranquility. In addition to the knowledge included within *The Holy Science* by Swami Sri Yukteswar and the knowledge included within the Vedas, the Upanishads were extensively used to identify these specific elements of transcendental knowledge. To elaborate upon each element, various discourses on chapters 4, 7, 8, 9, and 12 of the Bhagavad Gita, published by many authors, were extensively used to supplement other information.

Only spiritual ignorance keeps humanity from comprehending the almighty primordial force as the ultimate source of causations.

CHAPTER 11
PRIMORDIAL FORCE

Genesis

The primordial force separates the perpetual essence of the Creator, dark matter, into two parts: differentiated and undifferentiated. This gives birth to different forms of spiritual powers, which humanity identifies as the *divinity* (image of the Creator or the son of the Creator controlling the universal system), the *deities* (specific powers controlling the celestial part of the universal system), and the *godhead* (specific powers controlling the cosmic part of the universal system). Others at a lower level are identified as *demigods* (semi-manifested supreme powers controlling terrestrial regions of the universal system), the *archangels* (the seraphs helping living beings overcome difficult times), and the *divine envoys* (sanctified humanly souls enforcing codes of covenants).

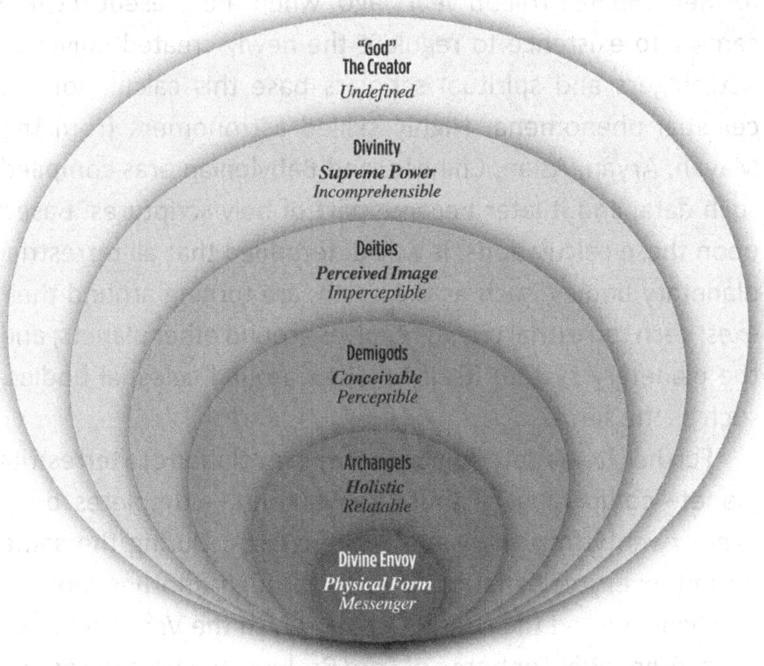

Illustration 9: Perceived Images of the Creator.

In addition the primordial force creates the "Wheel of Genesis" that generates its own powers, such as gravity, electromagnetic waves, etc., that cause the separation of differentiated matter into different spheres, forming a universal system, including our planetary system, where each planet is subjected to follow the defined path of equilibrium. It also causes each planet to go from unanimated to animated form, which is controlled by a cycle of revolution extending beyond many individual life cycles. The cycles in the Vedas are defined as *yugas,* and an invisible and unidentifiable supreme power regulates each life cycle, called *divinity,* which is directly controlled by the Creator, residing outside the universe.

Based upon astronomical calculations, the universe

formed 155.522 trillion years ago, when the present *divinity* came into existence to regulate the newly created universe. Astrologers and spiritual scholars base this calculation on celestial phenomena. Highly skilled astronomers from the Mayan, Aryan, Asian, Chinese, and Babylonian eras compiled such data, and it later became part of holy scriptures. Based upon these calculations, it was determined that all terrestrial planetary bodies, such as the earth, are turning around their axes; each terrestrial planet revolves around other planets; and the planetary system itself revolves around celestial bodies, such as the sun.

Further, it was determined that one revolution of a terrestrial planet—comprising all these movements—completes once every twenty-four thousand human years. During the same period, every celestial body goes through another motion, revolving around the Grand Center, which the Vedas referred to as *Vishnunabhi* or home of *Lord Brahma,* the progenitor and regulator of all living things on the terrestrial planets.

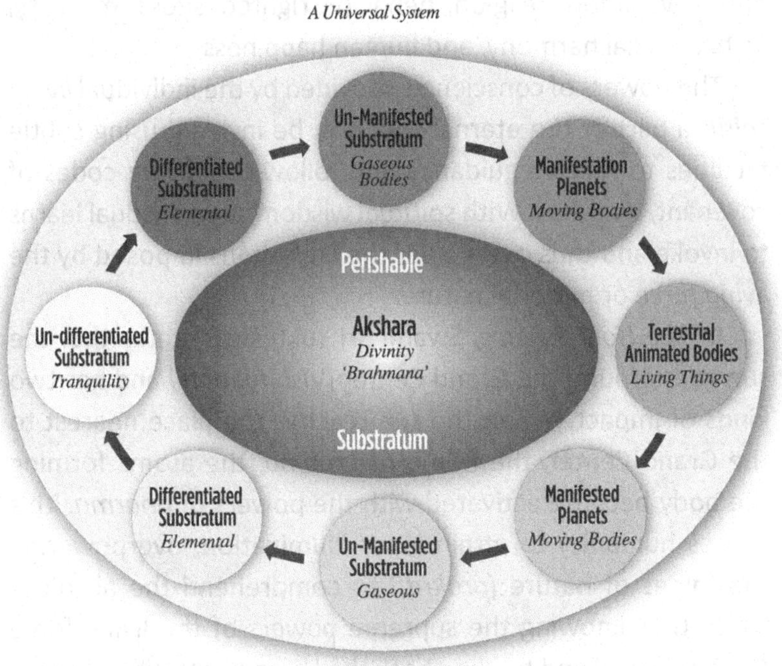

Illustration 10: Wheel of Genesis.

Equipoise

The principles of equipoise or the law of nature that upholds, supports, or maintains regulatory order of the universe, controls the existence of every creation. Equipoise, in spiritual terms, consists of two aspects called living force *(prakriti)* and eternal soul *(purusha),* which are also identified as *karma* (performance of obligatory actions and activity) and *dharma* (which are unlike *karmas* and are designated to regulate behaviors, necessary for the maintenance of the natural order of things or balance and tranquility). *Karmas,* at the humanity level, encompass performance of physical actions and activities; *dharmas,* at humanity's level, encompass individual spiritual duties, vocation, religion, behavior, righteousness, morality, justice, social harmony, and human happiness.

The powers of conscience, provided by the individual *living spirit,* a part of the eternal soul, can be invoked using subtle faculties to receive guidance and follow the divine codes of covenant, *dharmas*. With spiritual wisdom, an individual learns to invoke and thus overpower the limitations imposed by the *living force* or material nature.

In *The Holy Science,* Swami Sri Yukteswar states that the sun goes around the Grand Center *(Vishnunabhi)* and has two kinds of impact. When the sun reaches the place nearest to the Grand Center, the home of *brahma,* the atoms forming the body become activated with the powers of *dharma.* This causes humanity to attain inner illumination, overpowering the forces of nature *(prakriti)* to comprehend the absolute truth, thus knowing the supreme powers of the living force *(mahaprakriti)* and holding back the living spirit. When it goes farthest away from the Grand Center *(Vishnunabhi),* it causes darkness or generates spiritual ignorance within humanity. According to the Vedas, during the lifetime of a cycle of the planetary body, there are partial creations and annihilations. At the beginning of each day, defined as twelve thousand years, there is partial creation; at the end of each day, there is partial annihilation and a period of darkness (twenty thousand years). Each segment of twelve thousand years is called *daiva.*

Yugas

Each cycle is divided into four segments called *yugas*. Depending upon the duration and position, each *yuga's* name is based upon specific characteristics. Starting from the best to the worst, they are:

- *Satya Yuga:* This represents the Golden Age, and it lasts 1,728,000 human years, or 4,800 divine years. During this *yuga*, the majority of the population has acquired absolute truth or has gone beyond goodness, *sattwic guna*, and the average lifespan of a living being extends to 100,000 years.
- *Treta Yuga:* This represents the Silver Age and lasts 1,296,000 human years, or 3,000 divine years. During this *yuga*, the living beings have acquired transcendental knowledge, and more than 75 percent have already acquired godly qualities, *sattwic guna.* Individual lifespans are more than 10,000 years.
- *Dvapara Yuga:* This represents the Bronze Age, and it lasts 864,000 human years, or 2,400 divine years. During this *yuga*, more than 50 percent of the people have gone beyond *rajassic guna* and have acquired spiritual wisdom and thus acquired godly qualities, *sattwic guna*. They have learned to live in peace and tranquility, and the average life expectancy is more than 1,000 years.
- *Kali Yuga:* This represents the Iron Age, and it lasts 432,000 years, or 1,200 divine years. During this period, fewer than 25 percent of living beings have godly personalities, and the balance of the population is corrupted with materialistic desires, *rajasic guna*. Hypocrisy and egotism have overpowered society, which continuously faces unrest and upheavals. Individual life expectancy does not exceed more than 100 years. (As a reference, 360 days equals one human year; 360 human years equals one divine day.)

According to the Vedas, all material manifested bodies are created at the beginning of each day (consisting of several thousand human years); at the end of that day, there is partial to total annihilation. Each manifested body, in spite of all developments, modifications, and achievements, ultimately goes back to its original form to start again.

Living beings prevailing on the planet are subject to a shorter period of existence. Unless an individual living spirit is liberated prior to the completion of this cycle, during the period of less than one divine day, the living spirit helplessly comes into physical existence and goes through the physical annihilation of the physical body. These are called the cycles of birth and death.

As stated earlier, such existence depends upon the state of the individual's residual memories *(vasanas)*; each living thing continues this cycle of birth and death until the end of the divinity's life. At the end of the life of divinity, even the living spirits are liberated—along with their manifested bodies—and everything is annihilated until a new divinity is created to restart the universal system and restart the evolutionary process.

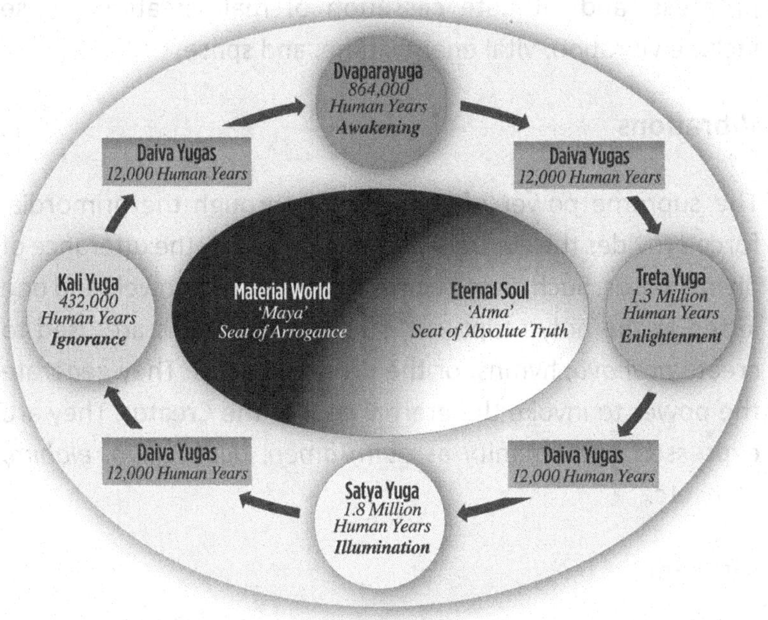

Kali Yuga	Dvapara Yuga	Treta Yuga	Satya Yuga
Iron Age	*Bronze Age*	*Silver Age*	*Golden Age*
432,000 Human years	*864,000 Human years*	*1.3 Million Human years*	*1.8 million Human years*
1200 Divine years	*2400 Divine years*	*3600 Divine years*	*4800 Divine years*
Average life span 100 years	*Average life span 1,000 years*	*Average life span 10,000 years*	*Average life span 100,000 years*
Decreased Godly qualities 25%	*Decreased Godly qualities 50%*	*Decreased Godly qualities 75%.*	*Decreased Godly qualities 100%.*
(Age of Ignorance)	***(Age of Awakening)***	***(Age of Enlightenment)***	***(Age of Illumination)***

Illustration 11: Yugas' Spiritual Life Cycles.

Four Elements

As briefly mentioned earlier, four main elements regulate the primordial force—with no beginning and no end. These four invisible elements act as the substratum for the process of creations, maintenance of sustainability, contribution toward progress, and ultimate cessation of manifestation. These include vibration, vital energy, time, and space.

Vibrations

The supreme power of the Creator through the primordial force provides the *vibration,* simply formed by the utterance of divine words. Such divine words consist of two vowels and one letter. In the holy scriptures, such combinations are used to create *pranava,* hymns, or the divine mantras. They generate the power to invoke the eternal soul of the Creator. They are expressed by humanity as *aum, amen, allab, allah, elohim, eloh,* etc.

Vital Force

The second element, activated by the forces of *vibration,* generates *vital force* that has the power of duality to transform an inert atom into a cosmic atom called *anu.* Within this process, the positive vibrations activate enough force to generate physical motion that generates a motion called attraction. As part of the duality, it also creates a force that produces a negative vibration to force and transform positive into repulsive motion. A combination of the two gives rise to the perpetual motion that ultimately produces illuminating forces, which in scientific terms relates to the origination of electromagnetic waves.

Time

As a by-product of the interaction between positive and negative forces, producing illumination creates darkness, called *kala*. The difference between illumination and darkness is measured in *time,* which becomes infinite in nature without light. Humanity uses this duality as a means to segregate time into smaller segments, such as day and night, as well as to calculate the evolutionary process commonly expressed as the geological time scale.

Space

The fourth element, the space, is defined as *desa.* It provides a measure to understand the universal system, astronomical structure, the ability to relate the creations with the Creator, and seek higher knowledge to go beyond intellectual knowledge to discover the unknown.

Though these four elements appear separate, they all operate in unity as one—as a means to unveil the infinite, invisible, indestructible, and incomprehensible nature of the Creator. One way to visualize the power of these four elements is through the process of elimination. For example, the stoppage of each aspect of attraction and repulsion will bring the universe to a standstill. Visualize that every little part of space that separates the object—and thereby creates distance—is reduced to nothing. Now, through mental powers, bring every segment of time that separates the past, the present, and the future to disappear. The only thing that will remain is a body smaller than a grain of salt. This is the true beginning of an ending—or you can imagine a fruit tree within a small seed.

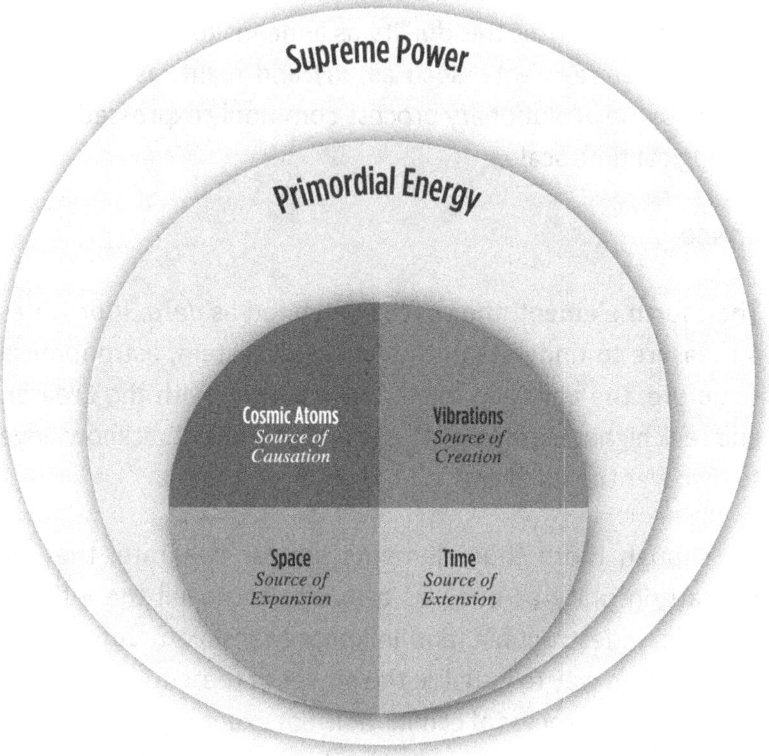

Illustration 12: Four Elements of Causation.

Eternal power that makes every ending a beginning and every beginning an ending is the living force.

Chapter 12
Living Force

Brahma

The second element of transcendental knowledge is the comprehension of living force, which is an integral part of the perpetual essence. It is the progenitor of all manifestations, both moving and nonmoving. The Vedas identify this as *brahma,* the creator of things moving and not moving. It has the ultimate power to prevail within the unmanifested—as well as the manifested—parts of the universal system. It resides at every level of the universal system and provides the vital force that all physical embodiments or dwellings require to survive.

At a higher level within the celestial part of the universal system, it provides the immense power to transform differentiated substratum into manifested physical bodies. It also acts as the source of all causation for mortal and immortal bodies.

Separation

Within the cosmic universe, the living force separates itself into two forms: an inert matter, *purusha,* consisting of atoms, and an omnipotent force, *prakriti,* which initiates the process of attraction and repulsion. This vital force is responsible for the collision of atoms to create gross mass and generate magnetic force.

Interaction

The gross mass over time expands to produce large physical bodies that generate magnetic forces, causing interaction among bodies to produce actions and activities. It is similar to how the physical inert matter of an engine and gasoline work together to make the automobile go. Similar to the automobile, the interaction between inert and vital energy causes physical cosmic bodies to move, rotate, and generate all other kinds of power, such as gravitation. It also forms the five great elements of nature: ground, water, fire, air, and sky.

Aspects

These five elements operate collaboratively to generate various forms of energy and produce specific aspects. These aspects are physical and nonphysical. For example, water is physical, but its ability to quench thirst is nonphysical. Fire is physical, but its ability to produce light is nonphysical. Air is physical, but its ability to cool is nonphysical; the ground is physical, but its ability to germinate is nonphysical; the sky is physical, but its ability to be infinite and invisible is nonphysical.

Impulses

These physical and nonphysical aspects of living force produce impulses that generate quests. There are two ways to fulfill such quests. One way is altruistic, and the second is egotistic. When a quest is fulfilled through the performance of actions in conformance with the covenant of nature, it becomes altruistic; when such a quest is fulfilled by the performance of actions in defiance of the covenant of nature, it becomes egotistic.

Attachment

Each quest originates the same way, but the nature of attachment creates the differentiation. If the nature of attachment is materialistic, it becomes selfish; if the nature of attachment is altruistic, it becomes selfless. The nature of attachment determines the negative or positive attitude. Developments of materialistic desire are of a negative nature. Material desires create mental anguish and anxiety and are considered to be of a lower quality. Altruistic desires are of a positive nature, as they generate long-term peace and tranquility. Therefore, they are considered to be of a higher quality.

Interdependence

Throughout life, every living thing on this planet is subject to physical and nonphysical aspects of the living forces. Since the nonphysical nature is imperceptible, it cannot manifest without a physical aspect of the living force, which creates the physical body. Similarly, physical nature, being inert, cannot show any opulence without nonphysical aspects of the living force nature. Therefore, without the presence of one, the other cannot actively exist.

All manifestations and creations therefore prevail together as one, and they stay as one in all aspects of changes in form within a form. For example, a beautiful snowflake appears as an individual, with form and shape of its own, but without its association with the spiritual aspect of divine nature, it is nothing but water molecules. These two aspects of nature, spiritual and material, interlock in such a way that brings out the splendor within the inert materials. For example, water by itself is inert; however, its combination with spiritual nature provides the water its unique ability to quench thirst. Similarly, the sun and moon are inert manifestations, but in combination with spiritual nature, they respectively produce effulgent heat and cool light to generate photosynthesis.

In written text, all syllables and words are inert, but their associations with spiritual nature transform them into sound through which one can communicate, produce music, and attain higher knowledge. Air by itself is spiritual in nature, but its association with inert matter transforms it into a roaring storm that can bring physical destruction and devastation. Elemental oxygen is of a material nature, but its association with spiritual nature transforms the breath into a life force.

Besides interdependence, a combination of these two aspects of living force generates a third aspect that is of paranormal nature and appears in the form of divine bliss. Only through personal experience is such bliss attained. It is a form of revelation called *vibhuti.* It is like acquiring the ability to comprehend the existence of multiple life cycles within a seed and an embryo by simply holding them or looking at them.

A person with such divine bliss can perceive within the physical body of a human the presence of infinite intellect and wisdom as well as see a multitude of attributes buried within all living things, moving and not moving.

Unique Link

The *living force* itself never changes; however, due to its association with *living spirit,* the aspects of primordial force, discussed in detail in the following chapter, go through changes, including physical, mystical, material, and spiritual aspects. These constantly interact to bring changes and generate new things with different characteristics or traits. All such changes are transient in nature. For example, soil in the process of germination produces multiple types of plants, fruits, flowers, and edibles, but the basic character of the soil and the basic process of germination never change.

The relationship between these two also continually brings change, which makes it even more difficult to identify the true link between them. The beginning can be seen as the ending, and the same ending becomes the beginning. For example, there is a tree (live) in the seed (inert), and there is seed (inert) growing within the tree (live), or there is an egg (inert) in the chicken (live), and a chicken (live) is in the egg (inert). Due to the complexity of this relationship, the human invariably wrongly assumes the living force itself to be of a transient nature. Living force is the substratum of nature bringing change in one form to another form. Living force is part of the immortal substratum of the perpetual essence. Any change experienced by living things is of a transient nature.

The interaction of five great elements of nature (air, fire, water, ground, and sky) to produce a unique link that causes changes, which affect the environment globally, regionally, and locally. They directly or indirectly produce associated impulses and stimuli (sound, touch, sight, taste, and smell) that can be observed through the five physical sensory organs (ears, body, eyes, tongue, and nose) to produce multiple combinations. In holy scripture, such multiple combinations are categorized as three traits called *gunas* or the traits of nature: *sattwa*, *rajas*, and *tamas*. *Sattwa* represents peace, tranquility, and contentment, thus producing a noble personality. *Rajas* represents passion, energy, and enthusiasm, thus producing an aggressive personality. *Tamas* represents a lethargic, manipulative, and cunning nature that produces a lazy, arrogant, and demonic personality.

These *gunas* influence an individual's personality; they remain independent of any activities performed by any living thing. These traits behave just like any metal or materials such as gold or clay, which can be molded into any size or shape and acquire certain characteristics; however, the underlying nature of the material or metal does not change regardless of what kind of jewelry or pottery is made from the material. With the melting of jewelry or the decay of pottery, the metal or clay goes back into its original form—as if it was never made into jewelry or pottery.

Likewise, the personality that originates from the interaction of material nature with spiritual nature only brings changes in form—but never in substance. Not understanding the true relationship between personality and temperament, individuals believe they can bring about changes to their own destinies. This delusion is caused by the power of nature *(maya)*, which is responsible for duality and multiplicity of a transitory nature. When these transitory delusions take on a permanent form, they cultivate ignorance. People are unable to understand, explore, or unveil how the supreme power impacts humanity. They end up acquiring malevolent habits and following the wrong ways of evil and demonic powers. Some even become aloof, are never satisfied with anything, and eventually end up following the wrong ways of life. They become victims of their own demonic or evil spirits. When this happens, they are never able to comprehend the true relationship between humanity, living force, and the Creator. Some even go to the extreme and end up not believing in the existence of the Creator.

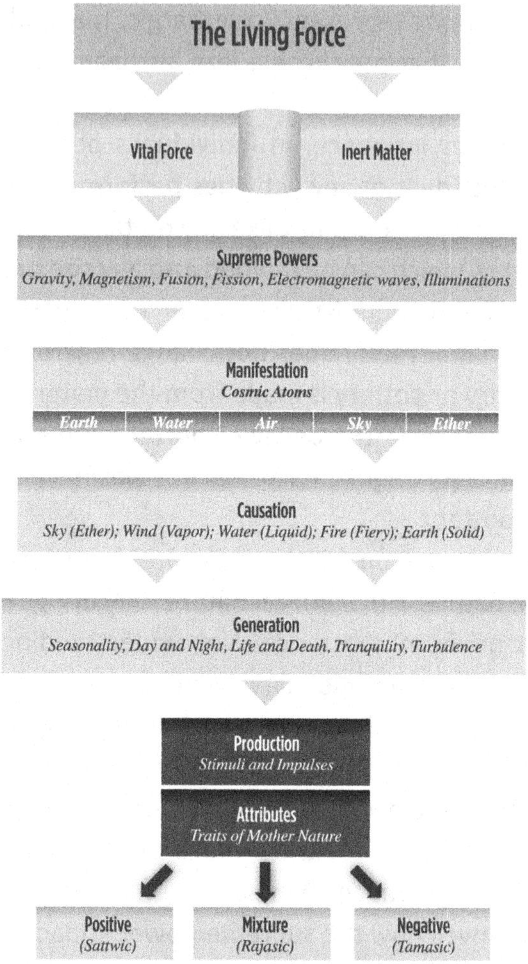

Illustration 13: Structure of the Living Force.

Categories

Those who understand the various aspects of living force, and can comprehend the true relationship between humanity and the living force, are grouped into four categories: the *curious*, the *selfish*, the *explorers*, and the *devotees*.

Curious

The first group includes those who are *curious.* Such individuals become interested only when they are dissatisfied with their lives, and they feel compelled to seek help to resolve their immediate problems. They practice spirituality as a means to overcome personal dissatisfaction or delusion. They have no commitment or long-term objective; as soon as the problem or delusion is resolved, they immediately forget about seeking higher knowledge or spirituality. They go back to a normal state of ignorance. They repeatedly follow this technique and gradually become habitual with such a transient approach to knowing the supreme power of the Creator.

Selfish

The second group includes those who are *selfish.* Such individuals are not true devotees, but once they have acquired financial, social, and political success, they become insecure. They understand the temporary aspect of happiness and glory. Nevertheless, to protect their success for as long as possible, they elect to worship the Creator and practice organized religion. As a means to seek higher knowledge, they become active members of a church, temple, synagogue, or other place of worship. Their motives of worship are associated with selfish and short-term materialistic gains. They conduct acts of selfless service out of fear of punishment. They are only interested in protecting acquired wealth or deflecting the danger of losing power. They publicly demonstrate their commitment to the Creator alongside their arrogance of wealth and leadership roles.

Explorers

The third group includes the *explorers.* These individuals cultivate the quest to acquire higher knowledge and understand the supreme power of the Creator. They are committed to unveil the relationship, and they make a long-term commitment to attain spiritual wisdom. They devote time and make concerted efforts to study holy scriptures, and they perform prayers, worship, and meditation to comprehend various aspects of nature and the Creator. Through this process, they succeed in attaining spiritual wisdom; once they have attained it, however, they become content and elect not to pursue it further.

Devotees

The fourth group includes the true *devotees.* These individuals are born with spiritual souls, and they display an inherent desire to attain absolute truth from a young age. They become ardent enthusiasts from early childhood and start to perform selfless acts of service to attain divine blessing and enlightenment. They demand nothing, expect nothing, and are the true spiritual scholars; they seek spiritual wisdom to attain the ultimate union with the Creator. They understand that comprehension of spiritual wisdom is only an intermittent path to the ultimate wisdom. They respect the individual soul residing within the body as an integral part of the eternal soul, and they seek purification through renunciation. They learn to surrender themselves to the Creator and nothing else. With a steadfast mind, they make a firm commitment, at any cost, to sacrifice all materialistic needs and to detach from any kind of selfish activity. They devote all their energy to performing selfless acts; any wealth they acquire through their own services, including material and nonmaterial things, they contribute toward improving the social conditions of deprived beings. They become committed to the supreme goal of attaining freedom from this material world. With the renunciation of the material world, such devotees receive rewards by the supreme powers of the Creator. They acquire mystical powers through which they are able to invoke the divine love in others. As enlightened souls or as a great soul *(mahatma)* they receive honor from society. They go through many births, serving the cause of the Creator with love and devotion to ultimately attain eternity and join the supreme power. According to the Bhagavad Gita, such great souls *(mahatmas)* are very rare to find.

The attainment of enlightenment is not the final stage. Some great souls, not realizing this fact, after attaining spiritual doctrine, become attached to their achievements and are unable to handle such glory. They have corrupted minds and believe there is nothing above enlightenment. This brings spiritual ignorance, and they become indecisive and continually change their methods of worship. Their minds are persuaded by material gains and materialistic desires, and they end up falling back on the path of ego.

Some, with the help of inner power, individual mind, and thought, come back into focus and regain inner peace and happiness. Even though such individuals are able to regain peace and tranquility, these individuals find it difficult to attain ultimate freedom from the cycle of life and death because of an inner weakness.

Masquerade

The ultimate power of the living force is *maya,* which at all times creates an invisible veil to protect true nature and the workings of living forces, including *vital force (prakriti)* and *inert matter (purusha).* This masquerade, *maya,* creates the duality, seen by living things in the form of illusion, delusion, arrogance, transitory blindness, or darkness, *kala*. Through this power, *maya*, a physical activity, is transformed from good action, *karma,* into wrong actions *(akarmas),* righteous morality *(dharma)* into immorality *(adharma),* and thus brings imbalance within equilibrium, resulting in the transformation of neutral phases of actions into evil, good, and divine.

Because of this masquerade, even at the highest level—transcendental wisdom—only a fraction of the eternal truth becomes apparent. Many great souls and spiritual scholars have been duped by this masquerade and have become victims to their logical ways of thinking. According to the Bhagavad Gita, many believe that after termination upon death, the inert matter and the vital force die. In truth, since both are part of the eternal living force, they just return to their original forms and reappear to create and support new embodiments. It is similar to the manner in which gold or silver jewelry loses its form when melted and then takes on new shapes and forms when redesigned. No matter how often gold is melted, it only loses its form—and not its substance.

The true source of absolute truth is the living spirit, residing within each living being.

Chapter 13
Living Spirit

The Soul

The other aspect of the primordial force is the living spirit that represents the third element of transcendental wisdom. It prevails as the eternal soul *(paramatma)* throughout the universal system and remains invisible at all times. Within a living being, it prevails as individual living spirit *(atma).* To perceive the existence of the living spirit, an individual has to cultivate an activated subconscious. This requires an individual to attain spiritual wisdom and, through the powers of such knowledge, invoke the inner conscience by piercing through the veil created by living force to protect the living spirit.

The living spirit's ultimate goal is to fulfill its responsibilities and guide living beings to attain freedom from the shackles of living force and free it to join with the eternal soul. The living spirit, being part of the eternal soul, remains the repository of wisdom, which living beings can use to attain final liberation and merge with the eternal soul. As part of this process, living things go through the process of spiritual and physical evolution; to accomplish such evolutionary process, living things go through cycles of life and death.

Every living being receives a basic code of covenants through the living spirit to stay in compliance with the laws of nature to maintain equilibrium and attain peace and tranquility. Through a well-defined process of self-perfection, individuals can learn to invoke the powers of the living spirit and go beyond the intellectual knowledge to attain spiritual wisdom. Some can even go beyond spiritual wisdom to attain divine bliss.

With the accomplishment of sanctity, an individual living spirit is able to establish a direct link with the eternal soul; the living spirit is able to move within the universal system without any limitations of time and space.

Embodiment

Through the interaction of two aspects of primordial force, *living force* and *eternal soul,* an embodiment is formed. The *living force* creates a manifested physical body, an embodiment, to provide a dwelling for the *eternal soul* to prevail within it as *individual living spirit*. The *living force,* by itself, is omnipotent; the *eternal soul* is omnipresent. Their relationship on an individual level is similar to the one between the automobile (living force/embodiment) and the driver (eternal force/ individual living spirit), where the automobile performs the actions while the driver provides the guidance.

Within the oldest scripture, *Enuma Elish,* the relationship between living force and living spirit is described. "Origination of life started when the Creator took the earthen material (clay) to form a dwelling and then introduced the breath of life to a fist of clay to start the process of pro-generation."

Similarly, in the Vedas, the *rishis* in the Himalayas determined the interaction of matter/inorganic and vital energy/organic, such as clay and water, created the embodiment of living things to house the living spirit of the Creator.

The Vedas further describe that the embodiments consisting of the living spirit receive support from the five great elements of nature: earth, water, light, fire, and sky. Cosmic bodies such as the sun provide direct light, the moon provides reflective light, and the planetary system provides seasonality. The terrestrial bodies, such as ocean water, transform into vapors, and vapors transform into rain to form rivers, lakes, and other bodies of water, providing life. The earth's crust transforms into mountains to germinate and produce nutrients.

At the same time, the physical transformation that takes place among these five phases of formation creates a delusion, or *maya*, that leads humanity to perceive each form to be an individual and independent entity. Thus, a change in form makes humanity believe they are all mortal, not realizing that, behind these interactions, an invisible power is providing the substratum (perpetual essence) that is indefinable—and cannot be measured, calculated, or scientifically proven.

Progression

The embodiment of living things, *jiva*, that first developed as a single cell further developed to form the vegetation kingdom and remained stationary; they were primarily created to provide nourishment for living beings. Later, there was the development of sensory organs, complete with physical features, such as the eyes, ears, nose, mouth, and skin. There was further advancement in the physical body to create limbs to go with the causal body, including glands and a functioning nervous system, which led to the evolution of the animal kingdom.

The ability to move about and travel long distances to

seek food heightened their consciousness to become aware of their surroundings, which spurred the acquisition of instinctive powers to protect themselves from external threats and challenges.

The advancement of the physical and causal body caused the development of the astral body, *lingasarira*, including the mind and intellect. This caused the evolution of the first primate to gradually evolve into a human and acquire the ability to understand the powers of nature and to interpret the supreme powers that caused mystical phenomena in the form of divine revelations.

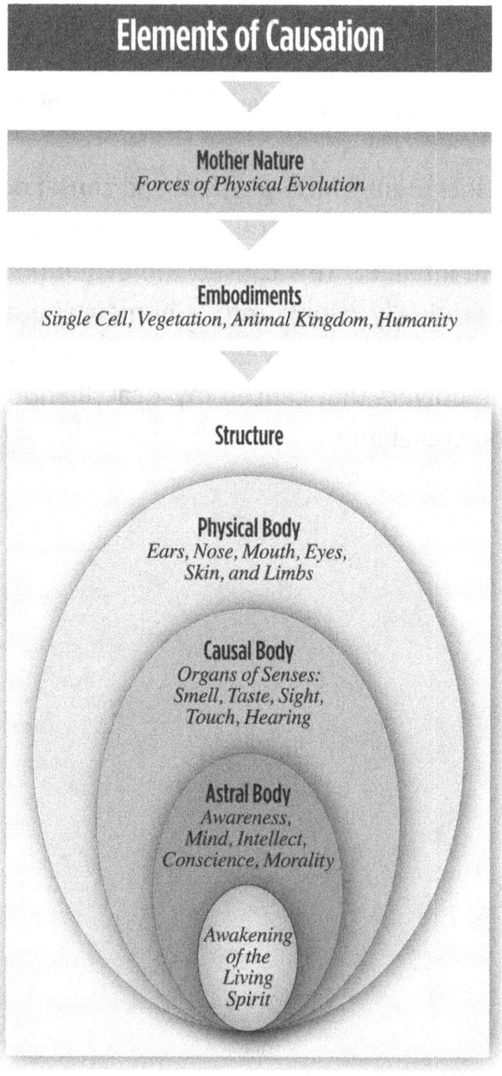

Illustration 14: Evolution of Embodiment.

Conscious Mind

With greater advancement in invisible subtle faculties, intellect of living things transforms into a conscious mind and thus acquires consciousness, *spiritual awakening* of the individual living spirit. With this conscious mind, living things—especially humanity—came to realize that each embodiment contains a living spirit, which could be inactive, awakened, or vibrant. Humanity first learns to invoke this conscious mind to acquire intellect. With further advancement, selected members of humanity learned to go beyond the practical knowledge or intellect to explore the invisible powers of nature. Spiritual scholars by now identified five regions that have the ability to receive and interpret sensational vibrations, a very low intensity of electromagnetic waves, which they defined as *pancha tattwa.* Each of these regions is controlled and managed by a subtle faculty of conscious mind and is regulated through five sets of internal invisible body parts. Depending upon the source of influence, they can be grouped as follows: *karmaindriyas, jnanendriyas*, and *sukshmasarira*.

Karmaindriyas

External forces *(prakriti)* produce impulses that directly or indirectly are influenced by material nature. They are received through the organs of the physical body, including the eyes, ears, nose, mouth, skin, arms, and legs and are directed through subtle faculties to produce activities that an individual uses to fill obligatory responsibilities called *karmas*. These impulses are of a material nature and are called *karmaindriyas*. They are responsible for the generation of physical actions and activities—with the desires to explore the world of nature. They directly influence an individual's ability to perform actions and activities. There are three traits of *karmas*—lethargic, energetic, and mystic. All three are influenced by the traits of nature *(gunas)* and determine individual temperament, personality, and character.

Jnanendriyas

Internal forces are regulated by the invisible and incomprehensible astral body. These sensations or *dharmas* generate mystic auras and produce pure inner impulses that can direct codes of covenants. These impulses originate from the living spirit and are processed through the causal body to produce smell, taste, sight, touch, and hearing—and thus impact individual actions and activities.

These then generate fountains of altruistic thoughts and desires. Depending on the conditions of the individual astral body, they counterbalance the external impulses and generate desires to seek higher knowledge. They create a quest to go beyond and acquire higher spiritual knowledge. These impulses are of subjective nature and are called *jnanendriyas.* These sensations transform the innate material quest into a spiritual quest and selfish desires into selfless and altruistic desires.

Sukshmasarira

When the mystic aura of morality overpowers the sensation of immorality, common personality transforms into noble personality as they develop perceptive powers to comprehend the transcendental knowledge. With the overpowering of one's carnal nature, the royal secrets of supreme power are revealed, and the individual achieves enlightenment, expressed in spiritual terms as *nirvana.* Such state is defined as *sukshmasarira,* where the astral body is able to establish a direct link with the perpetual essence and is able to access the powers of the eternal soul *(prabhuatma).* The individual living spirit attains liberation and humanly love; *chit* is transformed into divine love, *chitta.* The individual cosmic atom energizes to become a spiritual atom. All such transformations occur in the form of inner illumination; the magnetic aura or gamma rays pass through the body, creating a very low level of reaction, such as electromagnetism to produce eternal light or illumination. The individual living spirit becomes free of cycles of life and death. This state of being, defined in the holy scriptures as *kaivalya*, the state of no return, is commonly referred to as eternity or *moksha*.

Eternal Truth

Spiritual scholars have determined that, based upon the impact of these activities, the astral body could be transformed to perishable, semi-perishable, imperishable and immortal.

Perishable

Perishable embodiment includes creations in which the living spirit has not fully energized, and the embodiment acquires eternal truth through the physical part of the embodiment. These embodiments are subject to cause and effect, growth and decay, spoil and rot. The working of the living spirit within such embodiments can only be understood through the study of vibrant energy generated by these bodies in the form of changes in color, shape, form, and size. Flowers, vegetables, chemical compounds, and even different kinds of brilliant rocks or minerals go through various phases of existence (just as humans do), including origination, growth, production, and reproduction. They eventually go through a drop-off or fading phase where they return to their true inert forms. These physical objects provide the resources necessary for the survival and existence of other living things.

Semi-Perishable

Semi-perishable embodiment includes humanity and selected advanced-stage animals and other creatures. In these embodiments, the eternal truth is acquired through an energized conscious mind where living spirit plays an active role. It provides the physical embodiment necessary guidance that causes living beings to go through cycles of the physical evolutionary process, which occurs from birth until death. Within this phase, the embodiments also go through a series of spiritual changes. Each change represents liberation of the living spirit from the shackles of living forces. The individual living spirit passes from a physical body (visible form) to an astral body (invisible form), and from an astral body (invisible form) to a physical body (visible), until the astral body becomes purified from the blemishes it acquires through its affiliation with the living force or material nature.

Imperishable

Imperishable embodiment includes human beings who have attained self-perfection through the process of purification and receive eternal truth directly from the perpetual essence of the Creator. With the sanctified body, the living spirit gains full control of the embodiment, such as archangels, demigods, and deities. Such embodiments can prevail within the material world by remaining totally unattached or unencumbered. The embodiment can move into the past or the future; it can travel freely within the universe without any limitations created by time and space. Since their living spirit becomes a divine messenger, they use their embodiment to bring harmony and peace into the lives of others who are being victimized, such as

Mahatma Gandhi, Mother Teresa, Martin Luther King Jr., and Abraham Lincoln.

Immortal

Immortal is the final phase of an embodiment, where the individual living spirit finally leaves the astral body to become part of the eternal soul and lose its identity forever, which is commonly referred to as *the resurrection of the individual living spirit* or *attained eternity.* At this stage, the living force is no longer subject to cycles of life and death.

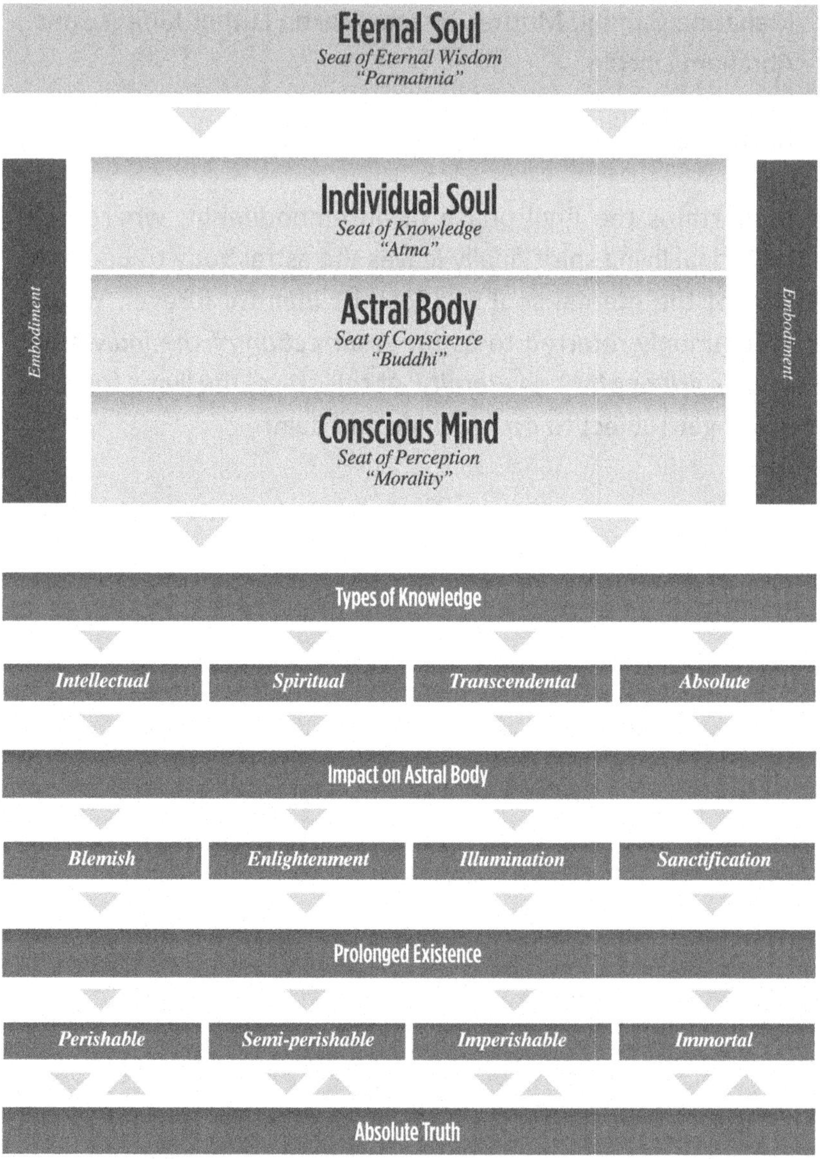

Illustration 15: Source of Absolute Truth.

An invisible link connects every creation with the Creator; in spiritual terms, this is called the Trinity.

Chapter 14
Invisible Link

Trinity

The fourth element of transcendental wisdom is comprehension of the invisible link among the three aspects of creation: Creator, creations, and power of creation. In spiritual terms, it is described as *Trinity* or as the union of the Father (the Creator or the supreme power, *divinity*), the Son (the *living force* creating the living things), and the Holy Spirit (the *living spirit* or individual soul). The process of attainment or comprehension of this invisible link is referred to as *sanctity*. With *sanctity,* individual doubts are abolished, and the true nature of the divine unity becomes apparent.

As we discussed earlier, the eternal soul of the Creator prevails throughout the universe, and part of the eternal soul resides within the embodiment of every living thing created by the living force. At all times, the individual living spirit remains connected to the eternal soul through this invisible and incomprehensible link. The ultimate goal of every individual spirit is to attain liberation from the powers of the living force to merge with the eternal soul called *eternity*.

The powers of the *living force* create a divine veil, called *maya,* that humanity recognizes as Mother Nature creating different kinds of phenomena that generate duality, multiplicity, illusion, and delusion. They create spiritual ignorance and limit an individual's ability to comprehend the true relationship between the Creator and its creations. It is only through supreme power or eternal wisdom that an individual can pierce through the veil to comprehend the true relationship between the Creator and its creations.

To reach such a stage, an individual goes through a series of inspirational, mystical, perceptive, and intuitive experiences. A devotee's conscious mind takes full control of all the sensory organs of perception, and the devotee feels embodiment, is liberated, and experiences inner freedom, like a leaf flying in the air without being tangled in the wind or becoming part of the air. Unless a devotee reaches such a state, the existence of the *Trinity* remains a mystery.

With the comprehension of the powers of the *Trinity,* a devotee comes to witness how the infinite can pervade the finite while remaining infinite, never becoming a part of the finite form. The demise of the finite has no impact on infinite form. This is likened to comprehending the infinite life cycle hidden within an egg or seed, or how the finite form exists because of its infinite nature. Without the infinite nature, the finite forms cannot exist.

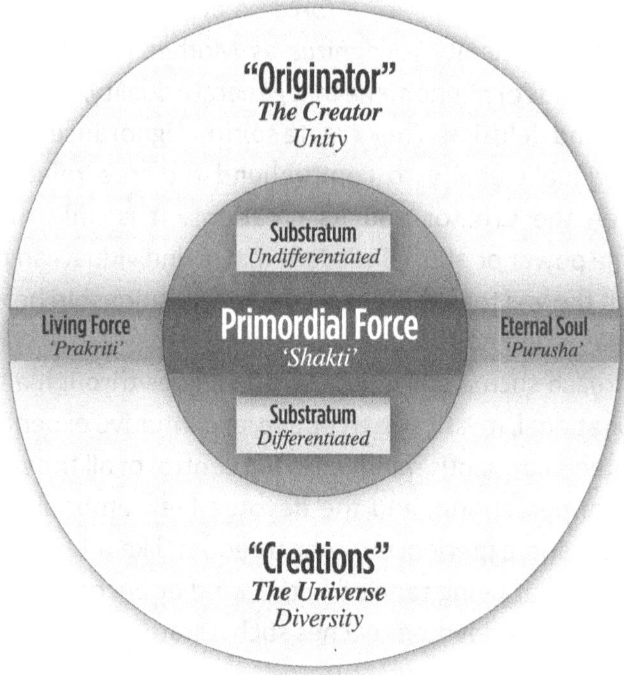

Illustration 16: Unveiling the Law of Creation—Trinity.

Visualization

The best way to comprehend the existence of living things in relation to the Creator is through the visualization of knots in a rope. These knots are formed from the rope itself, but they can exist only because of the rope itself. Similarly, the waves in the ocean can exist only because of the ocean. Likewise, an ocean can only exist because of nature. Nature can only exist because of the living force; the living force can only exist because of the perpetual essence of the Creator.

A true devotee understands that the Creator or supreme power is the immortal form that cannot be subject to annihilation. Therefore, even if manifested bodies are formed from its immortal form and appear to be an integral part of the substratum, they always remain separate from its substratum. The demise of the manifested forms does not mean the demise of the substratum or the Creator.

Another way to comprehend the concept of the *Trinity* is through examination of the process of individual dreams. All dreams are by-products of the individual's mind. Physically, the individual dream never becomes part of the individual; it remains together only as long as the dream continues. When the individual awakes, the dream is over—and it no longer remains part of the dreamer. Therefore, there are two aspects of the dream: the manifested and the unmanifested. When we are awake, dreams become unmanifested; dreams manifest and appear as if they are real only when we are asleep. Subjectively, both are related, but physically, they are not even connected.

With the comprehension of the *Trinity,* the power *divinity* becomes *reality*—and vice versa. With such understanding, one can comprehend how the inconceivable nature of the supreme power or Creator can go from conceivable to inconceivable or vice versa.

Tributes

Once the devotee is able to comprehend the powers of the *Trinity,* the devotee can confirm the inner conviction that the *living force* (embodiment), the *living spirit* (life), and the *primordial force* (divinity) are all part of the Creator. They are all one and only one. The Creator controls every aspect of the universe through the powers of its perpetual essence—manifested and not manifested. Through the power of primordial force, it enforces the evolutionary processes; through the powers of living force, it causes the manifestation of physical bodies; and through the living spirit, it enforces the code of covenants.

Humanity honors and respects various attributes of the Creator. They offer oblations to the Creator for providing the primordial force without which no living being could exist, progress, or serve individual obligations. They offer tributes to ancestors for providing heritage—without which the perpetual cycles of life would not prevail. They offer tributes to the eternal wisdom provided through the living spirit—without which no living thing could ever uncover the mysteries of the universe.

Humanity also offers tributes to other divine creations—like a mother providing milk for a newborn. They offer tributes to living things, including the lower animal kingdom, which sacrifice their lives to other animals to survive and serve humanity. They also offer tributes to the vegetation kingdom that provides healing and nourishment for the body as well as acting as a medium for purification. They offer tributes to rhythmic sounds—such as hymns and mantras—that bring peace and harmony. They burn sweet, hard, fatty oils or mixed materials with low melting points—such as wax or butter—to invoke the powers of the eternal soul that prevail within every aspect of the universal system. They ignite mixtures of herbs or incense to offer tributes to fire that provide illumination and honor the powers to purify anything—including the inner body through inhalation.

In addition, humanity offers tributes to divinity for providing a shield by creating the sky to hold back cosmic forces from influencing terrestrial bodies and the powers of attraction and repulsion for splitting atoms to create motion and provide illumination.

With the offering of such tributes and undivided devotion, individuals are blessed with the divine nectar and identify the establishment of the divine link.

The ultimate reward of spiritual wisdom, serenity, is acquired through internal equilibrium.

Chapter 15
Serenity

Self-Realization

The fifth element of transcendental wisdom is the freedom of living spirit from the shackles of living force or the material world to join with the eternal soul and thus become part of the primordial force and lose its identity. To accomplish this, one has to learn to practice the disciplines referred to as *yogas*.

Sankhya Yoga

The first yoga *(sankhya yoga)* deals with understanding the purpose and function of the individual living spirit, *atma,* which resides within the embodiment. With this yoga, the seeker comprehends the existence of the living spirit; its purpose is to provide guidance.

Karma Yoga

The second yoga is called *karma yoga.* With this yoga, a seeker comes to understand the different kinds of actions. The individual also comes to learn how the powers of the living spirit can transform the nature of action from selfish, *akarma,* into selfless actions, *karma.*

Yajna Yoga

With the third yoga, the seeker learns to incorporate the renunciation of desires through performing sacrifices, works of charity, donations, and oblations to transform selfless actions into devotional actions.

Dharma Yoga

Once an individual has accomplished renunciation and the abandonment of individual desires or *dharma yoga,* he or she is able to invoke the powers of inner living spirit and practice devotional obligations by complying with the path of morality, humanity, and righteousness.

Buddhi Yoga

With the practice of *buddhi yoga,* an individual embodiment, including the physical, causal, and astral body, goes through a complete process of purification. Thus an individual receives divine bliss and starts to follow the path to attainment. The individual soul is transformed from *atma* into a *mahatma* or a transcendental soul.

Abhysa Yoga

With the completion of *abhysa yoga,* an individual attains enlightenment *(moksha)* and acquires paranormal powers of perception and attains freedom from the shackles of the living force. With the completion of *abhysa yoga,* an individual attains enlightenment *(moksha).*

Ishvara Yoga

Only a select few go beyond *abhysa yoga* to practice *ishvara yoga*. With *ishvara yoga,* an individual attains inner illumination, comes to realize the absolute truth, and attains eternity.

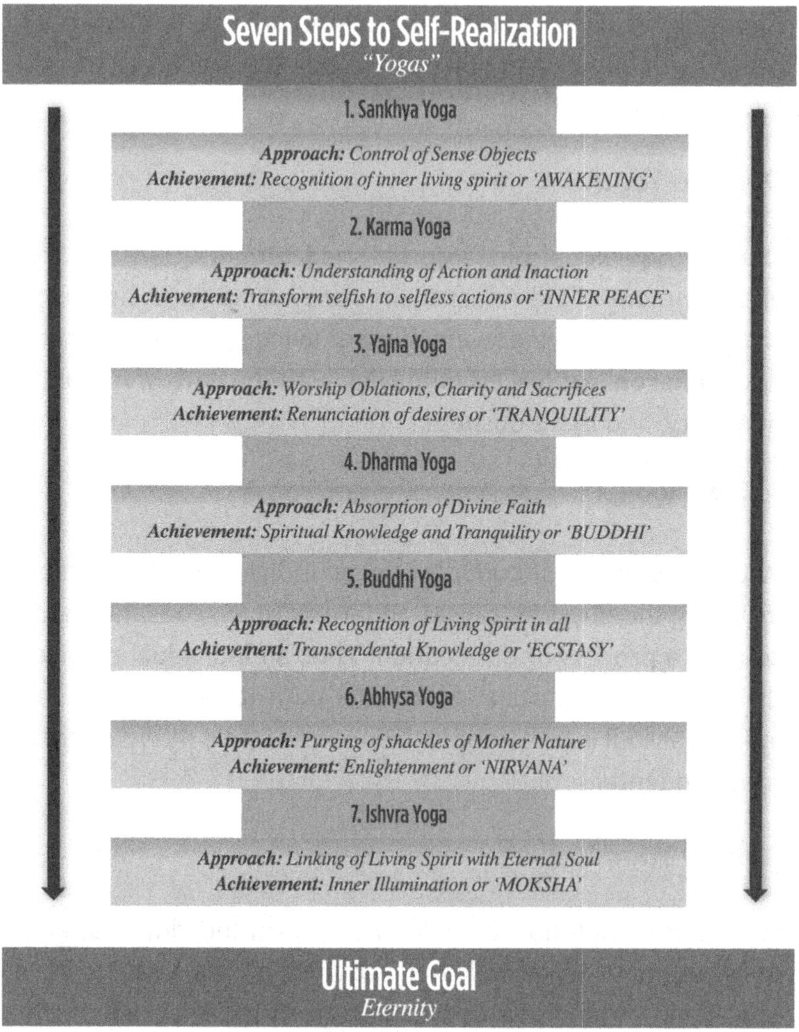

Seven Steps to Self-Realization
"Yogas"
1. Sankhya Yoga
Approach: Control of Sense Objects
Achievement: Recognition of inner living spirit or 'AWAKENING'
2. Karma Yoga
Approach: Understanding of Action and Inaction
Achievement: Transform selfish to selfless actions or 'INNER PEACE'
3. Yajna Yoga
Approach: Worship Oblations, Charity and Sacrifices
Achievement: Renunciation of desires or 'TRANQUILITY'
4. Dharma Yoga
Approach: Absorption of Divine Faith
Achievement: Spiritual Knowledge and Tranquility or 'BUDDHI'
5. Buddhi Yoga
Approach: Recognition of Living Spirit in all
Achievement: Transcendental Knowledge or 'ECSTASY'
6. Abhysa Yoga
Approach: Purging of shackles of Mother Nature
Achievement: Enlightenment or 'NIRVANA'
7. Ishvra Yoga
Approach: Linking of Living Spirit with Eternal Soul
Achievement: Inner Illumination or 'MOKSHA'
Ultimate Goal
Eternity

Illustration 17: Path of Self-Realization.

Commencement

The process of attaining freedom for the individual living spirit requires the attainment of eternal wisdom called absolute truth or *Sat,* which resides within the eternal soul. According to the Bhagavad Gita this absolute truth, which is an immortal knowledge, was first passed down from an eternal soul to the incomprehensible form of the Creator, called *divinity.*

Using the eternal wisdom, the divinity controls and manages the undifferentiated and differentiated parts of the universe. The eternal wisdom passed from incomprehensible divinity to unmanifested *deities* assigns the responsibility to control and implements the principles of equipoise.

Later, this wisdom was passed down to partially manifested *demigods* who were assigned the responsibility to manage the operations of the cosmic part of our solar and planetary system.

This knowledge was later passed from *demigods* to *divine envoys, avatars,* or *archangels,* who were blessed to guide the imperial rulers and their successors who were responsible for the organization of the first civilization on earth. Later spiritual scholars acquired such knowledge through inner inspiration or directly from *archangels* in the form of holistic visions. This knowledge was recorded in epics and holy scriptures such as *The Rig Veda, The Epic of Gilgamesh* of Babylon or Mesopotamia, The Five Books of Moses, the New Testament, and many others.

During periods when the quest for spirituality is suppressed due to political disruptions, material desires, or other reasons, the living spirit goes dormant—but it never dies. History has proven that, when immorality takes over morality, the eternal soul manifests and appears as the *divine envoy* on the earth to reinstate the forgotten principles of morality through the resurrection of the quest for spiritual wisdom. No specific time, location, color, or physical body determines the manifestation of the eternal soul. This *divine envoy* or messiah appears with inherent powers to activate the living spirit. It prevails until the mission is accomplished. Before returning, the *divine envoy* transfers the eternal wisdom to other spiritual scholars or devotees to reestablish codes of covenant and bring in the balance of powers or equilibrium. Humanity again learns to seek higher knowledge, enlightenment, illumination, and sanctity. Even after its disappearance, it continues to prevail and guide humanity.

According to the Bhagavad Gita, even as an embodied living being, the *divine envoy* is not subject to the cycle of birth and death. The living being never appears in the same image as before. Several *divine envoys* have appeared on earth to enforce the codes of covenant. These include Abraham, Moses, Confucius, Buddha, Zeus, Zoroaster, Jesus Christ, Muhammad, Baha'u'llah, and Nanak.

Covenants

Humanity is required to follow two kinds of covenants: one includes covenants established by living beings or by the authorities responsible for the enforcement of law and order; the second includes covenants established by the primordial force to comply with the divine rules of equilibrium and balance.

Human Laws

Covenants established by human beings are based upon interpretations of existing situations and are expressed in terms of black and white. These covenants are of objective and subjective. They are based upon individual levels of authority assigned by the society or individual interpretations of acquired spiritual wisdom. Such knowledge or authority is used to determine what is right or wrong; what is acceptable or unacceptable; what is desirable or undesirable; what is legal or illegal. These covenants established by humanity can be partial, which makes something good for one and bad for another.

Ancient sages such as King Solomon, Philo of Alexandria, the Jews of Palestine, the Pharisees, and the rabbis compiled *Mishnah.* During the Axial Age, spiritual scholars from Greece, India, China, and the Americas determined that one does not need to exit the material world to become a spiritual person. Based upon their personal experiences, they established that one could become a spiritual soul while existing within the material world by not getting attached to the material world and restraining from becoming possessive of material objects and material power.

Socrates, Plato, Aristotle, Confucius, and Buddha further demonstrated that serving obligatory responsibilities, such as taking care of family, fulfilling societal obligations, and performing devotional obligations, are an integral part of spiritual life. The life histories of sages and their experiences have proven that this is not just probable; instead, it is quite possible to live in the material world and still attain liberation from the material world.

Spiritual Laws

The covenants established by the spiritual laws are based upon codes of equilibrium and balance and are defined by the powers of the primordial force and regulated by the living spirits residing within the embodiment. They fall into three categories: neutral, positive, and negative. Humanity has no control on such covenants, and they influence humanity and all other living things indifferently.

According to the Bhagavad Gita, attaining liberation from the material world requires that every living being must understand these covenants and come to comprehend their associated hidden virtues operating behind each action. To attain such wisdom, a seeker has to come to understand the true nature of one's actions before and during the process of performing those actions. Once an individual acquires this ability, the individual can easily pursue every action with selfless motives and avoid any attachment to the results of those actions. It requires understanding the true differences in *action*, *no action*, and *inaction*.

It is not an easy concept to understand; even highly learned devotees are continually baffled by such a distinction. Understanding these concepts requires grasping the subtle aspects of every action and determining whether those aspects are masked within the action. For example, understanding and grasping the fact that there is taste hidden within the fruit, and there is no way to know the taste unless one bites the fruit. Moreover, two pieces of the same fruit do not have the same taste.

Process of Enactment

Based upon the nature of motion, the process of enactment includes three kinds of actions: inert, motion, and motionless. They in turn produce three types of activities: ineffective, physical, and spiritual. Irrespective of the type, in every activity, there is a hidden truth. The hidden truth is working all the time behind or within every action. The hidden truth differentiates one action from another—just as a sweet, juicy orange is different from a sour, dry orange. Depending on the hidden truth, the same physical or verbal action performed in a similar manner can have very different results. For example, one human being might consider a pat on the back a sign of encouragement; another human being could view it as a sign of aggression. The only thing that differentiates actions is the underlying truth or the hidden motive. Whether the action is supported by the living spirit determines the true virtue of an action. Based upon individual virtues, the actions fall into one these categories: inert action, neutral action, selfish action, and inaction.

The actions can be classified as inert, neutral, selfish, passive, worship, aspirant, devotee, or steadfast.

Inert

Inert action produces no physical or spiritual reaction. Such actions produce nothing except a show or demonstration.

Neutral

Action that produces motion generates a reaction to overpower the action itself. Any action performed in conformance with the laws of divine nature has neutral reaction. It follows the natural path and generates neutral virtue. Such actions are called spiritual actions, as they are in compliance with the laws of nature. Therefore, they follow the "natural path." They are humanly acceptable and considered constructive, righteous, and moral. Reactions produced from such actions are soothing and joyful.

For example, a mother giving birth and taking care of a child is in conformance with the laws of nature; a mother takes care of a newborn—if the mother is animal or human.

Similarly, leaves, flowers, branches, and trees float with the current of the river; such actions bring tranquility. Any action performed in conformance with—or according to—such reactions are neutral; therefore, they create pleasant or no residual memories.

Selfish

When an action is performed in a manner that does not conform to the laws of nature, it follows the path of abnormality—and its virtue becomes self-induced. Such actions are performed to fulfill personal goals and, therefore, are of a selfish nature. Such actions produce negative reactions. An innocent child's behavior demonstrates this. When a mother performs actions with love and emotion, a child's response is positive. When a mother elects to ignore a child to pursue her own chores, the child's behavior immediately changes. The child shows resentment by crying or biting. Similarly when a tree log elects to go against the flow instead of following the flow of water, it gets caught against a rock or along the embankment. That creates disruptions within the flow pattern, and it ends up accumulating debris and generating an unpleasant situation.

Passive

Passive actions are inactions that do not produce a visible or measurable counteraction; therefore, they are sometimes confused with no action or inert action. Inaction is an active action that produces mystical reactions, which create a subtle reaction in which the physical body remains completely dormant, but individual subtle faculties or the sensory organs of perception—awareness, mind, intellect, wisdom, and inner conscience—move at a speed that cannot be physically observed, measured, or properly recorded. Such actions include daydreams, thoughts, desires, focus, meditation, contemplation, and devotion. These actions—realized through internal experiences—produce inner satisfaction, tranquility, and peacefulness. Such actions leave no residual memory or blemishes on the individual's subtle faculties. There is, however, *inaction* within *action* and *action* within *inaction*. Upon gaining this unique ability, an individual is able to comprehend these aspects of inaction.

Worship

The method of devotion or worship used to honor or invoke the living spirit varies depending upon individual commitment and ultimate goals in life. Broadly, they could be grouped as follows.

Aspirant

At the lowest level, individuals study the scriptures or seek spirituality as a means of supplementing their desires for sensual gratification, accumulation of material wealth, or gaining power over other living beings. Such individuals usually worship divine idols (images of *demigods*) or even some living spiritual icon (far removed from *divinity* or *absolute truth*) to seek guidance. To support their egocentric and glorious personalities, they conduct pretentious prayers, offer ostentatious material sacrifices, and publicly display faith in the form supported by *maya* or the illusion created by the powers of nature. Even though such individuals follow spiritual practices, they remain spiritually ignorant in spite of their efforts.

Devotee

In the middle are those who passionately follow the path of enlightenment, develop inner quests to attain higher knowledge, and pursue the path to know the supreme power of the Creator. They make a firm commitment to become open-minded and approach everything with an open and receptive mind, and they explore different avenues to understand nature and acquire higher knowledge about the supreme power of the Creator.

They soon understand their shortcomings of their old convictions, and they learn to avoid such convictions through a completely purified mind. They accomplish inner purity through practicing renunciation of attachment. With purified minds, they perform daily prayers, make personal sacrifices, and conduct oblations by worshipping the Creator. They understand you cannot fill a jar if the lid is closed.

Steadfast

Through a continued process of devotion and dedication, many devotees become committed to realizing the divine truth and attaining the inner ability to differentiate between illusion and absolute. They overcome all the barriers created by the powers of living force; with steadfast mind, they acquire inner peace. With inner peace, they develop an unbound quest and joyfully perform selfless deeds. Ultimately, they acquire absolute truth and unveil the supreme power of the Creator.

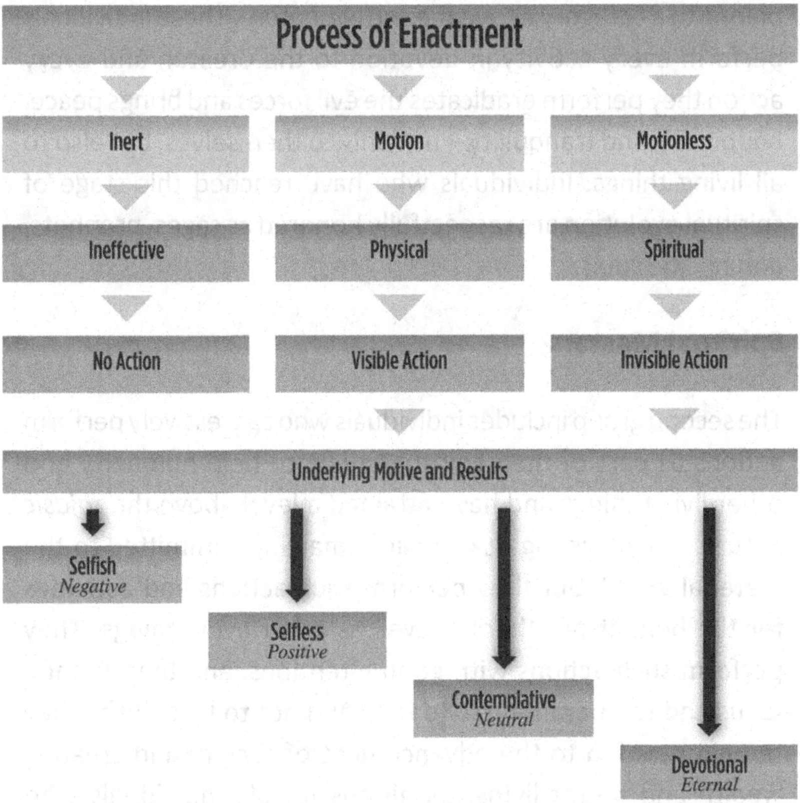

Illustration 18: Types of Action and Activities—Karmas.

Classification

Based upon individual actions and activities, individual temperament or the state of individual nature can be classified as follows.

Mystic Souls

The highest among this group includes the spiritually evolved souls who have succeeded in attaining unadulterated minds and consciousness to generate pure and divine thoughts that belong to a category above the *sattwic* nature. These individuals perform every activity in devotion to the Creator, and every action they perform eradicates the evil forces and brings peace, happiness, and tranquility—not only to themselves, but also to all living things. Individuals who have reached this stage of spiritual evolution are respectfully honored as sages, prophets, and mystic souls.

Spiritual Masters

The second group includes individuals who aggressively perform actions as part of their spiritual quest to help humanity and other living things and have attained a level above the *rajasic* nature. They take big risks while remaining committed to the material world, but they perform such actions and activities for the benefit of others as well as other living things. They perform such actions with good intentions, and their mental focus and temperament is to help and not to be selfish. They remain devoted to the advancement of society and creating wealth and better living conditions for all. Individuals who have reached this stage of spiritual evolution are respectfully honored as moral emperors, kings, industrialists, leaders, traders, and politicians.

Moral Warriors

This group includes spiritually passionate souls, which fight for righteous causes and even sacrifice their life for good cause. Others are moral fakers they use spirituality as mean to fulfill their selfish motives.

Faithful Servants

This group includes individuals who are faithful but not aggressive or true devotees. They are loyal to fulfill their obligatory responsibilities. They remain committed to their work, and they work hard to fulfill their obligatory responsibilities. Their temperament remains passive; they live happily and provide services and products for the betterment of humanity and other living beings. This group includes individuals such as farmers and service-providers.

Opportunists/Exploiters

This group includes individuals who are passionate and halfheartedly follow faith and spirituality but every action they perform is selfish in nature; they would not perform any activity that does not generate material gain for them. Their temperament remains aggressive-passive; they live happily within the material world and have no desires to know beyond intellectual knowledge or practical matters. This group includes individuals such as opportunistic business personas as well as farmers and service-providers.

Evil Souls

This group includes individuals who are selfish and whose temperament is controlled by demons. They perform actions and activities with the desires to hurt others. Their behavior is similar to animals; they have no feelings and never experience any form of remorse for their actions. This group includes ruthless businesspersons, robbers, thieves, murderers, and other criminals.

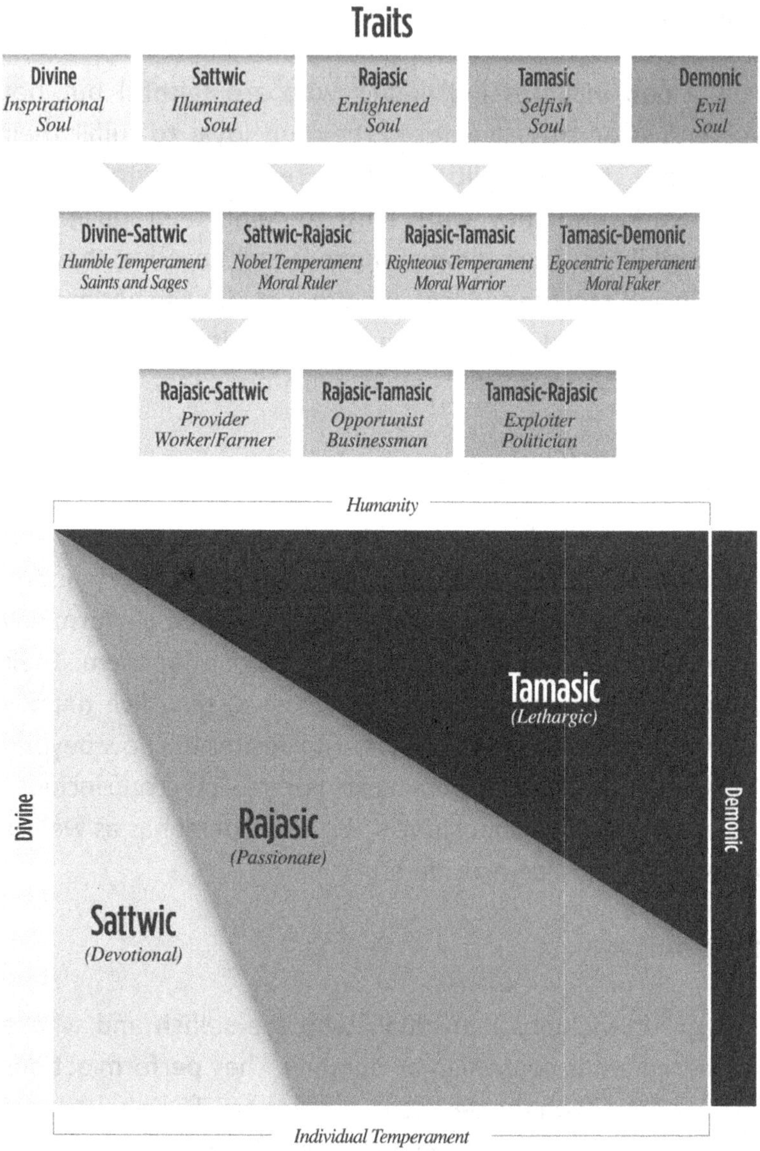

Illustration 19: Formation of Temperament and Traits.

Part 3: The Process of Self-Revitalization

The process of self-revitalization includes comprehension of five sheaths of embodiment *(koshas)*. An individual realizes the outer coating of the physical body is created to receive nourishment. The next sheath, the inner part of the physical body, regulates the life force, and it feeds the respiratory system and keeps the body fresh and active. The third sheath, the sensory organs of perception, collectively activate the subtle faculty called *manas* or mind and through their operations the embodiment comes to comprehend the powers of nature or intellect, called *chit*. Within the following sheath, with the activation of individual conscience, individual embodiment acquires perceptive knowledge *(buddhi)* and thus is able to comprehend the workings of the universal system and attain enlightenment. The last sheath through the invisible veil protects the individual spirit. It is through invocation of the living spirit that an individual experiences eternal happiness, inner peace, and tranquility. The individual's heart *(chit)* is transformed into *chitta* and acquires eternal happiness *(ananda)*.

The second aspect of revitalization is comprehension of the individual embodiment structure, which consists of three parts—the physical body, causal body, and astral body. To invoke the powers of the living spirit, every living being has to stabilize and purify each one of these three parts of embodiment. The knowledge retained within the physical parts of the body is of an intellectual nature. The knowledge stored within the causal body is in the form of experience, and the knowledge stored within the astral body is of a perceptive and intuitive nature, which is retained in the form of images or residual memories.

The third aspect of revitalization is the invocation of living spirit to acquire spiritual knowledge. Any living thing can become *cognizant,* which represents the lowest level of knowledge. Living beings, such as animals and humans who have fully developed subtle faculties, can acquire the next level, *commonsensical* knowledge, receive specific training, and make practical judgments. The next level of knowledge, *intellectual*, requires thinking, dealing with data, and the interpretation of data. The next higher level, *philosophical*, requires comprehension of subjective knowledge and cultivation of perceptive power to comprehend concepts not supported by scientific methods. At the higher level, *spiritual,* it requires comprehension of covenants such as ethics, truth, nature, morality, and divine laws. The next higher level, *transcendental*, involves comprehension of powers of the invisible forces responsible for all causation. To comprehend such mystic or divine knowledge one learns to unveil the relationship between living beings and the Creator. With such mystic powers, an individual can overpower every aspect of life, including the powers of the living force. Every living being has the ability to acquire every level of such knowledges, but—due to greed, ego, and attachment to materialistic things—

most individuals advance to intellectual knowledge, become content, and see no need to go any further.

Invocation of Inner Spiritual Power

An individual's ability to invoke spiritual power, the eternal soul of the Creator, depends on the continued process of conformance with the natural path of action and undivided devotion to the Creator. By conforming to the natural path, an individual diverts energy normally lost in daydreaming into potential energy. This continually transforms actions into inactions—*karma* into *dharma.* Instead of producing active and aggressive motion, actions are diverted, which transforms aggression into nonaggression. In this process, transformation of *karma* into *dharma* takes place. Here, an individual first completes the performance of individual obligatory responsibilities and then progresses to perform devotional responsibilities. The specific steps followed to attain this transformation are described within illustration 20.

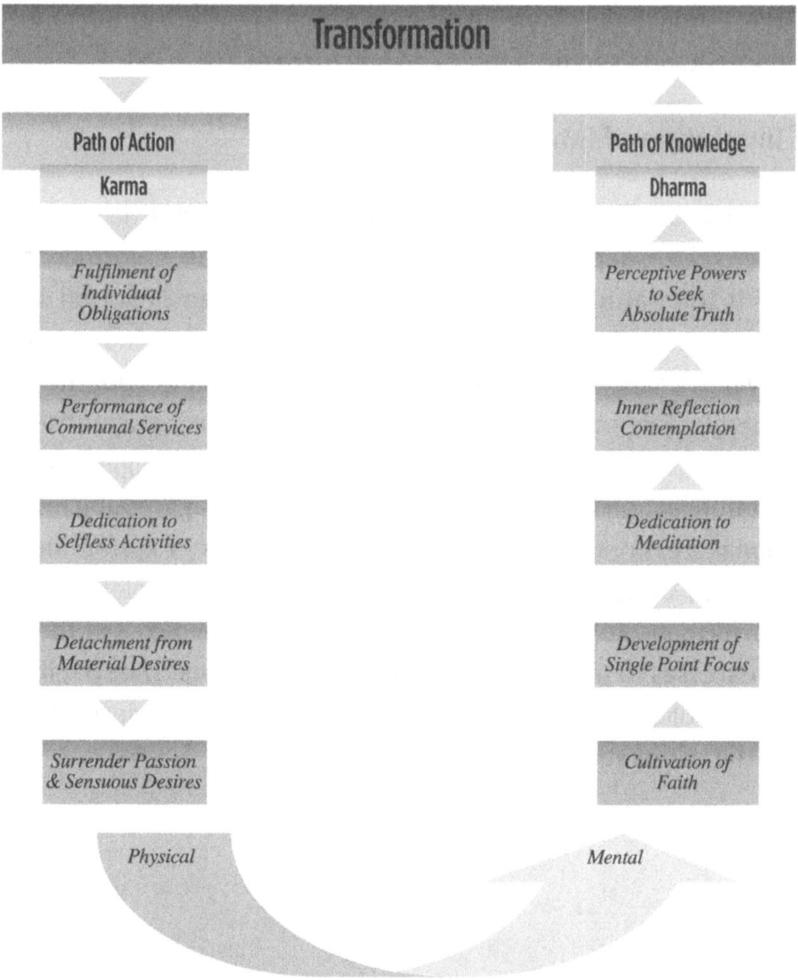

Illustration 20: Process of Transformation of Obligatory Actions to Devotional Activity.

Once an individual has transformed embodiment to perform *dharma*, in order to progress and move freely within the material world—without any strings attached—devotees learn to control the mind, intellect, and inner realm of consciousness to a level where the astral body is no longer controlled by human nature and the physical body goes into a trance. Individuals thus acquire the unique ability, *bliss*, to look at good and bad, gain and loss, love and hate—all in their neutral forms. Without any form of duality, they acquire the indefinable faith and no longer see the difference between good or bad. They accept both as gifts that have a purpose for occurring. With the elimination of duality, the mind and intellect are liberated from bondage. The living spirit takes charge of the embodiment to deflect the influences of the powers of nature. Such transformations in spiritual terms are called *eternal bliss, divine blessings*, or even *true gifts from God*.

To attain such *bliss*, devotees worship and thank the Creator for prevailing and controlling the universal system in its different forms. Some offer reverence to the *divinity* or Brahma, the supreme power of causation. Others offer reverence to each individual *deit*y controlling different aspects of planetary bodies and operating as part of the planetary system. They worship the *demigods* who control the immediate surroundings and the formation of different traits of divine nature that continually influence every living thing.

They both offer reverences to each of the five great elements of *divine nature*: air, water, fire, earth, and sky, followed by offering sacrifices of material things, such as food and material objects produced from the earth. They offer personal sacrifices in the form of selfless acts and participation in charitable functions and offerings follow this. The devotee understands that each oblation is different, serves a specific function, and cannot substitute one for another. There are some who offer personal oblations in the form of surrendering or restraining oneself from activities and actions, such as the practice of silence or the observance of selected days of fasting, including giving up eating meat. Others offer oblations by sacrificing indulgences, such as restraining from having sex or limiting material possessions, as well as practicing true detachment from all material and nonmaterial things. This includes the practice of controlled breathing with the goal of regulating or channeling oxygen to purify internal organs and attain direct access to the individual soul. Many practice austerity or personal inconveniences, such as pilgrimages, fasting, or letting the hair grow long as a symbol of sacrifice. Some genuinely part with wealth by giving everything to charity or other good causes.

The process of invocation of spiritual power is like going up several floors in a tall building. A hidden path connects each floor. You have to explore each floor in its entirety to find the path to the next level. You cannot skip and go to the top of the building unless you have fully explored each level and found the secret path to the next floor. With each level, the devotee acquires a specific aspect of spiritual wisdom, which leads the devotee to learn, identify, and explore hidden virtues that are not physical or apparent. They perceive these first by intuitive knowledge and then by perceptive power. Thus, at each step, the individual acquires personal experience and virtuous wisdom. The astral body becomes purer and more superior as the individual explores it further.

It is important to understand that offering oblations and performing sacrifices is of no use unless the individual is able to unveil the hidden virtues within each aspect of *yajna.* Without understanding the hidden virtues, it only fulfills an individual's desire to feel good and nothing more. It is important to remember that the Creator has no desire or need to exist in any manmade dwelling. Offering oblations in the form of building temples, mosques, or churches—or offering food and material things—is of limited value. They merely fulfill the human desire to feel good.

Some devotees who are unable to uncover the hidden virtues seek help from a spiritual master or teacher. According to the Bhagavad Gita, once the devotee has found a true spiritual master, the devotee has to demonstrate the longing for spiritual wisdom to the teacher. Only if a teacher who has attained spiritual wisdom accepts such a request, the devotee must make a pledge to obey and serve the teacher in order to gain the teacher's full grace.

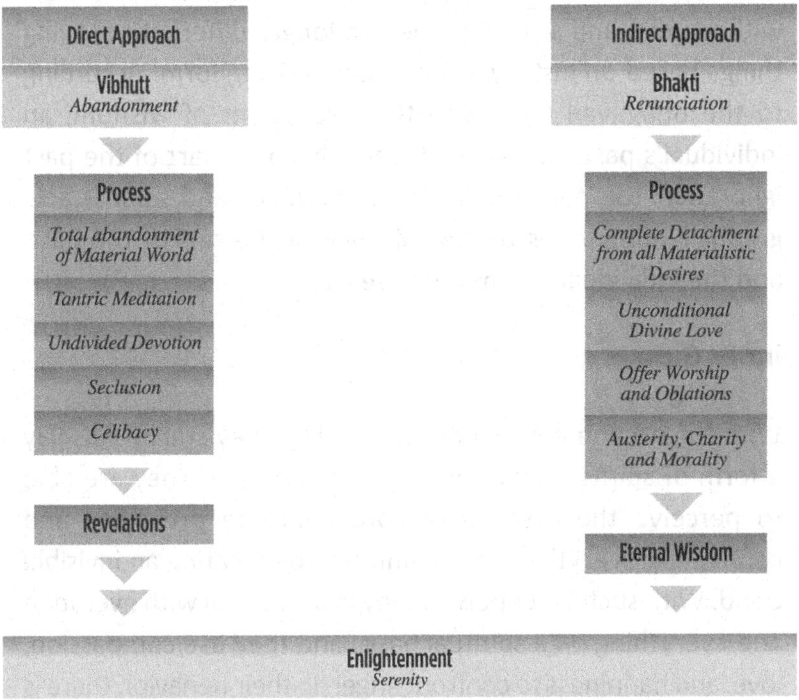

Illustration 21: Invocation of Spiritual Power.

Spiritual power in the form of eternal wisdom flows like water. Water can flow only from a higher level to a lower level. Therefore, the student has to place the teacher at the highest place in his or her mind and accept—irrespective of individual knowledge—that he or she is there to attain higher wisdom from the teacher. Moreover, spiritual power is not only eternal; it is also infinite. The spiritual power of the Creator is acquired by continually asking questions and challenging every answer from the teacher until one's longing is satisfied. The role of the master is to transmit this vast knowledge operating behind the supreme powers to the devotee based on the devotee's ability, desires, and capabilities.

Once the illusory difference disappears, devotees develop an eternal love for all living things. They learn to treat them with respect and affection; they no longer differentiate living things based on history, color, class, or living form. According to the Bhagavad Gita, with the attainment of wisdom, an individual's past sins and sinful acts become part of the past ignorance; the performance of good deeds and selfless acts gradually diminishes the significance of the sins of the past, and the individual attains inner peace.

Inner Glow

With the attainment of inner tranquility, they start to display a form of spiritual glow, an inner illumination. They are able to perceive the essence of Lord Supreme prevailing and connecting everything in the universe by creating an invisible bond. With such inner power, they learn to deal with everyone and everything on a spiritual basis, and they use compassion, love, and happiness to confront anger. In their behavior, there is a total absence of hatred or bad feelings. They view all material and nonmaterial things with altruism instead of egotism.

They examine things without duality or multiplicity; therefore, they are not deluded by the dual opposites and can see everything in balance—in physical and nonphysical forms. For them, pleasure goes together with pain, happiness accompanies sorrow, birth is tied to death, affection is linked to rejection, happiness leads to gloominess, and gloominess always follows happiness. With such understanding, they handle dual opposites and develop an ability to balance emotional behavior with calm composure. They display a true passion for any change in circumstances, knowing well that everything is transitory—and everything will pass.

Inner illumination also provides them with the understanding that individual behavior is a reflection of circumstances. The individual is not good or bad; circumstances change the individual's temperament. With such knowledge, they learn to differentiate between an individual's actions and being; they learn to follow the principle of "hate the sin and not the sinner." They become forgiving and hold no grudges or any kind of bitterness against individuals or other living things. Through the ongoing practice of meditation and contemplation, they develop absolute internal contentment and bliss—and they learn to develop self-control. With firm convictions, they enjoy undefined happiness without any material, natural, or physical requirements.

They realize the purpose of the physical body is to perform specific actions and activities to fulfill their functions in life; as embodied living beings, they recognize that they are here only for a defined time and purpose. They develop uniquely perceptive personalities so that they are not agitated easily or affected by the world around them; they do nothing to agitate others. They become free from any kind of mental anguish and gain the position of being truly neutral; they are able to help solve difficult situations within society by acting as peacemakers.

They understand the principles of performing actions in

accordance with the laws of divine nature *(dharma)*, and they are able to live in conformity with those laws. They learn to easily survive and live comfortably within the material world. They enjoy and participate in all activities without any form of attachment. Through their righteous and moral behavior, they earn the status of being icons of morality within society.

Emotionally, the soul continues to join the eternal soul of the Creator; they draw all their inspiration from this single goal in life. They become detached from normal human characteristics, such as rejoicing, grief, desire, hate, good, or evil, and they attach only to desires of purely spiritual activities and *inactions*. They become divine messengers; their relationships with other living beings change because they no longer recognize the difference between foe and friend, honor or dishonor, cold or warm relationships, or pleasure or pain. The ability to feel an experience no longer prevails; for them, all aspects of feelings—including praise, criticism, honor, and dishonor—are equal. After death, they attain the ultimate union with the Creator and become eternal, invisible, and indestructible.

Divine Union

The ultimate goal of every human being is to follow the path of spiritual evolution and attain divine union. In the Bhagavad Gita, two approaches to attaining serenity or ultimate union are described. One approach is called *ishvara yoga*, and the second is called *akshra yoga*.

Ishvara Yoga

In *ishvara yoga*, a devotee worships the Lord Supreme in its formless, imperishable, indefinable, and unchangeable nature.

This is called *Avyakta,* meaning not manifested. In the Quran, it is called *Allah*; the Old Testament refers to *El*; and the New Testament refers to *Lord Jesus*. To practice *ishvara yoga,* a devotee selects a sacred place to meditate and uses mystical powers to control unwavering thoughts. Devotees discipline the senses and sensory organs through meditation, contemplation, and single-point focus. By practicing undivided devotion, they learn to abandon the materialistic life and attain celibacy. The devotees follow the path of complete renunciation by fixing the mind on something inconceivable, such as immortal power, prevailing beyond the universe. Many elect to live in isolation away from humanity. There is no doubt that *ishvara yoga* is by far the most difficult yoga; it requires more than unconditional or blind faith, *shradha*, which is beyond comprehension.

Akshra Yoga

In *akshra yoga,* a seeker focuses upon Lord Supreme in a form selected by an individual to create or select an image of the Creator, such as *divinity, deity, demigod,* or even an *archangel* to worship. Such imagery is called *vyakta* and is perceived in the form of a living being or a physical object. Most who elect to follow *akshara yoga* remain actively involved within the material world; however, they learn to restrain the senses, mind, intellect, and awareness, just like a devotee following *ishvara yoga*. They use the conscience to overpower individual thoughts and desires concerning the material world and material things.

According to the Gita, it does not matter which approach an individual selects because each approach arrives at the same point—inner happiness and contentment—and cultivates genuine concern for the welfare of all living beings—no matter what deed is performed. The critical element is to overpower or abandon material desires and eliminate all blemishes and residual memories in order to gain the full support of the perpetual essence and attain *moksha,* which is freedom from all forms of attachment to carnal human nature.

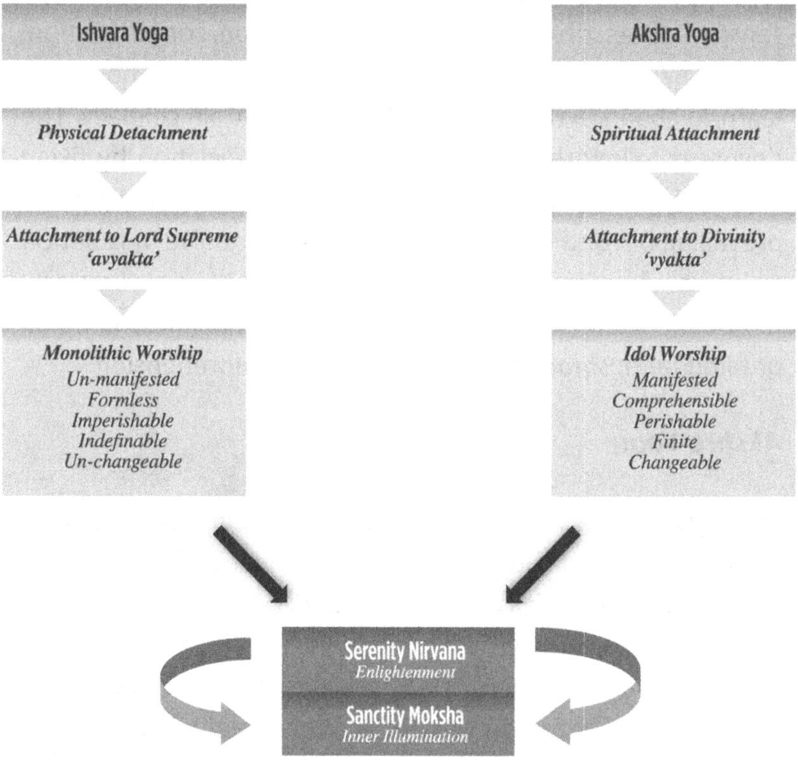

Illustration 22 Attainment of Sanctity—Divine Union

As part of the self-revitalization, after realizing the transitory nature of intellectual knowledge, some elect to seek higher knowledge while remaining active in the material world. They perform obligatory responsibilities and abide by the covenants of morality, humanity, and righteousness. They attain lower spiritual knowledge. A select few go beyond the lower spiritual wisdom to seek freedom from the materialistic world and elect to follow the path of a monk or *sanyase*. Through undivided devotion to the Creator, they seek the divine powers to break through the shackles of divine nature and achieve nirvana. Some, even after attaining nirvana, devote their lives to serving humanity by teaching others about the divine covenant. These individuals become prophets. To seek final unity with the Creator, they continue their devotion and attain total freedom from the cycles of life and death. In society, such noble souls are recognized by society as the messiah whose soul has merged or will merge at death with the eternal soul. The process of transformation starts with the cultivation of faith and ends with attaining inner illumination and the ultimate liberation of the living soul.

Spiritual Evolution

The process of spiritual evolution involves the transformation of individual embodiment through faith, spirituality, purification rejuvenation, enlightenment, and illumination to finally arrive at a state of being where the human body is no longer controlled, managed, and directed by the powers of the living force. The individual body, at its fully evolved state, is directed by the living spirit or the eternal force and in its liberated state the living being is no longer bound by the limitations imposed by the living force, such as time or space, gravitational and magnetic powers, and thus humanity can do things that are incomprehensible under the current state of mind.

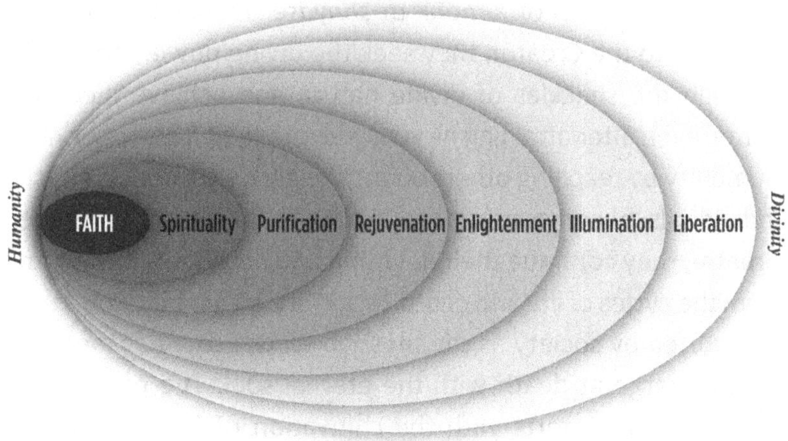

Illustration 23: Path of Spiritual Evolution.

The next five chapters describe in detail the process of self-revitalization and understanding the underlying principles influences of the process of spiritual evolution. These chapters are based upon information published within the discourses covering chapters 3, 5, 6, 13, and 14 from the Gita. In addition it does include information within the second part of the book *Mysticism* by Evelyn Underhill and several other books on Sufism.

The invocation of spiritual wisdom encompasses a seeker going through various stages of development and can be grouped into five categories: awakening, detachment, renunciation, revelation, and enlightenment. The purpose of all these is to eliminate blemishes that individual astral bodies have accumulated over time.

Section I: Invocation of Spiritual Wisdom

According to Vedanta philosophy, the very first living beings started with pure and uncontaminated subtle faculties and organs of sensory perception (*subtle faculties*). They received pure guidance and wisdom from the living spirit residing within the embodiment. Therefore, their actions and activities were always in compliance with the code of covenant, and they followed the principles of humanity, morality, and righteousness.

Over the years, as living beings acquired exposure to materialistic things, they cultivated materialistic desires, cultivated attachment to materialistic life, and acquired associated greed. They learned to abuse worldly things to fulfill selfish desires. These actions and activities generated images and impressions that contaminated their subtle faculties and ultimately left residual memories on their astral bodies. Continued buildup of these impressions resulted in the development of blemishes or residual memories within the astral body *(vasanas)*. The residual memories thus became an integral part of the astral bodies, which passed from one life to another, just like DNA.

These blemishes started to show up in the form of individual characteristics, temperaments, and personalities. In some cases, they even developed into instinctive powers that modified individuals' life patterns or resulted in influencing the physical evolutionary process.

Humanity's astral bodies are now preconditioned with the residual memories. The actions and activities they perform—or individual temperament—reflect selfish and egotistic natures. Now it has become necessary to survive in this materialistic world. In spite of the contaminations of the astral body, the individual living spirit remains pure, unaffected, and ready to provide guidance. Unfortunately, blemishes and residual memories are overpowering individual subtle faculties; the individual is constantly being subjected to delusion and illusion created by duality and multiplicity. The guidance from the living spirit is either deflected or obstructed; individuals have become victims of materialistic things, and the associated attachments. As a result, the nature of humanity has been guided by demonic nature; in many situations, possessiveness has caused humans to come under "satanic" powers that in spiritual terms are defined as the epoch of *Kali Yug,* or a dark era.

In spite of the current situation, every human is still blessed with powers of conscience that provide the ability to invoke the living spirit to rejuvenate the inner powers and attain spiritual wisdom. This phenomenon of invoking the living spirit is called self-revitalization. This process brings changes in individual temperament, personality, and character and results in a peaceful means of material success, inner peace, happiness, and inner contentment.

Awakening is an initiation to the path of inner illumination.

Chapter 16
Awakening

Initiation

As part of the self-revitalization, an individual comes to understand the underlying forces responsible for actions and activities performed and the blemishes that develop when actions are performed against codes of covenant. To initiate self-awakening requires acceptance of the existence of the Creator and the development of an inner desire to know the mysterious powers of the Creator.

Therefore, to start this process, an individual has to cultivate a true faith in the Creator and make a firm commitment to follow the codes of covenants. This process cleanses and creates a quest for self-revitalization and the need to acquire spiritual wisdom. Most individuals do not realize that the encrustations created by residual memories are making the individual's subtle faculties insensitive to morality and righteousness. Therefore, they have become unappreciative of others' feelings as well as having become ignorant of the divine powers that are prevailing and operating to keep universal equilibrium and balance within society.

The best way to visualize the impact of such encrustations within the subtle faculties is to imagine clogged plumbing. The purpose of self-awakening is to realize and appreciate the significance of this invisible blemish that influences every living being.

It creates an unyielding desire to acquire spiritual knowledge that shifts individual thinking from materialistic to spiritualistic. This simple change in the thinking brings changes to an individual's way of living; the personality moves away from selfishness toward the altruistic. Individuals find interest in following the path of humanity and righteousness; negative attitudes caused by inner demons overpowering the intellect are replaced by positive attitudes. It starts to make space for morality by giving up immorality. It is like a person emptying a full cup full of tea to make space for milk.

Understanding

Even though actions performed by the embodiment are neutral, it is the anticipation of the fruit of an action that determines if the action is truly an "action" or "inaction." An action that produces a reaction makes an action "active" like running water. Even when there is a delayed reaction, the actions are considered active, but it is recognized as transitory or temporarily inactive—like a volcano. An active action that produces an immediate reaction full of life, vigor, and energy is called energetic—like fire or electromagnetic waves. The actions produce visible movements, but the virtual energy remains invisible. Such actions are called latent actions—like water flowing in a river creating waterfalls and floods, ocean water creating tsunamis, and the drifting of continents.

Living things display similar personalities. For example, when individuals with lethargic temperaments perform dormant actions, they are physically and intellectually lazy. They have no desire to work hard or explore spirituality; therefore, they remain spiritually and intellectually ignorant. However, being lazy does not mean they do not have potential. An individual with a lively temperament produces physical results; they show great interest in acquiring knowledge and exploring unknown fields. Individuals with latent temperaments produce no physical results, but they do perform activities that are subtle or subliminal. Their activities are not physical; therefore, the activities remain invisible. They perform meditative and contemplative actions. They remain engrossed in following codes of covenant and live with inner peace and tranquility.

There is an anticipation of reward that underlies every action performed by living beings. This anticipation of the reward makes it extremely difficult to separate performance of actions from the underlying motives or contemplations. The underlying motives transform individual needs into greed. Even if an individual gives up the materialistic life and elects to live in the wilderness—away from all materialistic things—or adopt celibacy, the individual still cannot get away from the underlying powers causing attachment and the desire to anticipate the reward of individual action.

The path of physical action and the path of contemplation are integral parts of spiritual evolution. They are just like two hands of a clock; they appear to be separate, but both are needed to determine the time. The paths of *karma* and *dharma* are similarly designed just like in a clock; the small hand, *dharma*, moves in tandem with the large hand, and the movement of the smaller hand is fully recognized only when a full cycle of the larger hand has been completed. The manner in which an individual performs obligatory responsibilities, *karmas*, in turn determines the movement of *dharma*, the devotional responsibilities performed to attain freedom of living spirit or eternity.

There is another aspect of self-awakening that relates to the invocation of the powers of the eternal soul through which the humanly heart or *chit* is transformed into the heavenly heart, *chitta.* Such transformation is referred to as *shraddha* in the Vedas, where *dharmic* actions are transformed into *devotional* actions. Individuals follow this to invoke the powers of the eternal soul or the powers of perpetual essence to uncover the mysteries of *absolute truth*.

There are two paths identified to attain absolute truth. One is called *bhakti,* and the other is called *vibhuti. Bhakti* is practiced by remaining active in the material world and following the principles of detachment, and *vibhuti* is often practiced by following celibacy or living in seclusion to seek divine bliss. These two paths are discussed in more detail in the following section.

Because of misunderstanding that the path of action leads to attachment, many spiritual seekers elect to refrain from performing actions and run away from obligations and responsibilities. They abandon their normal lives and live in seclusion. Such misunderstandings only make them victims of demonic activities; ultimately, these seekers end up living in misery and grief.

Perception

In addition to understanding the relationship between action and inaction with spiritual awakening, the relationship of action, activities performed, and Mother Nature becomes apparent. Individuals come to understand that any action or activity performed by a living being is directly or indirectly influenced by the traits or *gunas* of nature.

These traits, as discussed before, transform cosmic atoms into five great elements: earth (solid), fire (fiery), water (liquid), wind (vapor), and sky (ether). In their manifested forms, they create different phenomena, such as windstorms, lightning, thunder, rain, earthquakes, asteroids, meteor showers, and volcanic activity that influence the physical part of each creation.

In the unmanifested form, they influence the causal part of each creation; in the ethereal form, they influence the astral part of each creation. In combination, they all cause circular motions and create various kinds of activities that can be observed by creations and perceived through sensory organs, such as the beginning of a day or night, changes in season, or eclipses.

The impulses produced are received by living beings as sensations, which are perceived in five ways: sound, smell, taste, vision, and feeling. The sensory organs receive these senses to cause awareness of the surroundings and generate thoughts, ideas, and desires, which ultimately cause the physical embodiment to react. Every action is directly or indirectly influenced by such activities of the great elements of Mother Nature. This circular reaction becomes responsible for the spiritual and physical evolutionary process.

Unfortunately, humans—due to a lack of understanding—believe that all things happening around them are being caused by an individual's actions or by the actions of other living things. This false idea leads humans to believe that individuals—or humanity in general—are responsible for all such actions and activities; therefore, an individual or individuals as a group are entitled to the rewards and benefits associated with such actions, the source of materialistic ideology.

Foresight

Another aspect of spiritual awakening is the ability to comprehend the inconceivable aspect of action and activities, that every action and reaction does create an image, and that—like a photographic process—every image creates a shadow that is recorded within the subtle faculties and leaves an inconceivable impression. Depending upon its nature or traits of action, these inconceivable impressions generate a form of blemish on the sensory organs of perception.

These inconceivable blemishes recorded within human subtle faculties start out to be very mild, but a continued process of similar activities transforms blemishes into a residual memory. The residual memory over time converts into inconceivable encrustations that obstruct the ability of subtle faculties to perform their functions. Ultimately, the building of incrustation even influences the purity of the astral body that directly or indirectly affects the development of individual character, personality, and temperament.

In holy scriptures such as the Vedas, the Vedanta, and the Bhagavad Gita, the creation of blemishes, impressions, memories, and their transformation into residual memories is defined as *vasana. Vasana* transforms *karma* into *akarma* or selfless action into selfish action; it transforms *dharma* into *adharma* or altruistic nature into egotistic nature.

Due to lack of scientific proof, such as DNA, the concept of residual memories remains inexplicable for most human beings. With spiritual awakening, a seeker of higher knowledge comes to accept this relationship—and its impact—without any scientific evidence. This allows the individual to overcome the critical aspects of spiritual wisdom and come to unveil the true relationship between actions, reactions, residual memories, and individual temperaments.

All living beings are created to perform actions. Every living being's subtle faculties are subject to the production of images, which create blemishes, leave residual memories, and influence individual temperaments. The nature of an action determines the nature of the impression.

If an action is performed in conformance with divine covenants, it neutralizes and becomes inaction and creates no reaction. If an action performed is immoral and against the divine covenant, it generates negative reactions; it leaves deep negative feelings or impressions within the astral body. This produces a negative temperament. If the actions are performed with devotion, they generate positive feelings, good memories, and positive residual memories.

The most important thing to remember is that individuals will continue to produce blemishes as long as the shackles of Mother Nature bind individuals to the material world.

An individual has a choice to pick from three ways to survive in the material world: *competition, cooperation,* or *compassion.* The choice an individual makes influences the development of the individual's temperament—for this life and future lives.

Competition

The first approach, *competition,* requires aggressiveness with a goal to acquire material wealth, power, and control, or to fight hard to preserve possessions and power. Such actions impress long-lasting and deeply rooted evil memories on the subtle faculties, along with a deep-seated desire for revenge.

Cooperation

The second approach, *cooperation*, requires give and take from both parties. The objective of this second approach is to "live and let live" and to seek win-win solutions. Such actions may leave some hard feelings—but not long-lasting or deep-rooted evil memories. Any negative impression left on the subtle faculties should wash away with time.

Compassion

The third approach, *compassion*, requires selflessness and every action to be performed without expectations, and each action must be performed with a commitment to follow the path of morality. Such actions leave pleasant memories and bring peace and tranquility to all.

Endowment

With spiritual wisdom, individuals come to comprehend the divine endowment, called the codes of covenant established by the perpetual essence to help living beings overpower the source of long-lasting blemishes. They are designed to maintain equilibrium and generate tranquility and balance among all divine creations. In the Bhagavad Gita, it clearly expresses that every living thing is created with a purpose to support another; therefore, everything is dependent upon another creation. A divine axiom says, "Giving is divine, and grabbing is demonic."

Individual Level

On an individual level, the codes of covenant abolish the

individual desire for an attachment to the fruit of action that are responsible for the transformation of selfish desires (negative) into selfless desires (positive). This brings inner peace and tranquility and causes an individual to perform *dharmic duties,* such as helping society or others needing help to survive, grow, and prosper.

Performance of *dharmic duties* can expedite the detachment process and cause an individual to become big-hearted. He or she treats others with more kindness, and the individual's doubts about the existence of the supreme power are removed. The desire to perform obligatory responsibilities with love increases. The individual learns to share love while acquiring inner peace and contentment. With further enhancement, the longing for personal gains and material objects diminishes. An individual feels the urge to share spiritual thoughts and recognizes that sharing this knowledge with others multiplies and enhances the ability to acquire higher knowledge through interaction. With higher knowledge, individuals feel the support of the supreme power and acquire eternal truth. With detachment, an individual realizes that this principle has been in operation since the time of creation. It is responsible for the propagation of our universal system, and it is the responsibility of humanity to propagate this and make it an integral part of life.

Terrestrial Level

At the universal level, each of the five elements of nature sacrifices itself to support the universal system. Fire gives out light and heat in the form of a sacrifice to give inherent powers to germinate. Wind, in the form of air, provides oxygen for living things. Water gives away its inherent power to provide moisture to generate coolness and quench thirst. Earth, in the form of soil, gives nutrients that plants need to grow, and it provides food for other living things. The sky, in the form of a protective cover, saves life from external forces, such as ultraviolet light.

Universal Level

At a higher level, the living force provides electromagnetic waves, which create electromagnetic and magnetic fields. The magnetic fields create molecular vibrations and generate sound waves, which become the basis of communication and provide the living spirit a mechanism to transfer eternal truth in the form of knowledge. Living beings use such knowledge to learn codes of covenant and develop ritual sacrifices *(yajna)* to unveil the powers of causation, invoke the powers of perpetual essence, and attain eternity.

Ignorant souls who do not recognize or follow the divine covenants end up experiencing miserable internal and external lives. They also bring agony and misery to many others. They do not realize that receiving sacrifices—but electing not to offer one's own sacrifices—is a crime; any living thing not following the principle is subject to punishment.

Aversion

After experiencing the rewards of detachment, many individuals revert to their old personalities and end up using aversion as a means to overpower attachment, not knowing that aversion is equally as bad, since it only suppresses attachment. Suppressed desires ultimately surface and become more detrimental than attachment. They end up falling back to their selfish personalities by adopting hate as a means to detach from attachment.

Through overpowering attachment with aversion, individuals unknowingly change their personalities and temperaments. Without such changes, the desires of possession and associated evil thoughts continue to affect the individual's temperament; he or she can never transcend from a common human being to a nobleperson.

It is better to live a long-lasting life of detachment than to live a life of aversion—a shorter or transitory life only brings agony, grief, disappointment, pain, and sorrow.

Deception

Further, through the process of detachment, individuals understand that the desire hidden behind the action is the root of all sinful acts—whether it is an attachment or aversion. The deception created by the desire hidden behind the action appears in three forms: semi-visible, invisible, and inconceivable.

Semi-Visible

The lowest form of deception is called semi-visible. It is intermittent in nature; it is only covered or protected through a thin veil that lasts for a short duration. It is similar to fire hiding behind smoke, sexual desire hiding behind romance, or rage hiding behind anger.

Invisible

Invisible deception is entirely covered. It is only visible through the proper process of uncovering the desire that is rooted deep within the individual—acknowledging and asking oneself why he or she has a particular desire, such as wanting to control others.

Inconceivable

The most difficult is the inconceivable deception. It represents a desire that continues to grow and remain protected under a thick layer of inert matter. It can only be unveiled through the powers of nature. The development of a fetus in the womb, the germination of a plant from a seed, and the existence of the living spirit within the physical embodiment are all inconceivable deceptions.

Individuals realize that, of all three, inconceivable deceptions are the most difficult to conceive, but if they can be conceived, they can provide the ultimate power to attain eternal wisdom. With such power, an individual can come to understand how fire, if properly managed and controlled, can provide comfort, heat, light, and power; if not, it can engulf the individual and destroy the embodiment. Similarly, understanding sin is the action of the physical body, and it can misguide an individual's ability to attain tranquility if not understood. Mahatma Gandhi preached, "Hate the sin, not the sinner."

Controlling individual subtle faculties, which receive the external and internal impulses, is a fundamental aspect of awakening. It is important to understand that subtle faculties or the sensory organs of perception are superior to the physical faculties. Awareness is superior to the senses, the mind is superior to awareness, intellect is superior to the mind, and the conscience is superior to the intellect. The individual living spirit is the final divine authority that can overpower human embodiment.

Once a devotee is able to accomplish spiritual awakening, establish a link with the living spirit, and allow the powers of inner guidance to take hold of the individual's subtle faculties and guide the embodiment, the individual can follow the path of morality. This constitutes overpowering attachments (likes) and aversions (dislikes)—and the embodiment attains a neutral disposition. Once a seeker's embodiment attains a neutral disposition, the individual learns to live like a bird in the sky.

Every living being has its own true nature; if the individual conforms to this nature, life becomes easy and happy. By maintaining conformity to one's true nature, all attachments and aversions become neutral or dormant; they generate no friction or residual memories. Only an individual can bring a change to individual temperament; no third person can bring such changes.

Detachment from materialistic desires directly invokes the living spirit.

Chapter 17
Detachment

Transformation

Detachment from attachment to the fruit of actions prepares the living being to go through several stages of inner inspiration:

Method of Thinking

With inspirational thinking, an individual desires to transform from selfish to selfless. Methods of thinking transform linear into spatial thinking, intellectual into innovative thinking, and objective into subjective thinking. An individual's subtle faculties are able to access fields of knowledge that are beyond what is controlled by the carnal parts of the physical body.

Changes in Values

With such changes, individuals start to appreciate the values associated with morality. They learn to avoid negative thoughts commonly associated with selfish acts and are responsible for creating blemishes or forming residual memories. They cultivate faith by studying scriptures and building divine trust to transform individual temperament from egotistic to altruistic. Some seek a spiritual teacher in order to encompass such changes and learn the true relationship between the living spirit and the powers of the living force. With the help of a teacher, a seeker comes to understand that the living force and living spirit are both part of the same force—perpetual essence.

Selection of Dogma

With faith, a seeker comes to select dogma, such as believing that the Lord is the Creator or that the process of creation started through an unidentifiable supreme power like the primordial force, which through the combination of vital force *(prakriti)* and inert matter *(purusha)* created a dwelling to house the living spirit. Irrespective of the selection of dogma, most individuals come to accept that there is an eternal soul *(prabhuatma)* that prevails throughout the universe, and on an individual level, it prevails as individual conscience *(atma)*. The powers of living spirit provide the guidance to conform to the codes of covenant and the laws of equilibrium.

Higher Knowledge

With such transformation, individuals become seekers of higher knowledge and cultivate inner quests to explore nature, creation, and the true structure of all living things. With acquired intuitive power, they learn to research scriptures and learn to perceive how a combination of inert materials and vital forces forms the dwelling for the living spirit. They explore the physical evolutionary process to comprehend the physical advancement of individual embodiment.

Spiritual Evolution

Seekers come to accept that every living thing goes through a well-defined path of spiritual evolution as part of life. It starts with instinct-prompted activities, such as a child calling its mother for feeding and cleaning, and includes survival-prompted activities where one learns essential necessities for survival, including the harvesting of gifts provided by the five great elements of divine nature. Later it triggers the need to cultivate intellect and transforms raw materials into products and tools. They use them to construct dwellings and live free from fear and hunger. As part of the next stage of evolution, an individual learns to utilize subtle faculties to understand one's surroundings and to recognize individual responsibilities and obligations. Living beings learn to use instincts, such as love and intellect, to form family structures and build societies and organizations.

With further development, seekers come to comprehend the impact of materialism on humanity through three traits of nature—good, average, and bad—and how these traits cultivate a desire to gain wealth, power, and control and how desires prompted by a material nature transform needs to "wants." They come to understand that this process continues to generate unbound and unfulfilled desires to own and control. Thus, a living being becomes accustomed to demands being produced to create and acquire far more than what is needed. This leads to ego and selfishness. Ultimately selfishness becomes the source of the obsessive and possessive temperament; it is reflected as arrogance and ultimately leads to evil and demonic behaviors—ending in murder, war, and the demise of humanity.

Once a seeker recognizes the transitory nature of

materialism, the seeker learns to detach by getting involved in selfless and altruistic activities. A seeker focuses on invoking the powers of the living spirit residing within the embodiment for guidance and starts to learn to understand the codes of covenant. A seeker practices selflessness and finds passive and peaceful ways to live.

Two Approaches

The practices of detachment's two approaches, *vibhuti* and *bhakti,* are described in the Bhagavad Gita.

Vibhuti

This approach requires complete isolation; sages have practiced this for centuries. This approach requires a seeker to leave behind everything and find a remote area to establish a private, sacred place of worship. The seeker practices undivided devotion and focuses on the unmanifested nature of the Creator—and nothing else. A person who follows this method is called *sannyasi.*

Bhakti

Since the isolation method requires extensive training and commitment, most seekers elect to use the participative method. This method requires the seeker to remain actively involved in the material world; however, it requires an individual to shed his or her old desires of attachment to the fruit of actions and attain freedom from the material world by unconditionally practicing the codes of covenants and cultivating undivided devotion to the Creator. A person following the participative method is called *devata.* This method of participation is based on the individual's dedication to remain a part of society, eliminate duality and multiplicity, and convert all selfish actions into selfless inactions. It requires the seeker to overpower desire by replacing selfish actions with selfless actions and avoiding attachment to any visible or hidden selfishness. Through this process, the seeker purifies his or her subtle faculties to receive pure guidance from the living spirit. With continued practice, a seeker learns to receive pure guidance from the living spirit. This method is also referred to as baptism. This process is similar to a snake giving up its dead skin to expose new skin—without dying.

Both approaches follow the underlying principle of purifying individual subtle faculties as well as the astral body to attain purity or start a new life. With both methods, seekers realize the presence of a living spirit in every other living being and cultivate devotional love for all other living things. By either method, a seeker gains additional strength to overpower the impure impulses generated by residual memories. The humanly love *(chit)* is transformed into divine love *(chitta)*.

The Gita states that these paths may be different, but they ultimately lead to the transformation of the living spirit into transcendental spirit. The two paths are like traveling to a city by air or by bus. You end up at the same place; the only difference is the nature of the experience.

Holy scripture states that, in order to go beyond spirituality and attain eternity, one must learn and practice the process of participation before electing to move on to the process of isolation. A person cannot give up something that an individual has not acquired or experienced.

The Gita further states that, without first experiencing attachment to the material world, a seeker's journey remains incomplete. The process of isolation leaves all dualities and material bondages suppressed and not truly eradicated. This is why direct abandonment often ends up in disappointment.

The individual who seeks isolation after participation receives a long-lasting reward in the form of everlasting divine bliss (eternal ecstasy). Sages, saints, and blessed souls who have experienced such divine bliss describe such ecstasy as a level of spiritual experience where one is no longer able to make a distinction between pairs of opposites, such as love and hate, friend and foe, or good and bad.

The seekers learn to treat both aspects of these ostensibly opposite pairs as the same; they become unbiased and can experience the presence of the divine everywhere and in everything. A seeker blessed with such eternal ecstasy can acquire special mystical powers to see divine manifestations in their true realities and equality without any kind of divine illusion or delusion. With such mystical powers, seekers come to understand that divine bliss is not the end—it is only a means to the end. Seekers develop an unbound quest to know the supreme power and the Creator.

Conscious Mind

After developing a link to the living spirit, an individual realizes the awakening of inner conscience; many seekers return from their spiritual journeys to serve the community or other living beings. With their inner subtle faculties purified, they can be actively involved in worldly activities—just like any other human being—but they are able to control the influence of external or internal impulses because of the inner purity. As the living spirit directs the subtle faculties, no form of attachment taints their actions. They acquire the ability to detach from any physical or emotional feeling that may generate due to an association with the material world. They live like petals of a rose, which never get wet from the raindrop.

Their personalities become transcendental and take on

humble, unpretentious, and noble characteristics. They accept that all activities performed by the physical body—thinking, seeing, hearing, touching, smelling, eating, walking, sleeping, breathing, speaking, controlling, holding, letting go, and even blinking—are the outcome of the living spirit moving within them.

Such purified souls perform righteous actions and denounce evil actions; therefore, every action they perform has no root and generates no residual memories. Such souls understand that true detachment from desire is not practical; therefore, they override such impulses through acts of devotion to the Creator. By doing this, they offer oblations to the powers of causation; desire becomes attached to the devotion itself, and they remain purified and uncontaminated.

These individuals remain impartial and live like monks or yogis. They perform only noble activities while living in peace and tranquility. Through the support of their bottomless faith and devotion, they remain unattached. It is important to understand that the process of becoming a monk or yogi is not just a physical detachment—it is a true mental transformation. A devotee with this inner experience gains control of the senses and impulses responsible for desire. They learn to renounce physical joy and replace it with spiritual joy.

The monk or yogi realizes the true human being is not the body; the eternal soul, in the form of the living spirit, resides within the embodiment. The embodiment by itself is inert. It can only perform actions through its association with the living spirit. The embodiment experiences this as pain and pleasure—or joy and sadness—because of the presence of living spirit. Once this association between living spirit and embodiment is finished, the embodiment loses its life force.

The physical body becomes unconscious and can no longer experience anything.

A seeker with this knowledge fully understands that action depends on the embodiment's reaction to internal impulses originating through the residual memories and external impulses generated through the traits of divine nature. The living spirit has no relationship to the action and activities or the outcome or rewards of those actions. In truth, there is no direct relationship between the action, the living spirit, the living force, and the Creator; they are all affiliated, but each operates independently and does not share the result of its actions or the reactions generated by them.

Knowledge and ignorance cannot coexist; spiritual knowledge dispels spiritual ignorance. With the attainment of wisdom, many sages, saints, monks, and yogis have transcended from illusion and delusion to a realization of the absolute truth.

Renunciation is the process of eradication of residual memories, the barrier to eternity.

Chapter 18
Renunciation

Process

Many individuals, in spite of isolation or participation, face a constant onslaught of thoughts arising from personal fancies, imaginations, and emotional upheavals. To overcome this dilemma, the Bhagavad Gita suggests the individual follow the path of renunciation—an enhanced state of detachment that eliminates unwanted thoughts that give birth to such desires. The process of renunciation is not physical; therefore, it does not require or generate any form of physical movement. It actually brings the physical body to rest to experience tranquility.

Selection

It starts with an individual selecting a place to sit that is comfortable and free from distractions. The place should be clean, stable, not too high, and not too low. The individual selects a seating arrangement that is suitable for a long-time stay without any discomfort. Complete solitude is achieved by selecting a place free of any kind of physical activity that could restrain the individual from cultivating a single-point focus, and the place provides a peaceful environment. The place could be in a house or outside. The main point is that the place provides a proper environment to maintain seclusion for a given period and to carry out devotional practices with secrecy and inward stillness.

Concentration

To carry out the process of yogic concentration, the individual should avoid any kind of public display or attracting any form of outside attention. The prime objective of concentration is to acquire inner peace and to free the mind from external impulses that generate thoughts that lead to materialistic desires, greed, lust, anxiety, and selfish expectations. The process of concentration also requires a calm attitude to accomplish single-point focus. The individual holds the head and neck in an erect position and firmly controls the position of the physical body to focus on the tip of the nose without looking around to attain single point focus.

Meditation

Firmly situated in such a posture, the individual brings uncharted thoughts into a single point, shutting down the powers of awareness by uttering internally a *mantra* (a holy word or divine name) for hours. Sometimes, a string of beads (either a rosary or *mala*) is used to develop single-point focus. Some individuals even use spiritual music to continue the single-point focus. Through these practices, the body enters a transcendental state of being—eliminating or overpowering the origination of thoughts that are not divine or moral.

Contemplation

Attainment of contemplation is similar to the process of tuning a stringed musical instrument. If the string is too tight, it breaks. If it is too loose, it produces no music. It is probably the most difficult stage of renunciation, especially in today's world; many individuals are unable to make a firm, long-term commitment to maintaining moderation in life. They find it difficult to maintain proper diet, sleep, recreation, enjoyment, and attitude habits; this inability to abstain from indulgence makes it difficult to achieve this level. There is a great deal of misconception regarding the anticipated rewards of such practices. As a result, many spiritual scholars become disappointed and lose confidence in the ability to attain such a level. They end up prematurely terminating the good start they have made in following yogic practices.

Spiritual Energy

Through yogic practices, including single-point focus, concentration, meditation, contemplation, and personal sacrifices, a seeker learns to bring lower subtle faculties under the control of higher subtle faculties. Then, it allows the inner conscience to eradicate the impulses responsible for agitating the mind and awakening the coiled spiritual energy.

Eradication of Duality

Once that is accomplished, the individual learns to overpower the duality operating within nature *(maya)* and then is able to observe *inaction in action* (hidden powers operating behind the action) and *action in inaction* (hidden actions contemplated behind a specific motive)—even when they are performed as selfless activities. They attain freedom from the powers of living forces responsible for the causation of traits of Mother Nature.

Unity

The individual makes an unconditional commitment, without any cavil, to follow the path of self-perfection and dedicate his or her life to performing every action full of devotion, love, and elation—and for the betterment of other living beings. With undivided devotion, the individual embodiment transforms from being a doer into an instrument of living spirit. The individual physical body, causal body, astral body, and living spirit all start to operate in conformance with divine covenants of morality, thus bringing the three bodies of the embodiment into balance with the universal system.

Mystic Power

Once individual faculties become allies, individual living beings acquire the powers to transform enemies into friends as well as to transform demonic forces into divine powers. Individuals are able to confront any internal or external stimuli on a head-on basis to overpower wavering, wondering, and turbulence created within the mind by such stimuli. An individual with an internally balanced personality becomes cognizant and is able to overpower the impact of physical feelings, such as hot or cold; emotional unrest, such as pleasure or pain; intellectual challenges, such as honor or dishonor; and egotistical conduct, such as winning or losing. They are able to limit the mind from fluxing and provide the ability to attain a state of tranquility.

Trance

With an intensive amount of internal strength and yogic practice, an individual goes through a very deep trance (*nirvikalpa Samadhi*). This occurs when thoughts merge with the inner consciousness to unite in the living spirit. Through this union, the devotee is able to grasp the true distinction between the *knower*, the mystical soul or individual temperament; the *act of knowing*, the burning quest to know the powers of causation; and the *object to know*—the ultimate supreme power or *divinity*.

Spiritual Energy

Individuals experience the unfolding of an immense inner power of affection and love for every living being and individual humanly love. *Chit* is permanently transformed into divine eternal love *(chitta)*. The individual experiences eternal love for all creations—irrespective of situation, color, shape, form, or type. The individual experiences the unfolding of coiled or quiescent energy as it starts to flow within the embodiment without any interruptions or blockage.

Awakening of *kundalini* is the unwinding of coiled spiritual energy as it starts to run through the bottom of the spinal cord to the medulla oblongata. In the brain, it passes through five barriers referred to as *chakras* in spiritual terms. These five *chakras* include the cervical *(vishuddha)*, dorsal *(anahata)*, lumbar *(manipura)*, sacral *(swadhishthana)*, and coccygeal *(muladhara)*. The experience is similar to a wave relinquishing its acquired transitory power to become a part of the ocean and starting to flow in tandem with the ocean currents. In spiritual terms, this is referred to as spiritual revelation.

Godly Personality

Those who are able to awaken the coiled spiritual energy acquire a state of being wherein the individual living spirit establishes a link with the eternal soul and attains direct access to higher eternal truth. While remaining in their physical bodies, they experience sovereignty from the powers of nature.

Disentanglement

The personality becomes totally absorbed with the supreme power and loses individuality as individual living spirits come under the control of the eternal soul. Individuals become disentangled from the material world. The individual is no longer agitated or subject to anger, anguish, or recklessness. Any longing for wealth or materialistic possessions dissipates; moreover, the individual's personality transforms into a godly personality. This state, in the Vedas, is defined as *brahmavastha*. In society, this personality is recognized as a great soul or a divine soul.

Ability to Distinguish

One of the unique characteristics of a godly personality is its ability to discern *sankalpa*, the root of evil within thoughts that are associated with desires responsible for causing want, greed, arrogance, and ego. With such discernment, the godly personality is able to block these thoughts and renounce them at the point of origination, which shields the individual's mind from drifting away from the path of liberation and returning to the shackles of human nature.

Immortal Wisdom

With the attainment of a godly personality, the individual easily comprehends the different form of immortal wisdom that is retained by the embodiment and passed from one life to another. Passing of such wisdom remains a big unsolved mystery within the scientific and intellectual communities. One of the reasons that most intellectuals and scientists are unable to comprehend the transfer of such wisdom from one life to another is due to a lack of understanding of the differences between types of wisdom.

Intellectual Knowledge

Intellectual knowledge is personal and is of a practical nature that is acquired by the physical body. It relates to understanding of the material world; therefore, it requires scientific justification. Because of its material nature, it is transitory—and retained for a limited time. For example, with the loss of brain function or lack of constant activity, intellectual knowledge disappears temporarily or permanently. Intellectual knowledge generates instant or immediate gratification; it can be measured in tangible forms, such as material wealth, tangential opulence, or material personal gains. It is measured with defined, finite values.

Inspirational Knowledge

Inspirational knowledge is impersonal and of a subjective nature. It is acquired through personal relationships or direct guidance. This knowledge is acquired by the subtle faculties and is retained within the causal body. Remaining in the form of memory and personal experience, it survives even after death and remains alive among living beings for some time. It fades and eventually disappears. Such knowledge in the form of intuitive power is passed from one generation to another. A baby lion is born with the intuitive power to hunt. A bird is born with the intuitive power to fly. A fish is born with the intuitive power to swim. Even humanity is born with the intuitive power to use common sense and logic to think and grow.

Spiritual Knowledge

Spiritual knowledge is part of the eternal truth and is immortal. This immortal wisdom was first received by divinity from the Creator and then—over the course of centuries—was passed down to humanity. Spiritual knowledge in the form of absolute truth or *Sat* is not acquired and never becomes part of the physical organs (such as the brain or heart) or the subtle faculties (such as the mind, intellect, and conscience). It originates from the living spirit and resides within the astral body. It leaves the physical body as an invisible force and remains unmanifested until the living spirit is blessed to be embodied again.

Recap

According to the Bhagavad Gita, such a link is attained by taking small steps; therefore, one must not become impatient. The attainment of a godly personality within a single life cycle is not practical; therefore, some have a difficult time accepting such ideology. History has shown, however, that some human beings have succeeded in attaining godly personalities. In spite of this fact, the majority of humanity is not prepared to take on such an extensive mission on faith and hope to go through a lifetime commitment to attain godly personality. Therefore, attainment of a godly personality requires unconditional or blind faith in the Creator, the supreme power of causation, and the ability to offer undivided devotion to or reverence of the Lord Supreme.

Selected individuals who are spiritually evolved accept this ideology without cavil and willfully follow the process of self-revitalization. These individuals comprehend the true nature of the individual embodiment, and their true purpose in life is to attain balance and tranquility through control and discipline of the subtle faculties. They accept that time and patience are required; therefore, they do not get discouraged in making long-term commitments to attain this.

They are not afraid of the loss of acquired eternal wisdom with the termination of life or premature death. These individuals accept that death of the physical body is a transitional phase and is not the ultimate ending of the individual spirit. They accept that death is a transitional part of the spiritual life and is no different from sleep. For such individuals, activities performed during the previous day determine the quality of the upcoming day; after dying, activities performed during the previous life determine the quality of the upcoming life.

Such spiritual seekers accept the doctrine that the beginning of a new embodiment is predetermined based on the nature and qualities of the blemishes or the wisdom carried as part of the astral body from the previous life. In other words, the blemishes or residual memories within the astral body influence the ability of the living spirit to guide the living beings. Natural instincts and internal impulses determine behavior patterns.

They accept that the living spirit remains protected from such blemishes. An advanced stage of spiritual evolution occurs when an individual's astral body is purified. Thus, the living spirit is blessed to be born within a family that is devoted to advancement in spiritual practices to provide the necessary environment to enhance and attain eternity without much hindrance. Ultimately, the individual soul merges with the eternal soul and loses its individuality—just as the air inside a balloon merges with the atmosphere when the balloon pops.

The ability to pursue one's own destiny—no matter how imperfect it may be—instead of chasing another's destiny—no matter how tempting—leads to divine revelations.

Chapter 19
Revelation

Unveiling

Revelation is an advanced stage of an individual's spiritual evolution. During this stage, a seeker becomes free of the shackles of nature—continually influencing every living being by transforming neutral powers into good (divine) or bad (demonic) ones. Seekers with godly personalities come to comprehend the underlying structure of the cosmic universe and the nature of the supreme power that is controlling its operations and affecting individual lives.

Validation

Based on such wisdom, godly personalities come to accept that the power of perpetual essence, *brahma,* is the true source that controls the environments surrounding living things. They experience validation of individual dogma. Lord Divine in its manifested form *(avatar)* is Jesus, Buddha, or Krishna. In its unmanifested form *(brahma),* such as El or Allah, it is responsible for the manifestation of all the physical bodies. All these physical bodies are formed through the combination of inert matter *(purusha)* and vital force *(prakriti)*, which prevail within defined cosmic spheres, resulting in separating Creator from its creations.

Separation

As described before, there are at least seven spheres identified as *lokas* that separate creations from the Creator. Within these spheres, the eternal soul of the Creator prevails and implements the laws of equilibrium to provide balance among divine creations as an absolute truth *(Sat)* that all living things are controlled and managed by the eternal soul *(parambrahma)*, prevailing within each living thing as living spirits *(atma)*. Any manifested body not conforming to the code of covenants is destroyed by demonic powers.

Attainment

The godly personality understands there is only one established means to attain eternal truth. They understand the source of eternal truth is beyond reach because it resides outside the universe. It is not possible to perceive or comprehend the unmanifested powers of causation without divine bliss—attained in the form of ecstasy.

Substratum

The godly personality accepts without any doubt that the Creator in its undifferentiated form provides the substrata for all differentiated, unmanifested, and manifested forms—as well as all physical bodies, moving and not moving. At the cosmic level, the perpetual essence prevails as the living force forming the planetary system. Around terrestrial bodies such as Earth, the perpetual essence prevails in the form of an embodied living spirit, *paramatma*, which transforms living things into living beings that live, grow, and prosper on the surface of the terrestrial bodies. The eternal spirit—in the form of the individual living spirit, *atma*—prevails within each living body.

Wheel of Genesis

The godly personality accepts without any cavil that, upon death, the living spirit leaves the body or embodiment to be reborn or to create a new embodiment. The living spirit, being part of the eternal soul, never becomes part of any embodiment. Through its association with inert matter and material embodiments, the living spirit develops a close affinity with material things and enjoys the benefits of actions performed by the embodiments; however, it never attaches to or becomes an integral part of an embodiment. The living spirit in the embodiment is similar to how air trapped inside a balloon behaves differently from air outside a balloon.

Collaboration

Finally, the godly personality comes to accept that all activities performed by the embodiment represent a coordinated effort of all parts of the three bodies acting in tandem. The development of organs of cognizance is largely reflective of the development of the physical body. The development of sensory organs of perception or subtle faculties largely reflects the development of brainpower and the transformation of the living spirit from its dormant to its illuminated state, which represents the intuitive and instinctive powers. The level of collaboration among body parts becomes complex as the embodiment structure transforms from simple to complicated.

For example, the vegetation and flora consist of a simple physical structure along with simple-impulse stimuli to cause responses. Small crawling creatures and insects have a visible structure that is limited in types of body parts. Animal kingdoms have established body structures along with conscious minds; some have an intellect that permits them to move, run, or fly. There are a wide range of human beings with intricate physical body parts and vital subtle faculties of stimuli, mind, intellect, awareness, and conscience. They display different levels of intellectual knowledge when working together.

Elucidation

Over the centuries, many godly personalities have gone beyond spiritual wisdom to unveil the absolute truth. It requires a type of astuteness that extends beyond spiritual wisdom to encompass various aspects of absolute truth that are part of the eternal truth—the immortal and indestructible supreme powers of the Creator.

Before comprehension of absolute truth through inner inspirations, humanity acquired absolute truth in the form of bliss. Such revelations were worshipped as divine or holistic visions or as direct messages from God. Sacred scriptures, such as the Holy Bible, the Rig Veda, the Bhagavad Gita, the New Testament, the Quran, and many other holy books were based upon absolute truth attained through holistic visions or through inner inspirations. For centuries, humanity has sought eternal peace and tranquility in following absolute truth.

With absolute truth, scholars have found that individual temperaments have become forgiving, upright, honorable, and respectful to all—irrespective of age, position, or condition. An individual overcomes weaknesses such as selfishness, egotistical nature, and hypocritical thoughts. In many cases, individuals even gain control of instincts, such as the fear of getting old, getting sick, dying, or having accidents. An individual cultivates a lifestyle of purity, cleanliness, consistency, and self-control.

Of all the creations, only humanity is blessed with advanced subtle faculties to acquire the absolute truth to move to the highest level of the spiritual evolutionary process. Humanity can perceive the eternal soul residing within all living entities, ready to empower the embodiment and fight demonic powers. Humanity can also experience the supreme power of causation prevailing everywhere. Some can even acquire mystical powers to visualize the underlying forces of causation operating within all forms of manifested entities—both moving and not moving.

With the attainment of such powers, humanity can come to comprehend the interrelationship of the living force and the living spirit and come to realize that pleasure and pain are perceptions or reflections of responses caused by the powers of attachment and aversion. The living spirit is never responsible for such reflections or ever becomes part of it or gets involved.

The living spirit and the eternal soul jointly form a linkage to create a network through which all living things appear to be separate and different, but they remain connected at all times. Even though each of the segments is perceived to be truly independent, with its own character and physical form, and each can enjoy the same character as the source, they may appear separate, but each remains an integral part of its source in absolute sense. For example, snow, ice, rain, steam, and moisture all represent the ultimate source—water.

At the end, everything loses its individuality when it merges with the source. A sandcastle loses its form and identity as soon as the force of a wave strikes it. Similarly, living spirit loses its individuality when it merges with the perpetual essence or the eternal soul of the Creator. At the time of death, a purified individual spirit goes back to its original form, and the two aspects of inert and vital forces return to their original forms, thereby losing their individuality. Only living spirits contaminated by an association with material nature are subject to the cycles of life and death.

Triumph

Revelation requires the completion of four basic responsibilities.

Obligatory Responsibilities

First, the seeker has to perform and complete the process outlined within *karma yoga* and learn to use his or her lower subtle faculties of the mind and intellect to fulfill obligatory responsibilities without generating attachment to the results of those specific actions. This is a basic process of detachment where an individual concentrates on gaining control of the senses. Individuals learn to perform all actions with goodness in their hearts so as not to become attached to any anticipated rewards for those actions.

Social Responsibilities

Next, the seeker has to perform and complete the practices outlined within *jnana yoga.* Through these yogic practices, they learn to use the subtle faculties of intellect to invoke the living spirit, *atma.* Individuals who practice *jnana yoga* attain perceptive powers to comprehend subtle and invisible aspects of powers operating within and outside the embodiment. With such knowledge, they come to understand the powers of duality that cause delusion, or *maya*. They come to comprehend the evolution of the human ego and its influence on human character and personality.

Devotional Responsibilities

Seekers modify their lives by incorporating proper devotion and worship by performing activities for the betterment of others. Even while living within the material world, one must attain stillness of mind, purity of heart, and develop faith and internal love for the Creator. With the practice of *dharma yoga*, the spiritually evolved seeker learns to control desires and live an altruistic lifestyle. They perform all actions and activities in conformance with the laws of the divine covenants. They accomplish this by following the path of morality and righteous living by treating all other living souls with compassion. They develop inner peace and happiness. They are no longer influenced by external or internal stimuli.

Eternal Responsibilities

After *dharma yoga*, one must follow and complete the activities outlined within *buddhi yoga*. This requires single-point focus with undivided divine devotion to attaining freedom of the living spirit to join with the eternal soul. When individuals reach this level, they proceed to attain enlightenment.

When the living spirit attains freedom from the shackles of material nature, an individual attains enlightenment.

Chapter 20
Enlightenment

Liberation

The ultimate goal of the living spirit is to attain liberation and join with the eternal soul. Every godly personality understands this ultimate goal. In spiritual terms, it means individual living spirits must reach or go even beyond the seventh sphere *(swarloka)* to establish a contact with the eternal soul. To reach even the sixth sphere, the living spirit has to be free from all external influences generated by the powers of living force. As defined earlier, as long as the individual embodiment continues to be influenced by the powers of nature *(gunas),* the individual living spirit *(atma)* cannot attain freedom. Even at the highest level of purity *(sattwa),* only through inner illumination is the individual spirit able to establish a direct contact with the eternal soul. During the process of inner illumination, the living spirit goes through a progression (enlightenment).

Transcendental Phase

During the initiation phase, living beings establish contact with the eternal soul, and it starts to gain freedom from external illumination that is received through the cosmic universal system. At this stage, the living spirit becomes free of the limitations imposed by the powers of *prakriti* or Mother Nature.

Neutral Phase

By attaining such freedom, the living spirit attains neutrality and is no longer subject to living forces responsible for creating electromagnetic fields. The powers of causation, attraction, and repulsion—responsible for the creation of duality—diminish. The living being is able to access the eternal truth, *Sat,* and unveil the mystery of causation. This process of inner illumination is expressed in spiritual terms as enlightenment or *nirvana.*

Independence Phase

The living spirit continues to remain embodied; however, it attains the power to stay or leave the embodiment at any time. Individuals experience the physical body going through a process of spiritual evolution, an out-of-body experience, where the embodiment comes under the control of the eternal soul. Devotees transform and use their own experiences to help others follow the path of self-illumination. In the Bhagavad Gita, it is illustrated when Lord Krishna (appearing in the image of God) guides a human being, the warrior Arjuna (appearing as the true devotee facing anguish).

Equipoise

With inner illumination, the individual is able to go beyond the *sattwic guna* and transcend beyond the fifth sphere. With such transcendence, the embodiment is no longer influenced by the powers of negative forces that are responsible for pain, anguish, and the creation of the inner fear of decay, death, and annihilation. An individual's temperament becomes free from the shackles of living forces and attains *moksha,* a state of being where the living spirit is no longer required to coexist with the living force. This state of being happens when an individual has fulfilled its purpose and accomplished its mission on earth. An individual's living spirit no longer needs to remain attached to the material manifestation to prevail. The living spirit becomes a form of vibration that does not need any instruments to produce music.

This state, *moksha,* is where the physical body attains absolute mental equilibrium, cultivating levelheadedness that is free from hatred. All longing vanishes. The physical body remains steadfast in peace and tranquility. The enriched mind no longer feels any impact of stimuli or impulse generated by external sources. The personality becomes emotionally unyielding and can no longer be swayed or manipulated.

For such souls, love, hate, pain, pleasure, glory, defeat, happiness, and sadness become transitory, emotional experiences. They are not agitated or hysterical; they are only observers and not participants. In truth, they remain fully aware of the causes of events or situations. If needed, they get involved to bring stability to those situations. They use true devotion to seek the support of the Creator to overpower any evil forces.

Section II: Invocation of Eternal Wisdom

Eternal wisdom is a state of liberation where an individual experiences a new life—with or without experiencing death. It is similar to a snake dropping its old skin to acquire a new skin without ever leaving its body. In various religions, to express a change of such a status is accomplished through a sacrament. For example, it is called *baptism* in Christianity, *mikvah* in Judaism, *misogi* in Buddhism, and *ayushkarma* in Hinduism. This signifies dropping an old heritage to start a new beginning or getting rid of spiritual ignorance by attaining the eternal wisdom. The process of attaining eternal wisdom truly is acquiring the absolute truth, *Sat*; hence, everything unknown becomes known, and all the mysteries of the Creator are unveiled. Using the information included within the holy scripture, I have identified the following steps that encompass various aspects of eternal wisdom.

It starts with controlling the life force with proper breathing processes and channeling the life force to different parts of the body to provide the necessary oxygen. This process brings calmness to an individual's sensory system and helps overpower the sources of thoughts responsible for causing obstructions:

hatred, shame, fear, grief, condemnation, prejudice, pedigree, and uprightness.

With the overpowering of these eight barriers, the individual heart is transformed from a physical faculty providing the love of humanity to a subtle faculty and providing the love of God. A devotee becomes a disciple, *sadhaka,* recognizing the powers of the Creator operating within each living thing—moving and not moving. With the love of God, a disciple proceeds to complete his or her spiritual journey to attain eternity.

Mythical Gift

With the love of God, a disciple receives a mythical gift; this is also called the sixth sense. Through this gift, a disciple is able to visualize, analyze, and realize the presence of the Creator, operating at different levels and forming divine splendors. A normal human being only witnesses such splendors as miracles or mysteries of nature.

Salvation

After attaining the mystic gift of a sixth sense, a disciple hears a peculiar sound in the form of a message or divine calling. In holy scriptures, this is defined as *pranava* or *sabda,* a "divine calling" or "sense of conviction" to follow the path of salvation.

Sanctification

After following the path of salvation, an individual's living spirit merges with the eternal soul, individual embodiment is sanctified, and the individual attains divine personage or sainthood *(ahamkara).* After the disciple experiences the passing of the living spirit through the seven centers of the spine, the individual experiences the divine bluish light or the third eye. In the other holy scriptures, this phase is expressed as the passage of life through the seven stars, seven centers, seven churches, or seven golden candlesticks—illuminating the journey as the living spirit passes through different spheres to merge with the eternal soul and attain eternity. This process of unification is described in the Vedas as *kaivalya* and defines the ultimate goal of the individual living spirit, *moksha,* or eternity.

Unification

The eternal soul has no beginning or ending; therefore, the eternal soul is depicted in a symbol that has no beginning and no ending—a snake swallowing its tail, a circle or sphere, or a combination of two circles joined together to denote zero to infinity. Sometimes the eternal soul is depicted in geometric forms such as the Jewish Star of David, the Greek *Ichthys* symbol, the Maltese cross of the Knights Templar, and the Hindu/Buddhist Mandala.

As part of the invocation of eternal wisdom, living beings go through four stages of spiritual evolution, which represent the final journey to eternity. Based upon the information included within published discourses on chapter 10, chapter 11, chapter 12, and chapter 18 of the Bhagavad Gita and other knowledge acquired from study of different books and epics, I have developed the following sections that elaborate upon the final four steps.

*The ability to visualize divine splendors
only comes with the sixth sense.*

Chapter 21
Mythical Gift

The first stage of invocation of eternal wisdom brings the individual to recognize the divine splendors operating within and beyond what can be perceived by spiritual scholars or an enlightened soul through spiritual wisdom. Over the centuries, several highly evolved spiritual scholars (maharishis, seers, and prophets) have attained eternal liberation and acquired this mythical gift, sometimes identified as the sixth sense. Through such a mythical gift, individuals received eternal wisdom and thus were able to discover invisible divine splendors operating at different levels within our universal system.

Astronomers, physicists, and scientists are now using highly advanced technology to understand and scientifically explain such divine splendors. Some of the splendors envisioned by spiritual scholars that are described in the Bhagavad Gita are elaborated upon here.

Astronomic Level

On the astronomic level, the Bhagavad Gita describes the continuous transformation of inert matter into energy and the energy produced transforming inert atoms into cosmic atoms.

Even the process of encirclement, which causes these cosmic atoms to collide with each other to form a bond and create gross mass, is described. This process generates brilliance, radiance, and illumination. In the holy scriptures, such events are described as the creation of divine light or eternal light produced by the supreme powers of the Creator.

Einstein scientifically demonstrated this divine principle of encirclement. Einstein, based upon eternal wisdom, established a simple mathematical equation to define the relationship between mass and energy: energy (e) = mass (m) x speed of light (C^2). It is determined, at the celestial level, that the transformation of vital force generates highly effulgent radiance. It also produces vibrations that ultimately cause the formation of our universal system. Beyond this universal system rest the Creator (*hiranyagarbha*) the ultimate source of causation. The universe itself is consisting of three main regions including Galaxies, Effluent Radiance, and Constellations.

Creator *(Hiranyagarbha)*

The Creator or ultimate source of causations *(hiranyagarbha)* rests beyond the universal. The region between the Creator and the universal is separated by a region that produces effulgent radiance many times greater than the sun. By residing outside the universe, the Creator creates the ultimate substratum from which all forms of universal manifestations come into existence, and they disappear into nothing.

Galaxies *(Adityas)*

The effulgent radiance consists of twelve extraterrestrial bodies *(adityas)*. According to the Vedas, these *adityas* represent the beginning or the ending of our universal system and are identified to regulate the supreme powers, *brahma,* and an image of the Creator, which is worshipped as d*ivinity* and corresponds to the formation of the zodiac.

Effluent Radiance *(Marici)*

Just below this zone *(adityas)*, another zone *(marici)* has been identified. Within this zone, out of the effluent radiance, seven supreme powers transform to create violent thunderstorms, creating cosmic rain and showers. These supreme powers are individually named based upon their functions and are worshipped as *deities.*

Within these three regions, the universal system is formed. They are called constellations *(naksatranam).*

Constellations *(Naksatranam)*

Within this region, a transformation of unmanifested bodies into manifested bodies takes place to form a universal system like ours. Within this region, the power of attraction and repulsion—and the power of electromagnetism—produce cosmic bodies, emitting radioactive or ultraviolet rays. Twenty-seven *naksatranam* or constellations have been identified and worshipped as *demigods.* The lower part of this sphere produces luminous planetary bodies surrounded by cosmic storms, such as Saturn. They are identified as *maruts* and worshipped as *archangels.* The physical bodies that do not conform to the laws of equilibrium are subject to rejection and appear as shooting stars, asteroids, and meteorites.

Within the constellations, there are manifested physical bodies where the transformation of energy into mass has subsided to create environments that permit the formation and survival of living and breathing things *(jivas).* These living things survive on a secondary form of illumination called reflective light or soft light *(sasi)*. The reflective lights become the source of photosynthesis and mutation—an important element in the origin of life within terrestrial planets.

Terrestrial Level

The terrestrial level includes different zones identified as *loka*s or spheres.

> *Maharloka* is where the powers of *maya* produce duality, creating light and shadow or day and night.
>
> *Dasamadwara* establishes a barrier between the material and spiritual worlds, acts as a revolving door between the ethereal body (astral) and the material body (physical), and regulates the cycles of life and death, happiness and sadness, and gloom and doom.
>
> *Swarloka* surrounds the terrestrial planets and provides the magnetic aura experienced by living beings on earth. It also provides the necessary environments for the living spirit to prevail in its mystic form, without any embodiment, and be ready to appear on the planet in a fully embodied form. In spiritual terms, this is called *purgatory.*
>
> *Bhuvarloka* is where all living things in their embodied or semi-embodied forms prevail. It covers the region between the surface and the sky and is controlled and managed by the powers of lower

> gods or avatars. Humanity worships these powers as saints *(devam)*, prophets *(vasavah)*, illuminated souls *(indriyanam)*, enlightened souls *(viratwam)*, and departed noble souls *(mahatmas)*.
>
> *Bhuloka* covers the surface of the planet where gross matter, earth, provides a dwelling to house the living spirit and create living things, such as the single-cell kingdom, vegetable kingdom, animal kingdom, and the highly complex physical bodies forming humanity.

Spiritual scholars established that, within the terrestrial level, every living thing, irrespective of shape and size, was created to serve designated functions. Individuals perform actions and activities and are regulated and influenced by nature. Irrespective of the obligation, each creation is required to conform to the laws of equilibrium, and maintain, balance, and generate tranquility. Every action or activity produces images. The images created through these actions performed not in conformance with codes of covenant leave memories that generate blemishes that build up to create residual memories, causing the malfunction of subtle faculties. The malfunctioning of subtle faculties limits any transformation of guidance from the living spirit to an individual's body. Accumulation of such residual memories influences an individual's ability to attain guidance and access higher knowledge. Thus, the neutral nature of individual actions *(yakshas)* turns negative and becomes *rakshasas*. Individual actions transform from neutral to evil.

All natural resources, including metals, water, forests, land, and mountains, are created to fulfill the needs of living things. These resources by nature generate attraction and cause attachment *(kubera)*. When *kubera* is exploited to fulfill selfish needs, it takes on a demonic nature; instead of helping, it acquires demonic characteristics and brings the demise of living things, moving and not moving. The darker side of *kuberas* appears in the form of fires, floods, landslides, earthquakes, or massive freezes. On a higher level, they bring major upheaval, such as tectonic movements, volcanic eruptions, the churning of the ocean, massive meteorite showers, and asteroids.

Spiritual Level

Scholars determined that when the demonic forces threatened to end life on the planet during the upheavals, the living things were provided with the same eternal wisdom that had been provided to *divinity, deities, demigods,* and *archangels.* To fight back demons and evil forces and reestablish the equipoise, living beings were provided with the same knowledge in the form of nectar *(amrita).*

According to the Bhagavad Gita, during the churning of the ocean, with the powers of such nectar, living things acquired higher wisdom. With such wisdom, they evolved to a higher spiritual level. Exemplified as the water horse cultivating mythical wings to become a white horse, *uchaishravas* could fly out of the waters. The water elephant transformed into a mythical white elephant, *airavata,* who could rise up into the clouds. Similarly, the children of *avatar* prevailing within the oceans transformed into *manus,* which were spiritually evolved moral and ethical living beings who ruled the earth. The royal kings led to the development of civilization on earth and the creation and development of humanity. This spiritual evolutionary process is described below.

Divine Souls *(Manus)*

On earth, they first appeared as *avatars,* divine physical bodies, to initiate the development of living things. These physical bodies possessed primordial force and eternal wisdom; in the Vedas, they are referred to as *manus*. They were responsible for the establishment of the codes of covenants of morality and righteousness to help humanity control desire and overcome inborn demons.

Illuminated Souls *(Rishis)*

The same wisdom that *manus* had received from *avatars* was passed down to humanity. The wisdom remained dormant until selected individuals learned to invoke the inner living spirit through holistic visions or by inner awakening of the conscience. Such knowledge was documented in the form of epics such as the Vedas, the Bible, the Quran, the Five Books of Moses, the Confucian Analects, and the Mayan Book of the Council. Within these books, methods, rituals, processes, and practices that need to be performed to invoke individual consciousness were described.

Enlightened Souls *(Gurus)*

Enlightened souls outlined the process of selection of a place of worship, performing personal sacrifices and offering oblations. They created temples to worship and open spaces, such as under trees. In the Bhagavad Gita, for worship and for seeking higher knowledge, the tree of *Asvatha* or *pipal* was recommended. This tree was recommended for a number of reasons, including the shape, size, and long life. Other features include shiny leaves shaped like hearts, long petioles, linear lancelet tail like snakes, inherent powers to provide medicinal values such as treatment of skin diseases, inflammation, poison, neuralgia, constipation, and many gynecological problems. In addition, scholars recommend the performance of single-point concentration under such trees to establish a link with the eternal soul. For centuries in India, spiritual scholars have selected this tree for prayer, worship, and communal services and gatherings.

Spiritual Scholars *(Yogis, Munis,* and *Siddas)*

Spiritual scholars have discovered that by writing, playing, and listening to beautiful spiritual music, one can invoke inner consciousness. According to the Bhagavad Gita, the first person who was able to invoke the individual living spirit was *Narada.* Through beautiful music, he was able to rouse the primordial force and make his mind subservient to his consciousness. Through the awakening of primordial force, spiritual scholars experienced the flow of energy through the spinal cord; when it is properly channeled, the inner gland produces a special type of nutrient *(nectar)*—similar to one naturally produced by plants and flowers to attract pollinating insects and birds. Yogis have said, "One drop of such nectar is enough to conquer death and achieve immortality."

Physical Level

At the physical level, the divine splendors operate to protect and support living things, including humanity.

Thunderbolt

At the highest level, it is the thunderbolt. Hindu scriptures identify this as *vajra*, the indestructible weapon of archangels that can destroy anything; it can even cut though anything without being demolished. It has the ultimate power to bring living forces back into equilibrium and can pierce any protective shield, including the sky (which has the ability to hold back cosmic forces, radiation, and ultraviolet light).

Lightning and Rain

Lightning and rain join the windstorm and have the power to transform the immortal nature of living forces into mortal nature. They can even fight any evil force, such as fire or heat, to bring things under control. They also provide life to resources that allow humanity and other living things, such as nourishing trees and plants that supply consumable products, without losing life, such as fruit trees, flowering plants, and different forms of vegetation that produce nuts and other edible products.

Nourishing Foods

Similar to lightning, another splendor produces nourishing foods to save newborns and provide nourishment throughout life. Within Hindu mythology, *kamadhuk*, or milk-bearing animals—cattle, goats, sheep, and even women—possess the immortal power to supply enough milk to feed newborns. Such animals are worshipped within many religious groups for these reasons. Their milk is extensively used to produce other nourishing products, such as butter and cheese. Even their waste is used to produce fertilizer or as a source of fuel, and their skin is used to make leather clothing and other coverings.

Proliferation

Further, through divine splendors, the process of physical and spiritual evolution can be continued. There are two means of proliferation. The first is asexual *(kandarpa)*. The second is sexual *(vasuki)*. *Kandarpa* is the process of creation accomplished through a natural process of the division of a cell into two daughter cells. Asexual reproduction does not require two entities of compatible sexes. *Vasuki* requires two animals or other living things—typically of the same species—to reproduce. As part of sexual reproduction, spiritual scholars identified a tiny creature that plays an important role. This creature brings life within an inert cell; through the creation of embodiment, living things are able to experience physical and spiritual advancement. The tiniest creature remains dormant until birth when it assumes a latent position. In physical terms, sexual reproduction starts with the creation of affinity for a soul mate. This affinity leads to a union between the two, which develops into a sexual desire that ultimately gets satisfied by means of mental and physical activities. Sexual desire alone is not enough to spark reproduction; it only creates a passion until the union of two living spirits produces sperm *(kandarpa)* to initiate procreation. Unlike cross-pollination of plants or insemination for two animals, this process is defined as intercourse or the act of performing sex in scientific terms. Sanctified souls have named this *kamashastra*. The process of transforming passionate urges is generated through physical sensory organs. They are fulfilled through subtle faculties or organs of perception to produce sperm. *Kandarpa* consists of a head, a mid-piece, and a tail. The tiny sperm *(vasuki)* is depicted as a snake ring on the finger of Shiva. In terms of spiritual evolution, the tiniest creature is defined as the emergence of the living spirit within the embodiment. It goes through several stages of spiritual evolution: *chit, chitta, shraddha, sannyasa, nirvana,* and *moksha.*

Perforation

The divine power works through crawling creatures operating below the surface of the earth. They dig small holes to set up natural ecosystems. Through this system, surface water reaches the roots of plants and other vegetation. During the spring, these creatures come out of the ground as worms and create holes to allow rain and floodwater to seep down to roots and permit the vegetation to grow and prosper. According to Hindu mythology, during the churning of oceans, worms, eels, crawlers, snakes, fish, and reptiles created an ecosystem to transfer the water from oceans, rivers, and lakes to fertilize the land and cause vegetation to grow. Over time, these creatures evolved and transformed into different species that spread onto land and into the sky. The evolutionary advancement eventually established the substrata for the development of individual species with a predetermined temperament to sustain and grow. Even today, in many cultures, snakes, crawlers, and other animals are considered eternal spirits and are worshipped by humanity.

Environment Level

At the environmental level, spiritual scholars have identified divine splendors that provide protection to living things prevailing within different regions of the planet.

Within Oceans

Within the oceans, special marine creatures manifest in half-god and half-fish forms called *varuna*. This mystic power brings tranquility and calmness to the ocean. This sea creature, in mythical terms, is larger than any other fish or sea creature. It prevails within the ocean and remains invisible until it is needed. It manifests in the form of fish to provide protection to living creatures in the deepest parts of the ocean.

Below the Surface

The region below the surface is not subject to direct sunlight. A special creature called *anata* crawls and hides in caves and mineshafts. This creature—in the shape of a serpent—is known as the demigod of land. This creature has a very long body and one large or many small faces. The primary purpose was to protect natural resources from being abused by greedy living beings.

Above the Surface

The region above the surface receives direct light from the sun and reflective light from the moon. It is protected by living spirits called *pitranam* that are no longer manifested, such as our ancestors and descendants. According to spiritual scholars, they represent the astral body that has not yet attained complete liberation from the shackles of nature. These are sometimes referred to as *aryaman* or *archangels*. According to the Bhagavad Gita, ten divine angels make the final determination on liberation of a sanctified soul from the cycles of life and death to join the perpetual essence.

On Land/Air/Sky

In the Bhagavad Gita, when a mammal cultivates faith in the supreme powers, it is blessed with mystic wings to fly like a bird. It can see in the darkness and attain protection from evil spirits or vampires, such as mammals that turn into bats or *baku*.

Similarly, animals that cultivate faith in the supreme powers are blessed with unique powers to run faster than other animals to protect themselves from evil spirits or death, such as deer or tigers (*mrga-indrah*). A bird that cultivates faith in the supreme powers is blessed with the ability to fly high in the sky without any fear. The bald eagle *(garuda)* can see evil from long distances. People who cultivate faith in the supreme power acquire the unique power to overpower or kill the evil spirit.

Living beings who face challenges from evil powers are provided with mystic powers to destroy such evil—no matter how powerful the evil is. For example, *Prahlada* is a devotee who constantly faces challenges from *Hiranyakashipu,* his own father. The father—who had come under the influence of a demonic monster—was killed by the powers of *yamas* and *niyama.*

Similarly, in the fight between David and Goliath, *yamas* came to protect David from the evil powers of Goliath. According to the Vedas, during the war between *devas* (good) and *asura* (evil), the powers of *yamas* turned ocean water into *nectar* and destroyed the mystical monsters *(asuras)* that had gained control of the planet.

Beyond the Sky

The ethereal region is where no material object or embodiment can survive and where there is no beginning or end. After death, the astral body departs to become part of this region until the living spirit is liberated to go beyond to join the eternal soul. The astral body of a noble soul leaves behind nothing but memories that are expressed in the form of sadness, disappointment, depression, or melancholy; this period is called *kalah* or inner darkness. In such situations, the splendor of the supreme power appears by showering good news to shorten such sadness created by the death of a noble soul. However, when the astral body of egocentric or demonic personalities departs, it extends the occurrence of bad news *(kalayatam)*.

Devotional Level

At the devotional level, spiritual scholars have identified two kinds of divine splendor that provide individual peace and tranquility. One is of a transitory nature, and it lasts through an individual's life. The second is of an eternal nature that lasts beyond an individual's life. The first is of a physical nature, and the second is of a spiritual nature.

Physical Nature

As part of the physical nature, individuals can attain eight different levels of happiness and tranquility. These include fame *(kirtih)*, material wealth *(srih)*, fine speech *(vak)*, compassion *(nainam)*, memory *(smrtih)*, intelligence *(medha)*, steadfastness *(dhrtih)*, and patience *(ksama)*. A person who has accomplished all eight levels during life attains material happiness and is recognized in terms of honor, fame, nobility, and self-respect.

Spiritual Nature

As part of spiritual nature, an individual seeks everlasting tranquility. There are several levels of inner peace and tranquility. In everlasting tranquility, an individual experiences invisible mystic powers attained through invocation of the eternal soul.

Hymns

Individuals practice sacred hymns in silence or by chanting with true devotion. Each sacred hymn encompasses a small segment of the ultimate truth buried within each letter, vowel, and word. Through practicing each hymn, individuals uncover the divine messages and secret eternal wisdom that has been carried from one life to another. An individual ultimately acquires absolute truth through this process.

These sacred hymns are so complex that only a selected few can unveil the hidden eternal meaning of each hymn. In the Bhagavad Gita, *Bharat-Sam* has thirty-six meters. It contains the most sacred verse and is the highest level of eternal truth. A devotee who unveils the underlying message experiences flowing *nectar* in their glands; while chanting this hymn, the devotee goes through a series of revelations before attaining *nirvana*.

Prayers

In addition to these complex hymns, there are also simple hymns used by most devotees to cultivate faith and follow the codes of covenant to acquire spiritual wisdom and focus on immortal perpetual essence. In the Hindu faith, this hymn is called *gayatri mantra*. These hymns in the form of prayers are commonly practiced three times per day to promote inner peace and tranquility.

Rosary

Another simple method includes a garland of beads or stones and yarn or cord, with one hundred knots, constantly passing through the hand in a circular motion. Christians call this a rosary. Buddhists call it a *mala*. Middle Eastern faiths use a spiritual string.

Silence

Some elect to follow the path of silence. They maintain complete silence at all times to focus on the immortal perpetual essence.

Individual Level

At the individual level, divine splendors establish inner confidence and help individuals cultivate faith in the Creator during periods of constant change created to maintain equilibrium and balance within the universal system.

Seasonality

Seasonality generates curiosity within the human mind, especially during periods of gloom. To overpower any loss of confidence in the powers, divine splendor brings a period of happiness and joy. Ending such periods specifically creates activities to reinstate happiness and cultivation. For example, hot summers are followed by a loss of leaves and treacherous monsoons. Bugs, germs, and health epidemics bring periods of depression, but they are immediately followed by seasons of pleasure, happiness, and social gatherings. This period extends from late October until the end of December. These are the most auspicious months in every religion; this is when major days of divine worship, festivities, and religious holidays occur. Similarly, the second positive period is the spring season, which extends from the end of March through May. New life—in the form of fresh plants, flowers, and babies—begins once more. This period reestablishes hope for happiness, health, and a prosperous life. This period represents another religious holiday and brings people together to enjoy the changes in seasons.

Motivation

Another divine splendor identified is the anticipation of rewards for individual actions. Divine power in its invisible form, *maya*, cultivates never-ending attachment to the rewards for individual actions as the motivator for performing actions and activities. This underlying power of attachment to the expectation of rewards causes individuals to gamble, acquire ideas of grandeur, accumulate power and resources, conquer assets, develop business ventures, and attain personal accomplishments. Many individuals want to accumulate wealth without exerting energy or perform selfish and immoral activities to acquire material wealth that can quickly lead them to participating in fraudulent activities. When such activities are handled improperly, it creates disappointment, mental anguish, or melancholy. The invisible power also has the power to lead individuals to realize the transitory nature of material gain and wealth. Therefore, many cultivate quests to seek long-term peace.

Birth and Death

Another divine splendor remains unknown and unpredictable until it has already happened, which is defined as birth and death. This divine splendor is based upon the principle that a creation has to disappear in order to make a space for a new creation. A seed has to open and die to give birth to a new plant in the form of a seedling. This unpredictable power can be observed within the eternal love that produces a sperm to displace a living being.

Abandoning attachment to the physical body leads to salvation.

Chapter 22
Salvation

Physical Abandonment

The second stage of eternal wisdom is an individual's ability to abandon attachment to the physical body. It is accomplished by taking an individual's life through the performance of three contiguous acts of compassion, including sacrifice, charity, and austerity. Spiritual scholars have discovered that when individuals fulfill these acts with full devotion, which is beyond detachment from material life, they attain a state of salvation.

Individuals who—with full passion and devotion—elect to fulfill obligatory responsibilities and perform selfless services with true commitment and willing hearts—but for some reason are unable to go beyond to accomplish abandonment from the physical body—are still blessed and rewarded for their devotion. The astral body, in its purified form, attains salvation, but the individual living spirit is not freed to go beyond, and it remains part of the zone of magnetic aura called *swarloka* or the sphere of the great vacuum *(mahasunaya)*, heaven, or the highest region within the terrestrial zone.

Any individual who elects not to serve family and society and decides to follow the path of desertion experiences delusions and never attains the true benefits of salvation. The astral body remains blemished with residual memories that prevent them from prevailing within the zone of fine matter *(bhuvarloka)*.

Those who are able to attain salvation acquire the unique ability to be in a state of contentment regardless of their surroundings. They do not feel miserable in distasteful situations or express delight in pleasant environments. They continue to perform their duties peacefully irrespective of whether the duties are agreeable or not. For them, the peak of happiness and the valley of sorrow do not prevail. Maintenance of equilibrium becomes part of life.

Affinity

As stated earlier, every living thing has to perform actions to survive; therefore, even the smallest organism cannot attain salvation without absolute abandonment or liberation from the powers of living forces or the physical body. Physical bodies generate a longing for material things and develop personal feelings for other living things. Especially among humanity, the longing continues to grow and develops an affinity for material things and an attachment to the results or rewards of actions. Thus, images of those actions continue to accumulate on the subtle faculties of the mind; they leave impressions that influence the temperament and personality.

Over the centuries, the materialistic desire to own and control objects—as well as the desire to manage and control other living beings—has created so many blemishes that an individual's living spirit is unable to provide guidance on morality. As a result, humanity in general is born with blemishes carried with the astral body from birth; thus the physical body continuously influences the individual's thought processes. Greed overpowers our inner impulses; this generates unbound thoughts and desires to cling to material gains and acquire powers to control and manage other human beings and living things at any cost.

For centuries, possessive traits have influenced the human body to such an extent that humanity of today is dominated by *rajasic* temperaments. Morality is masked—and sometimes even overpowered—by the abundance of intellectual and practical knowledge. Many individuals live without knowing there is a higher knowledge than intellectual knowledge, and they believe there is nothing beyond the current physical existence. They only see the physical body with a defined life and nothing else. They don't accept or understand the immortal living spirit. They cannot even comprehend the subjective aspect of actions because they cannot observe those actions with the physical senses. Therefore, they live in spiritual ignorance, not knowing that every action leaves an impression on the subtle faculties and sensory organs of perception. Moreover, due to spiritual ignorance and lack of divine wisdom, many individuals do not realize that such memories leave footprints that do not disappear with the ending of life. In reality, as part of the astral body, such footprints are transferable; they become the substrata for the temperament of the newly created living being.

Insight

Through the process of salvation, the individual physical body comes under the full control of the eternal living spirit, which gains control of internal and external stimuli generated through the powers of the living force. The sensory organs of perception, the nervous system *(indriyas)*, and individual thoughts and desires all come under the control of the eternal soul. According to the Bhagavad Gita, when the physical body attains such a level, the embodiment *(kshetrajna)* generates radiant and inner illumination *(tadvidah)*. This union of three parties *(tripuri* or *triad)*, perceived with salvation, helps the individual witness the three powers of causations working together. The embodiment goes through a process of harmonization and equilibrium, and then an individual is able to look through the infinite field of knowledge *(kshetrajna)*, operate the powers of the living force, and unveil the ultimate powers of the causations.

Many living beings have acquired such powers through devotion—and they have acquired the innovative wisdom to unveil the ultimate powers of causations. Well-known sages, prophets, and enlightened souls have used such powers to uncover secrets of a divine nature—recognized as revelations. Similarly, many others have used such devotion to unveil creative and innovative discoveries. For example, Newton discovered the laws of gravity from the infinite field of nature. Likewise, Leonardo da Vinci unveiled different aspects of life, and Gautama Buddha used these powers to uncover the powers of *nirvana* and *moksha*.

Transcendent

With salvation, an individual comes to comprehend the difference between physical transformation, spiritual transformation, and transcendental transformation. Physical transformation represents the changes in the physical body in birth, childhood, adulthood, and old age. The spiritual transformation represents the changes in an individual's causal body that transform spiritual ignorance into spiritual realization, enlightenment, and inner illumination. Transcendental transformation represents the purified individual's astral body from encrusted residual memories to liberate the living spirit from the embodiment.

The power of salvation provides an individual the supernatural powers to transform work into worship—and affinity for action into devotion—and the ability to watch the result of actions like an observer and not as a participant. The power of salvation is available to all living beings on an equal basis, but the ability to attain salvation depends on an individual's approach toward methods of living, dealing with others, and the level of devotion and dedication to follow the path of morality. Those who comprehend the structure and inner workings of actions and learn to relinquish any attachment to the results of those actions are blessed. They are able to enjoy the inner support of the living spirit. Others who are able to accept divine power and transform the living spirit into a transcendental soul go beyond the three levels of divine nature (good, bad, and average) to attain true liberation. Once they attain liberation through acquired mystic powers, they can negate or eliminate any negative forces obstructing them from performing righteous acts. If needed, they can even kill any evil force acting against them and restore righteousness. Any killing they perform for such a divine cause becomes divine; therefore, it does not leave any residual memories.

Endeavors

In the process of attaining salvation, the path of salvation varies, depending upon the source of inner inspiration. An individual passes through three stages of development, depending upon if the source of inspiration is external or internal.

External

When the process of salvation originates through the realization of the transitory nature of material nature, the inspiration is of an external nature. It is subjected to the traits of the living force—*sattwic, rajasic, or tamasic*—that influence the individual's temperament and determines the direction and nature of the path of salvation. Individuals whose inspiration is motivated by material nature do not attain purity in all aspects or attain salvation through difficulties, but they do achieve a certain level of purity.

Such individuals rise up to the level and become noble rulers, impartial kings, honest politicians, good industrialists, fair businesspeople, and merchants. Such personalities enforce and implement righteousness, peace, and tranquility as a way to improve before they ultimately attain liberation. Their inspiration, movements, and quality of faith remain dominated by traits of material nature, and they experience salvation in the form of ecstasy, which may or may not last long.

Internal

When the process of salvation originates through the realization of faith or the existence of inner living spirits, the individual is subject to trait devotion. All actions and activities are performed in accordance with the codes of covenant, such as morality and devotion. The path toward salvation varies widely, depending upon an individual's dedication and devotion. For example, one who cultivates the purest form of inner inspirations—without any attachment to fruits of actions—utilizes the utmost compassion in accomplishing assigned tasks and obligations and receives unique inner strength.

For such divine personalities, duality never becomes a

factor in life. They cultivate an enduring ability to overcome any hardship. The mind, intellect, and conscience work together in harmony to help them attain salvation. They quickly attain the status of a prophet, sage, or enlightened soul *(mahatma)*.

Ultimate liberation of living spirit from the astral body leads to sanctity.

Chapter 23
Sanctity

Adaptation

The third stage of eternal wisdom is sanctity—where individual living spirit attains the ultimate liberation from the living force—and the individual is able to pursue his or her ultimate destiny. As long as even a small part of the astral body remains associated with the matter or cosmic atoms, the merger of the living spirit with the eternal soul cannot take place. Therefore, attainment of sanctity requires an utmost purity of the astral body.

Once the living spirit *(atma)* becomes completely free from the astral body and merges with the perpetual essence of the Creator *(parambrahma)*, it loses its identity forever. The Bhagavad Gita states that the astral bodies of a demigod, archangel, and illuminated soul are not completely purified; therefore, they are not able to merge with the eternal soul *(parambrahma)*.

This process of conversion of living spirit to sanctified spirit cannot be observed by any means or measured by any scientific instrument. It is only perceived through mystical power, which the Bhagavad Gita calls the third eye, the higher sensory organ of perception, which remains dormant within the human body until it is invoked through continued persuasion of unconditional devoutness. According to the holy scriptures, it is extremely difficult to attain this level; therefore, only a select few have been able to reach this state of spiritual evolution.

In the Vedas, attainment of this stage is defined as *brahmana*. This inner glow electrifies the physical body and reveals the inner powers of illumination and the individual's state of serenity, self-restraint, austerity, purity, forgiveness, and uprightness. Such sanctified souls become invisible and can only appear as invisible rulers' *avatars,* divine envoys *(brahamarandhras),* or ascetic majestic powers *(aiswaryas).*

With such power, the physical body can appear in eight different forms:

> *Anima:* the power to make one's body as small as possible—to the size of a tiny cosmic atom—and lose one's manifested body
>
> *Mahima:* the power to magnify the body to make it as large as possible
>
> *Laghima:* the power to become as heavy or as light as needed
>
> *Garima:* the power to acquire knowledge and become a spiritual master
>
> *Prapti:* the power to acquire anything and become anything

Vasitwa: the power to overpower irresistible power

Kama: the power to bring everything under control

Isitwa: the power to become the supreme power and lose identity

Prerequisite

The evolutionary process of sanctity requires that an individual's mind is endowed to fulfill the basic requirements:

- Attain inner peace, maintain total self-control, and maintain complete inner silence
- Practice a strict diet to maintain purity
- Practice sanctuary in solitude
- Keep the individual conscience shielded from internal or external influences

As stated earlier, it is not practically possible for most people to reach such a level without major commitment and devotion. Over the centuries, only a few individuals have diligently followed such an evolutionary process to attain sanctity.

History shows that individuals who succeed in attaining sanctity earned the respect for living things, never assuming any position of superiority or performing any action out of greed, ego, or arrogance. Such individuals face every obstacle with faith and never resort to individualism or egoism. At all times, they know the divine powers that support the process of transformation from salvation to sanctity can turn into demonic forces and immediately transform any happiness into misery, ultimately punishing those individuals with pain and anguish. They remain bound by destiny and follow the path of self-perfection by fulfilling individual obligations and never attempting to be someone else. No matter how helpless the situation may seem, they maintain faith in the supreme powers. Even if they become victims of materialistic desires, develop greed, or elect to establish their own destinies, they receive the support of the supreme power to gain control of the situation by helping them destroy such desires and adhere to the codes of covenants.

Process

According to the laws of nature, each creation is created with the defined objective of performing a specific function in life. Stoic philosophers define this as the divine animating principle that protects individual rights and obligations. The Bhagavad Gita states that everyone is assigned to perform one's own duty, and the performance of one's responsibilities is protected by an invisible shield.

Therefore, it is a prerequisite that no one should abandon individual obligatory responsibilities—no matter how faulty they may appear. One should not be enticed by the activities of others or the associated rewards. Individuals should be strict in personal obligations and responsibilities and not be swayed by greed, ego, or personal gain. According to the code of covenants, if any individual approaches or exceeds such desires, the living thing is subject to punishments, such as agony, anguish, misery, and pain—and sometimes even with a miserable death. For example, fire is blessed with smoke as a shield to protect the innocent from its evil powers. The same fire is also blessed with the power to provide heat and light to serve living things. Similarly, the bee is provided with stingers for protection; at the same time, it is blessed with the ability to provide honey and beeswax.

Moksha

One cannot attain sanctity by running away from life or personal obligations. It can be accomplished only through participation. Sanctity is a state of *moksha*—when the living spirit is no longer subject to the cycles of life and death. At such a stage, the living spirit is no longer affiliated with embodiment; it is not subject to thoughts, desires, or the turbulence of fruits of individual actions and activities. It reaches a state of "action-less-ness."

Many people confuse ecstasy with sanctity; these individuals remain deluded. Attainment of sanctity is a long-lasting and permanent state of being. Ecstasy is impossible to maintain for a long period—or achieve on a permanent basis. Many attain ecstasy as an experiment or for transitory pleasures by using drugs and other intoxicating substances. Others are devoted and experience ecstasy through concentration, meditation, and contemplation.

Some use yogic practices and self-perfection to attain ecstasy. This provides tranquility and peace of mind for a longer duration, but nothing compares to the state of sanctity or *nirvana* attained through all-encompassing devotion to the Creator. This process requires commitment to sacrifice everything for the Creator—including one's life—purifying one's physical body of all greed, ego, arrogance, and anger, liberating the astral body from all sins of the past, and allowing the living spirit to be free and merge with the eternal soul.

Those who are devoid of austerity or devotion can never attain such a level. Those who do not render obligatory responsibilities or perform actions and activities in conformance with the divine covenants cannot attain sanctity. Those who elect to ignore the existence of the Creator and supreme power—or even believe they can overpower divine creations—also cannot attain sanctity.

A glimpse of the divine presence is the momentary gift received by only a few.

The ultimate mission of every creation is to face amalgamation, which no living thing is ready to accept.

Chapter 24
Unification

Trepidation

The greatest trepidation of all is death, which is part of the law of creation. Nobody has any control over it, and nobody has any clue as to what happens after death. Every living thing is apprehensive, worried, and scared of such uncertainty. Every sage, prophet, and enlightened soul is afraid; out of fear, they believe the Creator brings such demise. Therefore, to please such powers, they worship and offer oblations by singing hymns and giving personal tributes to please higher powers. Many even acquire higher knowledge to uncover the secrets of such powers. Even angels, demigods, and deities look up to the Creator out of amazement and respect. Even kings who served their kingdoms with morality and righteousness have been subject to death, and their kingdoms have been subject to demise. A cow that provides milk to a newborn, provides skin for clothing, and dung as a source of fuel is also subject to death. Similarly, many famous, righteous warriors who defeated their enemies and conquered everything within reach have ended up destroyed like moths that rushed hurriedly into a blazing fire.

The existence and demise of life—along with a multitude of factors that influence individual lives—generates unbound curiosity and fear within the hearts of all living beings. Knowing there is an ultimate demise, humanity has cultivated an extremely negative and fearful perception of the powers of the Creator. Throughout history, many have adopted methods of isolation to practice meditation and contemplation to overcome the fear of demise. Many have elected to follow myths, ideologies, and philosophical and ritual practices to please the powers of perpetual essence and attain tranquility and eternity.

Reassurance

Through attainment of inner illumination and eternal truth, sanctified souls have come to comprehend that the true nature of the powers of the Creator is fundamentally neutral and was created to preserve balance and equilibrium. However, its true neutral nature is transformed into the demonic or the divine by the actions of living things—moving and not moving.

By acquiring spiritual wisdom and furthering the attainment of absolute truth, it is revealed that the destructive nature of the Creator is a delusion based upon fear, ignorance, and arrogance. Understanding the true purpose of death—that it is a phase of a continuous process of physical and spiritual evolution—allows these powers to view things with respect, love, compassion, and devotion. This understanding helps attain tranquility and sanctity.

With the help of absolute truth attained by sanctified souls and other highly learned spiritual scholars, the true purpose of an individual's death is accepted as a means to enhance the path of spiritual evolution as well as to maintain balance in the universal system. Further, the transitory nature of each causation is accepted as the divine rule; it is commonly being applied to every material object, event, and happening.

Several spiritual scholars accept each transitory phase of life as a natural step toward ultimate eternity. With such knowledge, the causation and cessation of manifested bodies at the cosmic level is also accepted as a transitory phenomenon. It leads to the advancement of the physical body to attain its unmanifested form; at the terrestrial level, each birth and death represents the transitional level leading to the liberation of the living spirit to eternity.

Based upon eternal truth, sanctified souls come to comprehend that the fundamental aspect of the annihilation is to continue to make space for new creations. Each creation is on a path of physical and spiritual evolution; the ultimate goal is liberation. Every material and living thing has a defined life, and they all end at a specific, predefined time—irrespective of the presence of an observer. The deaths of our enemies, loved ones, and nobles are predestined and will happen whether we are there or not.

The Bhagavad Gita demonstrates that every creation will end at some time. At the time of death, some leave this world fighting and holding on to the ego and associated attachments. Others leave this world with knowledge, peace, and tranquility, knowing death is only the beginning of the new stage of the next development.

The life cycle of each creation is controlled by the divine laws of equity, balance, harmony, tranquility, and equilibrium. Individual existence, achievement, and dominion are pre-established; once the designated function is fulfilled, everything will face its demise—like a flower. The cause for death—as defined by humanity as an accident or incident and feared by humanity—is only due to spiritual ignorance.

In absolute terms, death is an instrument created by the supreme power to segment the four infinite elements of causation—vibration, time, space, and eternal force. It physically and spiritually supports the evolutionary processes.

Comprehension

After attaining sanctity, the living soul comes to accept the Creator as the ultimate power. It prevails beyond the universe to provide substrata from which everything originates and ends. It further comes to accept the Creator as beyond comprehension. In spite of all this, it continues to prevail to know the true nature of the Creator or the ultimate destiny of each creation.

In the Bhagavad Gita, the living spirit of King Arjuna, who had attained absolute truth, gained full control of his ego, eliminated every form of delusion, and shifted his mind into a trance ultimately attained sanctity. He maintained a longing to know the Creator and used his mystical powers to eliminate all shapes, forms, and colors by beholding and eliminating any space between manifested bodies. Arjuna, in his trance, witnessed the cosmic and celestial manifestations. By eliminating any space between them, he witnessed the unmanifested form of all bodies in the universal system—the original state that prevailed prior to the manifestation of all things.

In this mystical trance, Arjuna was able to bring the entire universal system into a single point where any form of individuality, duality, or multiplicity was eliminated by eradicating any space between the luminous celestial bodies *(adityas)* and the cosmic bodies *(vasus)*. He even overpowered all powers created by such manifestations: the powers of causation *(ruddras)* responsible for destruction, the powers of protection *(aswins)* responsible for mercy, the power of vibration *(martuts)* responsible for sounds and motion, and any other supreme power responsible for the source of creation. Arjuna, in spite of his effort and mental trance, was unable get a glimpse of the Creator.

No matter how much Arjuna tried, he could not get a glimpse of the Creator. He pleaded through Lord Krishna, an avatar of God, to help him experience the true nature of the Creator and the ultimate destiny of all creations. With the help of Lord Krishna, Arjuna practiced *yoga aishwaryam,* which is necessary to link oneself with the *ishvara*—the inconceivable form of the Creator. According to the Bhagavad Gita, Arjuna ultimately received the gift of divine bliss or the activation of the third eye.

Validation

According to the Bhagavad Gita, while sitting in a trance and using the powers of his third eye, Arjuna visualized the cessation of the universal system, including material manifestations and mystical manifestations. He finally saw the ending of all divine creation. Arjuna saw manifested and unmanifested forms fusing into a single, undifferentiated body. The physical bodies and their eyes, mouths, legs, and arms were crushed—and wearing ornaments and weapons. Everything was dissolved into the elemental phases of its existence. Every living thing—humanity, the animal kingdom, and the vegetable kingdom—were fighting back from the extreme calamity; nobody wanted to face death.

Arjuna experienced how humanity held on to its beautifully embodied inert material objects and wide range of luxury items—wreaths, necklaces, and clothes with fragrances and shining colors. They did not desire to part with the material possessions and hard-earned success, power, and control. This demise—including every living thing—came from every direction. The manifested physical bodies lost any opulence, duality, brilliance, power, and glamor as the living spirit departed from the manifestation. The manifested bodies merged to become unmanifested bodies. As they lost any individuality, they became a single entity—void of differentiation.

Arjuna observed every inch of space between all living and material things being eliminated. As everything collapsed into one consolidated mass, Arjuna realized that he was viewing the ultimate amalgamation of the celestial, cosmic, and terrestrial universe.

The magnitude of light produced exceeded the light that would generate from thousands of blazing suns in the sky. Arjuna came to accept that he was witnessing the unimaginable phenomenon; the entire universe formed one luminous cloud without any beginning or ending. Arjuna saw the mystical forces prevailing as angels, demigods, deities, and divinity merged into the perpetual essence of the Creator. After witnessing this unification of the universal system, Arjuna's hair stood up in horror. Arjuna could no longer cope with an experience so ghastly; he begged and pleaded to Lord Krishna to help end the terror.

After experiencing the ghastly image, Arjuna accepted the primordial dynamic force as the ultimate source from which everything evolves and dissolves. This primordial dynamic force has its beginning and ending within itself, which is the sole Creator. This provides a true substratum for all manifestations, moving and not moving. Our universal system is similar to small balls rotating within a ball bearing; each ball rotates individually, is formed from itself, and merges itself. The bearing acts as the substratum, creating and dissolving balls to end up becoming part of the same substratum.

Admiration

With comprehension of such absolute truth, sanctified souls suggest—instead of fear—that every human should always worship the perpetual essence and the supreme power by bowing their head to such powers with love, admiration, respect, and honor for the creation and enforcement of codes of covenants and for providing the powers of equilibrium, tranquility, peace, and happiness.

Humanity should worship and give thanks for the creation of divine and demonic forces. They have enormous powers—provided by the Creator—to maintain proper control. They respect the overpowering laws that keep demonic forces under constraint. With utmost devotion, humanity must express its gratitude to the Creator for its perpetual essence as the Guardian of life *(vayu)* and death *(yama)*. It is the true source of the link (Holy Spirit) between all creation (Son) and the source (Father). The heavenly manifestations include the sky, earth, fire, water, and illumination or sun. Humanity should appreciate the creation of the guardians (deities) of waters *(varuna)*, darkness *(sansanka)*, procreation *(prajapati)*, and ancestry *(prapitamahah)*.

Humanity must respect and express indebtedness for the creation of demigods such as the power of authority, the power of competence, and the power of equilibrium. The Creator operates behind the perpetual essence. The Creator never dies or is reborn. The Creator is a force that represents many, but there is one and only one. It has been given different names by many—*Ishware* in the Bhagavad Gita, Allah in the Quran, Holy Father in the Bible, Yahweh in the Book of Moses, and Elohim in the holy scriptures—but the ultimate Almighty God remains the same one and only one.

Summary

The Creator which humanity commonly identifies as God is an eternal force that is invisible, indiscernible, infinite, immortal, and indivisible, which prevails beyond the universe and has no beginning or end. The eternal force consists of a primordial force that has the ability to separate the undividable form of the eternal force into two parts, thus creating un-manifested substratum and manifested substratum, the two aspects of the universe. These two aspects, continuously changing, give rise to the phenomenon of each beginning being an ending and each ending being a beginning. Primordial force has the power to transform itself from extremely violent waves, such as electromagnetic waves, to brilliant illuminations, to tranquility, such as flowing water.

Comprehension of all such powers is the eternal wisdom of knowing the absolute truth. It starts with the cultivation of faith, which leads to spiritual wisdom, a subjective knowledge that is beyond the practical or the intellectual knowledge. It gradually evolves into transcendental wisdom. Ultimately it leads to comprehension of absolute truth, called the union of individual living spirit, with the eternal soul. Or it leads to subsidence of mental anguish, turning into a state of ultimate tranquility or a river merging with the ocean and losing its identity forever.

There are two kinds of evolution: physical and spiritual. Humanity represents an advanced stage of physical evolution and it represents the earliest stage of spiritual evolution. The process of spiritual evolution starts with humanity cultivating quest to know the Creator. Once a human body cultivates faith, and follows a path of spirituality and a process of inner purification and rejuvenation to attain eternal truth, it thus acquires enlightenment and illumination and attains freedom from the powers of living force, such as time, space, gravitational, magnetic, and other powers controlling the embodiments. The human physical body thus comes under the direct control of the eternal soul, where the human body becomes an instrument of the living spirit, also called resurrection, where the physical body can do things that, within the current state of mind, are incomprehensible and fall within the field of mystics.

Humanity believes we have come a long way toward knowing the truth, but in terms of spiritual evolution, the unveiling of the absolute truth has just begun, and it has millions of years to go.

Bibliography

Armstrong, Karen. *A History of God: The 4,000-Year Quest of Judaism, Christianity, and Islam.* New York: Gramercy Books, 1993.

______. *The Great Transformation: The Beginning of Our Religious Traditions.* New York: Anchor Books, 2006.

Auken, John Van. *Ancient Egyptian Mysticism and Its Relevance Today.* Virginia Beach: A.R.E. Press, 2002.

Berney, Charlotte. *Fundamentals of Hawaiian Mysticism.* Toronto: Crossing Press, 2000.

British Museum. *The Babylonian Legends of the Creation.* Miami, FL: Hard Press, 2010.

Capra, Fritjof. *The Tao of Physics.* New York: Bantam Books, 1983.

Chidbhavananda, Swami. *The Bhagavad Gita,* Commentary. Tirupparaithurai: Sri Ramakrishna Tapovanam, 2008.

Chinmayananda, Swami. *The Holy Geeta,* Commentary. Mumbai: Central Chinmaya Mission Trust, 1995.

______. *Talk on Sankars Vivekachoodamani.* Mumbai: Central Chinmaya Mission Trust, 2007.

Dalley, Stephanie. *Myths from Mesopotamia: Creation, the Flood, Gilgamesh, and Others.* New York: Oxford World's Classic, 2008.

Dimmitt, Cornelia, and J. A. B. van Buitenen. *Classic Hindu Mythology.* Philadelphia: Temple University Press, 1978.

Doniger, Wendy. *The Hindus: An Alternative History.* New York: Penguin Books, 2009.

Fox, Everett. *The Five Books of Moses: Genesis, Exodus, Leviticus, Numbers, Deuteronomy.* New York: Schocken Books, 1990.

Gandhi, Mahatma. *The Bhagavad Gita according to Gandhi.* Berkeley, CA: North Atlantic Books, 2009.

Goswami, Amit. *Physics of the Soul.* Charlottesville: Hampton Roads, 2001.

Govinda, Lama Anagarika. *Fundamentals of Tibetan Mysticism.* Boston: Weiser Books, 1969.

Heidel, Alexander. *The Babylonian Genesis.* Chicago: The University of Chicago Press, 1955.

Kabbani, Shaykh Muhammad Hisham. *The Sufi Science of Self-Realization.* Louisville: Fons Vitae, 2006.

Khan, Muhammad Zafrulla. *The Qur'an.* New York: Olive Branch Press, 2003.

King, L. W. *Enuma Elish: The Seven Tablets of Creation.* London: Luzac and Co., 1902.

Kushner, Lawrence. *The River of Light: Jewish Mystical Awareness.* Woodstock, VA: Jewish Lights Publishing, 2000.

Macdonnell, A. A., H. Oldenberg, and Max F. Muller. *The Golden Book of the Holy Vedas.* Delhi: Vijay Goel, 2007.

McDowell, Michael, and Nathan Robert Brown. *World Religions at Your Fingertips.* New York: Alpha Books, 2009.

Merton, Thomas. *Seeds of Contemplation.* Norfolk, VA: New Directions Books, 1949.

______. *Seven Storey Mountain: An Autobiography of Faith.* Orlando, FL: Harvest Book Harcourt, 1998.

Muktanand, Swami. *Where Are You Going? A Guide to Spiritual Journey.* South Fallsburg, NY: SYDA Bookstore, 1985.

Nikhilananda, Swami. *Bhagavad Gita.* Translated by Advaita Ashrama. Kolkota: India, 2008.

Osho. *Unio Mystica (Mystic Unity).* Vol. 1 and 2. Pune: Tao Publishing Pvt. Ltd, 2004.

______. *The Revolution Talk on Kabir.* Mumbai: Jaico Publishing House, 2007.

Power, Richard. *The Lost Teachings of Lama Govinda: Living Wisdom from a Modern Tibetan Master.* Wheaton, IL: Quest Books, 2007.

Prabhavananda, Swami, and Christopher I. Sherwood. *Songs of God: Bhagavad Gita, Translation.* New York: New American Library, 1972.

Prabhupada, A. C. Bhaktivedanta Swami. *The Bhagavad-Gita as It Is,* Commentaries. Mumbai: The Bhaktivedanta Book Trust, 1986.

Rajneesh, Bhagwan Shree, and Osho. *Sufis: The People of the Past.* Vol. 1. Pune: Tao Publishing Pvt. Ltd., 2006.

______. *Sufis: The People of the Past.* Vol. 2. Pune: Ma Yoga Laxmi Rajneesh Foundation Ltd., 1980.

Rama, Swami. *Living with the Himalayan Masters: Spiritual Experiences of Swami Rama.* Honesdale: Himalayan Institute Press, 2005.

Ranganathananda, Swami. *An Exposition of the Gita in Light of Modern Thoughts and Modern Needs.* Vol. 1–3 of *Universal Message of the Bhagavad Gita.* Kolkata: Advaita Ashram, 2006.

Sankaracharya, Adi Sri. *The Bhagavad Gita,* Commentaries. Madras: Samata Books, 2001.

Saraswati, Madhusudana. *Bhagavad-Gita.* Translated by Swami Gambhirananda. Kolkata: Advaita Ashrama, 2007.

Satchidananda, Sri Swami. *The Living Gita: The Complete Bhagavad Gita—A Commentary for Modern Readers.* Buckingham, VA: Integral Yoga Publications, 1988.

Sells, Michael A. *Early Islamic Mysticism.* New York: Paulist Press, 1996.

Underhill, Evelyn. *Mysticism: The Nature and Development of Spiritual Consciousness.* Oxford: Oneworld, 1993.

Vidyalankar, Pandit Satyakam. *The Holy Vedas.* Delhi: Clarion Books, 1998.

Waite, Dennis. *Back to the Truth: 5,000 Years of Advaita.* Winchester: John Hunt Publishing, 2007.

Wilkins, W. J. *Hindu Mythology.* New Delhi: Asia Book Corp. of America, 1989.

Yogananda, Paramahansa. *The Bhagavad Gita: Royal Science of God Realization,* Commentaries. Vol. 1 and 2. Los Angeles: International Publications Council of Self-Realization, 1999.

Yukteswar, Swami Sri. *The Holy Science.* Los Angeles: Self-Realization Fellowship, 1990.

Index

Advaita school of thought, 31, 32
aesthetics, 19
affinity, for material things, 257–58
Agams (inaccessible sphere), 83
ahamkara (sainthood), 234
Ahura Mazda (Creator), 7, 8
air, splendors in, 249
airavata (mythical white elephant), 242
aiswaryas (ascetic majestic powers), 265
Aitareys (eighth Upanishad), 21
akarma (selfish actions), 108, 136, 157, 164, 193
akarma yoga, 69
akshra yoga, 180, 181–82
Alcott, Amos Bronson, xxxi
allab, 122
Allah, 122, 181, 222, 278
allegories, 27
altruism, 72, 127–28, 178
altruistic desires, 128
amen, 122
amrita (nectar), 242
anahata (dorsal chakra), 215
Anama (sphere of universe), 82–83
ananda (eternal happiness), 171
anandamaya kosha (fifth sheath), 87
Anat (primordial force), 112
anata (demigod of land), 248
ancestry, 277
ancient Greece, 19–20, 24–25, 26, 112, 161
Andronovo, 13
anger, 69, 75, 78, 79, 90
Angra Mainyu, 8
anguish, xxiii, 2, 35, 78, 90, 128, 179, 216, 232, 253, 267, 279
anima, 265
animal sacrifices, xxii
anna (nourishment), 87
annamya kosha (first sheath), 87
annanda (eternal love), 88
annihilations, 118, 120, 273
Antu (earth), 6
anu (cosmic atom), 122
anxieties, restraint of, 73
apertures, of the human body, 49
Aphrodite (primordial force), 112
Apsu (fresh flowing water coming from the ground), 5
Arabian civilization, 112
archangels, 54, 60, 63, 114, 159, 239, 248, 264
Aristotle, 20, 161
Arjuna, xxix, 231, 274–76
Armstrong, Karen, xxviii, xxxi, 1
arrogance, 21, 34, 35, 69, 75, 77, 133, 136, 204, 216, 266, 268, 272
aryaman (archangels), 248
Aryans, xxiii, 112, 116
Asat (faith without undivided devotion), 65
ascetic majestic powers, 265
asexual proliferation, 246
ashwattha tree (eternal tree), 42–43

I

S

About the Author

Ramesh Malhotra was born in Lahore, undivided India, in November 1943* on the day of celebration of Guru Nanak's birthday. After partition in 1947, the author's family moved to a small town, Solan, in the Himalayas where he got his education. Later, his family moved to the newly built town of Chandigarh. He completed his master's degree in geology at Punjab University and worked as a geologist for the state government in Simla, Himachel Pradesh. In 1967, the author left India to work toward a postgraduate diploma in mining and prospecting from Mont. Hochschule Leoben in Austria.

In 1968, the author came to the United States for postgraduate studies. After receiving an MS in earth and space science from Stony Brook University in New York and an MSBA from Michigan Tech, he joined Columbia University to pursue a doctorate in mineral economics. In 1971, he joined the Illinois State Geological Survey as a mineral economist. In 1974, he entered the business world and worked for Freeman United Coal as assistant vice president. In 1981, he joined NERCO Coal; after six years as the president of NERCO, he left the corporate life to start his own business.

In 1987, the author established Coal Network, Inc. in Mason, Ohio. Over the past several years as an entrepreneur and

* Birthday record: 4th February, 1945

angel investor, he has been actively involved in seeding new business ventures, acquiring and expanding existing businesses to create new jobs, and supporting others in realizing their dreams. The author currently owns and directs the activities of more than seven different businesses in the fields of trading, manufacturing, import and distribution, innovative technologies, and brand marketing. As a group, his company ranks as one of the top 100 companies in Greater Cincinnati.

In 1991, the author became a patron of the arts and has been supporting budding artists and art galleries, and sponsoring other art-related ventures within the greater Cincinnati area.

The author's passion for exploring and acquiring higher spiritual knowledge started during the early 1990s. He has traveled in India and other parts of the world and visited spiritual centers to learn and experience spirituality. The author has used spiritual knowledge as an integral part of his personal as well as his business life. This is the author's first attempt to present his thoughts in the form of a book, and he is fully committed to acquiring higher knowledge and helping others in seeking such knowledge.

In 2011, the author initiated funding for an elementary school, located near where he received his early education. At this school, located in Himalayas near Sadhupul, Solan, fundamentals of higher knowledge are being taught and practiced. The author will dedicate the proceeds from the sale of his books to support this institute and similar organizations around the world.